THE GREAT HISTORIES series is designed to introduce the reader to the works of the most important historical writers from Herodotus to those of the present day. Each volume is devoted to the most significant works of a single author and offers the full scope of his contribution both to the study of history and to the development of historical writing. Edited and with a critical introduction by a distinguished scholar, each volume is devised for intelligent and enjoyable reading by the layman or the student.

The general editor of the series is H. R. Trevor-Roper, distinguished Regius Professor of Modern History at Oxford University.

MACHIAVELLI was edited by Myron P. Gilmore, Professor of History at Harvard University.

THE GREAT HISTORIES *Series*

HERODOTUS, *edited by W. G. Forrest.*

THUCYDIDES, *edited by P. A. Brunt.*

POLYBIUS, *edited by E. Badian.*

JOSEPHUS, *edited by Moses I. Finley.*

TACITUS, *edited by Hugh Lloyd-Jones.*

PROCOPIUS, *edited by Mrs. Averil Cameron.*

BEDE, *edited by James Campbell.*

AMMIANUS MARCELLINUS, *edited by Geoffrey de Ste. Croix.*

MACHIAVELLI, *edited by Myron P. Gilmore.*

GUICCIARDINI, *edited by J. R. Hale.*

SARPI, *edited by Peter Burke.*

VOLTAIRE, *edited by J. H. Brumfitt.*

GIBBON, *edited by Hugh R. Trevor-Roper.*

PRESCOTT, *edited by Roger Howell.*

MACAULAY, *edited by Hugh R. Trevor-Roper.*

BURCKHARDT, *edited by Alexander Dru.*

HENRY ADAMS, *edited by E. N. Saveth.*

THE GREAT HISTORIES

A series under the general editorship of
H. R. Trevor-Roper, Regius Professor
of Modern History, Oxford University.

MACHIAVELLI

THE HISTORY OF FLORENCE and Other Selections

Selected, Edited, and with an Introduction by
Myron P. Gilmore

Newly translated by Judith A. Rawson

Twayne Publishers, Inc.   ::   New York

*This Twayne Publishers edition
is published by special arrangement with
Washington Square Press, Inc.*

Standard Book Number: 671–48364–1.

Contents

INTRODUCTION   vii

NOTE ON THE SELECTION OF TEXTS   xxxv

BIBLIOGRAPHICAL NOTE   xxxvi

CHRONOLOGY   xxxvii

DESCRIPTION OF THE AFFAIRS OF FRANCE   1

DISCOURSE ON FLORENTINE AFFAIRS AFTER
THE DEATH OF LORENZO   15

THE LIFE OF CASTRUCCIO CASTRACANI OF LUCCA   29

THE HISTORY OF FLORENCE   55

    Book II   55
    Book III   117
    Book IV   167
    Book VII   214
    Book VIII   263

INDEX   319

Introduction

I

Foreword

Niccolò Machiavelli was sent by his father in June 1486 to bring home from the binder's a newly bound copy of the *Decades* of Livy. Nearly forty years later, in May 1525, he journeyed to Rome to present to Pope Clement VII the eight books of his *History of Florence*. Between these dates almost everything he wrote, whether public or private, reveals his passionate interest in history and his determination, as he said, to extract its "true meaning and the savor that it possesses."

In spite of this preoccupation, many would be disposed to contest Machiavelli's inclusion among the "great historians," arguing that he was too systematic, that he lacked a real sense of history, that he warped what had actually happened in order to fit preconceived theories of what always must happen. It is true that for Machiavelli history was a dimension of present experience; he had no use for histories that were not relevant to the present; his own pages become duller when he cannot endow an incident of Roman or Florentine history with contemporary significance. Nevertheless it would be a mistake to accept too simple and static a picture of Machiavelli's ideas about history. If he consciously sought in the past lessons for the present, it is also true that the events of his own life changed his perspective on the past, and provided the basis for those interpretations and insights on which in fact rests the greatness of his historical work. An understanding of this work therefore depends on some knowledge of the genesis and development of his ideas on the relation between past and present and the modifications which bitter experience brought to his conception of the uses of history.

II

The Background

Only in 1954, nearly five hundred years after Machiavelli's birth, was there published the document that tells us more than any other about his family background and early years. This was the *Libro di ricordi,* or journal, kept by his father Bernardo Machiavelli from 1471 through 1487. The manuscript of this work, unknown to all but the most recent biographers, was discovered on the eve of the war in 1939 and a transcript was prepared. When the war came, the journal was hidden in what the owner hoped would be a secure place in the Apennines. During the German retreat the hiding place was discovered and destroyed, and the documents it contained were left lying on the ground, exposed to the weather. Although the covers and parts of the manuscript were badly damaged, the editor, Cesare Olschki, was able to publish the text in 1954.[1]

From the daily jottings of this journal, there emerges a clear picture of the varied interests of Machiavelli's father, a Florentine lawyer of modest means. We see him worrying over his law cases, his taxes, the administration of his farm at Sant' Andrea in Percussina, buying and selling wine and oil, and arranging for his daughter's dowry and his son's schooling. Above all, we get some glimpses of those intellectual interests which were to be his most important legacy to his son. Consider the following account of his purchases of books in 1486.

> I record how on this 21st day of June, 1486, I have given to Francesco d'Andrea di Bartolommeo, the stationer of the quarter of San Giorgio in Florence, two books to be bound, one a reading by the

---

[1] Bernardo Machiavelli, *Libro di ricordi,* Cesare Olschki, ed. (Florence, 1954).

Abbot of Sicily on the fourth and fifth books of the *Decretals* [Nicholas de Tudeschis, 1482, Pavia], a folio, and the other three decades with the epitome of the 140 books of Titus Livy also in folio [Pavia, 1483]. He was to bind them well in half-leather with boards projecting and two clasps on each, and I agreed to give him for the binding of both of the volumes 4 lire, 5 soldi of which I was to give him [in] red wine, which he has tasted, at the rate of 50 soldi the cask. I carried the said books to him and he promised to give them back to me bound within eight days.

On the evening of the same day after the twenty-fourth hour he came with a porter and carried away one cask of red wine at the rate agreed upon of 50 soldi the cask.

On the 27th of the same month I gave to him to be bound the *Novella* of Gian Andrea on the *Sextiles* in the form in which I had bought it from Bartolo di Fruosino, the bookseller of Garbo, and from there I brought it to the said Francesco and he was to bind this together with the *Mercuriales* for which he promised to come here this evening as soon as he left his shop.

Later on that same day at the hour of the Ave Maria the said Francesco came here and I gave him to be bound the *Mercuriales* of Giovanni Andrea and instructed him to bind them with the *Novella* after the latter in a binding of wood covers with half-leather and two clasps for 40 soldi. I agreed to give him wine at 50 soldi the cask as above recorded.

I record how afterwards on the 1st of July Niccolò my son gave to the said stationer Francesco d'Andrea to whom I had given the said books to be bound one cask of the aforementioned red wine at 50 soldi the cask.

And afterwards on the 4th he gave to him 20 soldi in cash as he said he could not finish the work if he did not have 20 soldi to buy leather.

And on the 8th of this month Niccolò gave to him three flasks of the said red wine and one flask of vinegar which he came to fetch. This was in lieu of the 5 soldi. And on the same day the bookseller brought back to my son the said books bound, one well done according to his agreement, namely, the *Reading* by Niccolò l'Abbate, the other two badly done and not in accord with the specifications. And this happened while I was at my villa in the country.

Thus, amid the exchange of flasks of red wine and vinegar, we have what is very probably Machiavelli's first encounter with Livy.

Bernardo also records some of the uses to which he put his newly bound volume. One Niccolò Tedesco, "a priest and astrologer," commissions him to prepare a list of "all the cities, rivers, islands, mountains, and provinces" mentioned by Livy in the first three *Decades*. If the father thus spent his evenings compiling the topographical features unique or recurrent in Livy's work, it is perhaps not too fanciful to imagine that even at this early age there presented itself to the mind of the son the possibility of making generalizations about the men and events of Roman history. In any case, the picture of Bernardo, conscientiously studying his *Decretals* and his *Sextiles* and also reading his Roman history, not only provided his son with a convincing justification for the relevance of classical studies, but also reminds us of the relationship between the legal profession and the humanistic culture of the Renaissance.

This relationship goes back more than a century and a half before the time of Machiavelli. In the development of the pre-Petrarchan humanism of the north Italian towns, it is among the lawyers, judges, and notaries that we find the first self-conscious cultivation of an interest in classical civilization. It is perhaps natural that men who had been trained in the exegesis of the texts of Justinian's Digest should turn to exploring the meaning of non-legal classical texts. The social conditions of the Italian communes gave to these lawyers a certain amount of leisure, and the product of their new intellectual interests is to be seen in the *florilegia*, collections of bits of Latin history and verse, which prepared the way for the enthusiastic reception of Petrarch's ideas.

It is true that after the first conquests of Petrarchan humanism, Petrarch's followers often expressed scorn for the methods of teaching and exposition practiced by the lawyers. Petrarch himself had declared that he was disillusioned with the study of the law and advised a young friend to have nothing to do with it. The lawyers, he charged, had no real knowledge of language and were more concerned with commentators than sources. In spite of these attacks, however, and in part no doubt because of them, the lawyers began to apply in their own professional work the methods of understanding a text, the interest in history and in the writing of good Latin which the humanists had urged. The result was that by the second half of the fifteenth century a great part of the legal profession, especially in Florence, was not only master of the traditional professional knowledge but also actively interested in the newer humanistic study of Roman history and literature.

Such an interest is amply documented in Bernardo Machiavelli's *Ricordi.* In addition to the Livy, he records borrowings or purchases of numerous other classical and humanistic books and manuscripts. Among these were the *De oratore,* the *De officiis,* and the *Philippics* of Cicero, the *Nicomachaean Ethics* with the commentary of Donato Acciaiuoli, the *Historiarum romanorum decades* and *Italia illustrata* of Flavio Biondo.

Some of these works, including the Livy, were probably eventually inherited by Machiavelli from his father. We may also suppose that the young Machiavelli studied and perhaps copied some of the manuscripts in his father's library.[2] In any case, there is sufficient evidence

---

[2] In 1961, Professor Sergio Bertelli claimed that the Vatican Ms. Rossianus 804, which contains the text of Lucretius' *De rerum natura* and the *Eunuchus* of Terence, was in the hand of Machiavelli. *Cf.* Sergio Bertelli, "Noterelle Machiavelliane. Un codice di Lucrezio e di Terenzio," *Rivista storica,* LXXIII (1961), pp. 554–57. See also his "Noterelle Machiavelliane. Ancora su Lucrezio e Machiavelli," *Rivista storica* LXXVI (1964). This conclusion has been accepted by the majority of Machiavelli scholars and most recently by Roberto Ridolfi in *Bibliofilia* (1968), *di-*

to conclude that Machiavelli had in his early years a more thorough acquaintance with certain of the Latin classics than his older biographers supposed. Through Livy he may have been already attracted to that study of ancient history which he was later to try to make into a system like that of the law, "opening a path which no man had trodden before." The humanist vision of the greatness of Rome and the lessons to be learned from Roman history and literature provided the foundation for his later developed philosophy of history.

III

Experience

In June 1498, Machiavelli, twenty-nine years old, was elected Second Chancellor of the Florentine Republic. He perhaps owed this office to his association with Marcello Virgilio Adriani, who had succeeded to the first chancellorship a few months before. The functions of these two offices were no longer clearly distinguished. Their incumbents were the civil servants charged with carrying on the official correspondence of the elected magistrates who governed the city. Like other civil servants in other societies they had at times considerable opportunity to influence and even to make important decisions of policy. The Second Chancellor was also named Secretary to the Ten, the collegiate body in charge of the conduct of war.

Machiavelli held this secretaryship for more than fourteen years. He was deprived of his office by the newly restored Medici government on November 7, 1512.

---

spensa 2. Bertelli has suggested that Machiavelli's interest in Lucretius may have been stimulated by the political and philosophical ideas of the group opposed to Savonarola and that he may have undertaken the copying of these texts at the suggestion of Marcello Virgilio Adriani, who occupied the chair of poetry and oratory in the University of Florence and became First Chancellor of the Florentine Republic in 1498. Such a conclusion would confirm the passage in Giovio's *Eulogies* in which he says Machiavelli received from Marcello Virgilio "graecae et latinae flores."

During his fourteen years in office, he was constantly preoccupied with the problems of military and foreign policy which the Florentine Republic had to face in the critical period of the struggle of the northern powers for the control of the Italian peninsula.

The reconquest of Pisa, which had revolted against Florence at the time of the invasion of Charles VIII in 1494, was the most pressing task confronting the Signoria and the Ten at the time of Machiavelli's appointment. This was not accomplished until 1509, and the final success was in large part due to Machiavelli's contribution. In his first months in office he wrote a *Discorso della guerra di Pisa* which showed his ability to analyze a situation and present an incisive judgment on a course of action. He constantly urged upon the government the necessity of providing for a militia, and in 1505 and in 1506 recruited and trained the first battalions which were to play a decisive role in the final military action against Pisa. After the event, Agostino Vespucci wrote to him, "I would make bold to say that you, with your battalions, have produced so fine an institution that, not slowly, but rapidly, you have restored the dominion of Florence."

The fifteen-year campaign for the reconquest of Pisa had to be conducted under the pressures created by the constantly shifting alliances of the Italian powers and the threats posed by the new invasions from the north. Venice was always ready to take advantage of any weakness in the Florentine position. The alliance formed between Alexander VI and Louis XII of France created a particular danger as it was the basis of Cesare Borgia's aggressive attempt to impose his rule on the territories of the Marches and Ravenna. This crisis came to an end with the Pope's death in 1503 and with the consequent dissolution of the Borgian power, but a new and ultimately more serious threat to the Florentine republican government was posed by the election to the papacy of Julius II. The *"papa terribile"* was determined to reestablish his authority over the states of the Church. His conquest of Bologna in 1506 brought to the frontiers of the Republic a powerful potential enemy. As long as the Pope remained in alliance with France, Florence was safe. In fact, the formation of the League of Cambrai in 1507 and the combined attack of the Papacy, France, and the Empire on Venice gave Florence the opportunity to bring the war with Pisa to a successful conclusion. But when Julius II turned against the French in 1510, Florence remained faithful to the alliance with Louis XII, and the victories of Julius II prepared the ruin of Soderini's government and the restoration of the Medici.

Throughout these critical years, Machiavelli as secretary supplied his government with information, analysis, and advice. He was sent to the camp of Cesare Borgia in 1502, and received from the prince himself his account of the murders at Sinigaglia at the end of the year. After the deaths of the Borgia Pope and his temporary successor, Machiavelli made his first journey to Rome to report on the conclave which elected Julius II. He was ordered on a second legation to the same Pope after the conquest of Bologna. At the end of 1507 and at the beginning of 1508, he was one of the Florentine envoys to the imperial court, and three times, in 1500, in 1504, and in the critical year 1510, he carried out missions to France to the Court of Louis XII.

The dispatches which Machiavelli sent back to Florence and the reports which he drew up for the Signoria are brilliant examples of his powers of observation and analysis. His knowledge of men and affairs, his training in distinguishing the most important factors in a given situation, and his reasoning on the consequences which would follow from the adoption of a particular course of action provided the basis for his later interpretation of Florentine history. In fact, many of the documents of this period of Machiavelli's most intense political activity show how much he took account of history in explaining a present problem. Consider, for example, his description of the French monarchy and French society, the *Ritratto delle cose di Francia* composed in 1511 as a summary of the information he had acquired on his three missions to France. In this document he surveys the reasons for the present great power of the French

Crown, mentioning among other factors the Salic law, primogeniture, and the successful struggle of the Capetian kings with the great feudality. Similarly, in discussing French military strength Machiavelli draws upon the history of military institutions in France as well as upon what we would call social psychology. His accounts of France and Germany invite comparison with the famous dispatches and relations of the contemporary Venetian ambassadors. Machiavelli shares with the latter the ability to give a comprehensive picture of a country, including not only the ruler and the court and the institutions of government but also the attitudes of the people and the condition of the economy. In Machiavelli's analysis, however, there is not only more insight into the psychology of a foreign nation but there is also more awareness of the historical factors which condition the present. Even in the period of his greatest diplomatic and political activity, Machiavelli did not neglect the relevance of past events to an appreciation of a present situation. The *Description of the Affairs of France* was probably written early in 1511. Machiavelli's judgments on the military staying power of the French were confirmed in the following year. Although the French army under their brilliant commander Gaston de Foix fought bravely at Ravenna, after the battle, the French power melted away. Julius II was victorious, and in September the government of Soderini fell and the Medici were restored to power. Machiavelli was removed from office and forbidden to leave Florentine territory; in the beginning of 1513, he was unjustly implicated in an irresponsible plot against the Medici and spent February in prison, where he was tortured. He was freed in March in the general amnesty which followed the election of the Medici Pope, and he retired to his property at Sant' Andrea in Percussina. The speculations of the contemplative life succeeded the responsibilities of the active life. To this retirement from active participation in the political life of Florence, accepted at the time with bitter resignation by Machiavelli, who knew his own merits, the world nevertheless owes the masterpieces of the next decade.

IV

The Lessons of History and Experience

At Sant' Andrea, Machiavelli spent his days hunting and taking care of the farm. In the evening, as he tells us in the famous letter to his friend Francesco Vettori, he put on courtly robes to commune with the ancients, that is, he turned to his books. Among these books may well have been the Livy which he had been sent to fetch from the binder so many years before, and it seems plausible that, as Ridolfi suggests, he had already during his busy life as secretary begun to take notes and to compare what he could learn from Roman history with his experiences in Italian politics.

The successes of the Roman Republic contrasted with the failures of the Florentine Republic provided him with a great theme. In the first months of exile he began to assemble the material that ultimately took shape as the *Discourses on Livy.* This project was, however, suddenly set aside in July when Machiavelli saw an opportunity to make a practical application of what he called his "long experience of modern affairs and his continual reading about those of antiquity."

Leo X, Giovanni de' Medici, had been elected Pope in March. His younger brother Giuliano and his nephew Lorenzo were in control of Florence. This combination of circumstances recalled the position of the Borgia ten years before when Alexander VI was Pope and his son Cesare was in control of the Marches and Romagna. The Medici might succeed where the Borgia had failed, if they followed a resolute course of action based on precepts which both history and experience showed to be applicable to the establishment of a successful principate. Machiavelli wrote *The Prince* between July and December, 1513,[3] and it has been plausibly argued that he was

---

[3] This dating is now almost universally accepted. See Machiavelli, *Il principe e discorsi,* Sergio Bertelli, ed. (Milan, 1960), pp. 3–10 and the literature there cited.

principally motivated by the hope of entering the service of the Medici and particularly that of Giuliano, for whom the Pope was proposing to create a new principality, leaving Lorenzo in charge of Florence.[4] This would explain the original intention to dedicate *The Prince* to Giuliano, as well as the emphasis on the problems of a new regime. The Pope's foreign policy, however, never succeeded in establishing a new state for Giuliano, and on the latter's death in March 1516, Machiavelli finally dedicated his treatise to Lorenzo. It was first published in 1532.

The problems connected with the composition and date of the *Discorsi* and their relation to *The Prince* are more complicated and have been the subject of much recent scholarly discussion.[5] Those who maintain that the *Discorsi* were conceived and, at least in part, written before Machiavelli interrupted himself to write *The Prince* emphasize the unity of Machiavelli's thought. On the other hand, it is argued that if the *Discorsi* were entirely posterior to *The Prince*, then there can be traced a development of Machiavelli's thought from a "realistic" preoccupation with practical politics to a more "humanistic" approach to the problems which concerned him.

From the point of view of Machiavelli's attitude toward the study of history, these questions are academic. Both *The Prince* and the *Discorsi* draw on those sources in history and experience to which Machiavelli refers in the dedication to *The Prince*. Both works include examples from ancient and modern times and both illustrate the ideas that Machiavelli held in this period on the nature and use of history.

These ideas are most clearly stated by Machiavelli in the Introduction to the first book of the *Discorsi*. Here he proclaims that he is following a new route "which has not hitherto been followed by anyone." He registers his amazement that, considering the general admiration for antiquity and the price paid for a few fragments of an

---

[4] C. H. Clough, "Yet Again Machiavelli's *Prince*," *Annali dell'Istituto Universitario Orientale*, Sezione Romanza, Vol. 2 (1963), pp. 201–226.

[5] It is resumed in Bertelli's edition of the *Discorsi*, pp. 109–116.

ancient statue, more attention has not been paid to the wonderful examples which ancient kingdoms and republics present. He continues:

> When we see these examples more admired than imitated, or so much neglected that not the least trace of ancient virtue remains, we cannot but be as much surprised as afflicted. The more so as in the differences which arise between citizens or in the maladies to which they are subjected, we see these same people have recourse to the judgments and remedies prescribed by the ancients. The civil laws are in fact nothing but the decisions given by their jurisconsults, and which reduced to a system direct our modern jurists in their decisions. And what is the science of medicine but the experience of ancient physicians, which their successors have taken for their guide? And yet to found a republic, maintain states, to govern a kingdom, organize an army, conduct a war, dispense justice, and extend empires, you will find neither prince nor republic nor captain nor citizen who has recourse to the examples of antiquity. This neglect I am persuaded is due less to the weakness to which the vices of our education have reduced the world, than to the evils caused by the proud insolence which exists in most Christian states, and to the lack of a true knowledge of history, the true sense of which is not known or the spirit of which they do not comprehend. Thus the majority of those who read it take pleasure only in the variety of events which history relates, without ever thinking of imitating the noble actions, deeming that not only difficult but impossible, as though heaven, the sun, the elements, and men had changed the order of their motions and power, and were different from what they were in ancient times.[6]

Machiavelli concludes his Introduction by stating that he wishes to draw mankind from this error by comment-

---

[6] Machiavelli, *The Prince and the Discourses,* C. Detmold, trans. (New York, 1940), pp. 104–105.

ing on the books of Livy in order to provide a comparison between ancient and modern events. So he hopes to derive the advantages which should be the aim of all study of history, and he hopes also to carry his undertaking so far that little will remain for others to do.

This declaration by Machiavelli may appear astonishing at first. How was it possible to maintain that history and the examples of antiquity had been neglected when humanist educators for the last one hundred fifty years from Petrarch onward had done little else than reiterate commonplaces about history as philosophy teaching by example, recommended the study of Livy, and imitated him when they came to writing histories of their own? The key to Machiavelli's condemnation of all his predecessors, however, is to be found, not in what they professed but in what they had failed to accomplish. Looking at the disorder which had come upon Italy since the French invasion of 1494, Machiavelli was above all impressed with the contrast between what was preached and what was practiced. The easy confidence of the earlier generation that it was enough to discover the lessons of history and that they could be relevant to the present, equating knowledge with virtue, was beginning to crack. And it is in this connection most significant that Machiavelli appeals to the disciplines of law and medicine as those which represent the successful use of antiquity.

Machiavelli was impressed with the fact that in both law and medicine the particular case was assimilated to the general rule, and the general rule had been tested by many authorities of classical antiquity. Those who had studied the ancient historians, which for the Renaissance was the same thing as studying ancient history, had indeed found examples of virtue and vice, wisdom and foolishness, but these examples had never been reduced to a system; there existed no systematic body of knowledge which could be compared to that accumulated by the commentators on the civil law. This is the focal point of Machiavelli's criticism of his humanist predecessors, and this is why he felt that he was entering upon a path which no one had trodden before. In his definition of what history ought to be, Machiavelli realizes a new synthesis between those legal and humanist traditions which we have seen combined in his father's experience.

The Prince and the *Discorsi* were thus built on the conviction that there could be created a systematic knowledge of history. In 1519, Machiavelli essayed an extended practical demonstration of this new science. This was the *Arte della guerra* cast in the form of a dialogue imagined to have taken place in the Rucellai gardens in 1516.[7] In the dedication to Lorenzo di Filippo Strozzi, Machiavelli affirms the close connection between military and civil institutions. All the provisions for the common good in a civilized society, respectful of the laws and of God, would be in vain if there were no provision for the common defense. Where the latter is well organized, it can preserve even defective civil institutions and, on the contrary, the best polity without military defense is no better than a superb palace that is adorned with gems and gold but lacks a roof. This proposition is illustrated at length in the long and detailed exposition of Roman military institutions which Machiavelli gives in the form of Fabrizio Colonna's speeches to his friends in reply to their questions. There is the same concern as in the *Discorsi* with the analysis of the reasons for the Roman successes and the same hopes that the results of this analysis can be applied to contemporary conditions. The lesson is explicit that just as the Roman legions conquered the Macedonian phalanx, so with a proper military organization the Italians could conquer the Swiss infantry who had been so decisive in the campaigns of the first two decades of the sixteenth century.

In his long speech at the end of the dialogue, Fabrizio summarizes the generalizations which he has learned from the study of the ancients and from his own experience. Among these are many aphorisms which have come to be associated with all that is most characteristic in Machiavelli's philosophy. It is more important than any-

---

[7] For the date and circumstances of the composition, see Roberto Ridolfi, *Life of Niccolò Machiavelli*, Cecil Grayson, trans. (Chicago, 1963), pp. 177–179, and Sergio Bertelli, "Introduction" to Machiavelli, *Arte della guerra e scritti politici minori* (Milan, 1961), pp. 309–320.

thing else to recognize one's opportunity and seize it. Nature produces few strong men; hard work and training make many. In war, discipline counts for more than fury. Men, weapons, money, and bread are the nerves of war, but of these four the first two are the most necessary because men and weapons can procure money and bread while bread and money cannot provide men and weapons.

Fabrizio's speech concludes with reflections on the contemporary scene. Through Fabrizio, Machiavelli renews his condemnation of mercenaries and summarizes again the reasons for the success of the Swiss and the Spanish and the failure of the Italian princes. The tone of confidence, however, in what can be accomplished in the future is no longer as strong as it was in the *Discorsi* a few years earlier. There is a bitter characterization of the Italian princes who in the period before the shocks of the invasion had thought it sufficient to invent a clever reply, to write a graceful letter, to live in luxurious style, practice treachery, lord it over subjects, award military offices as favors, disregard good advice—thus preparing the way for their destruction. From this situation came the disasters of 1494, and it has subsequently come about that the three most powerful states in Italy have been sacked and laid waste. What is still worse is that there has been no change in the mental attitude of the Italian rulers, and they take no account of the fact that those who in ancient times intended to maintain their rule prepared themselves by disciplining body and mind. Caesar, Alexander, and other great leaders may be condemned for too much ambition but not for luxurious living. If the princes of today read and believed these things, it is impossible that they would not change the form of their lives and the fortune of their states. Here is Machiavelli clearly reiterating the proposition that men of capacity and with the courage to act are more important than institutions and that one has only to study their lives to find lessons to be applied. He who disregards these reflections, if he be a prince disregards his principate, if he be a citizen disregards his city. But then comes the change of tone. "I am now old," says Fabrizio. "You who are young will be able to counsel and aid your princes, and do not be dismayed because this province seems born to resuscitate dead things, as we have seen in poetry, painting, and sculpture. But as regards me, I am discouraged, being advanced in years. Truly, however, if fortune had given me in the past enough resources for such an enterprise, I believe I would have demonstrated to the world in the shortest time how much the ancient institutions are worth and without doubt I would have either enlarged the state gloriously or lost it without shame."

Reading these words, we can perceive that Machiavelli's confidence in the new understanding of history, in the "path that no one had trodden before," was no longer so firm. It was a confidence that was to be still further shaken in the final years of Machiavelli's life.

V

The History of Florence

By 1520, Machiavelli's friends had made some progress in restoring him to favor with the Medici family. Lorenzo Duke of Urbino, to whom *The Prince* had been dedicated in vain, died in 1519, leaving an only daughter, the future Catherine de' Medici. Pope Leo X was uncertain about the dispositions that should be taken for the government of Florence, which he had temporarily entrusted to Cardinal Giulio. It was represented to both the Pope and the Cardinal that Machiavelli was a man of great talents, whose knowledge of history and politics might be put to good use.

On April 26, 1520, Battista dalla Palla wrote to Machiavelli from Rome, giving an account of an interview with the Pope. He reported that he had discussed Machiavelli's situation with His Holiness, whom he had found so favorably disposed that he suggested taking up with Cardinal Giulio the possibility of bestowing some patronage on Machiavelli and commissioning him to write for the Medici. The Cardinal who was favorably inclined to this suggestion was then serving among his other capacities as head of the Florentine *Studio*, and by the autumn an agreement had been reached on the terms of Machiavelli's employment. He was engaged by the officers of the university for two years at a salary of 100 florins *di studio* (devalued florins) *"inter alia ad componendum annalia et cronacas florentinas et alia faciendum."* Prior to the signing of this contract on November 8 and during the summer months while his employment was being discussed, Machiavelli had had an opportunity of giving to his friends a little demonstration of his ideas on historical method and style.

He had been sent to Lucca in July to represent the creditors of a banking house which had failed. During the month which followed, in the intervals of transacting business, he composed *La Vita di Castruccio Castracani di Lucca* and sent it off to his friends Zanobi Buondelmonti and Luigi Alamanni to whom it was dedicated. This work was based on a life of Castruccio written by a Lucchese, Niccolò Tegrimi, and published in 1496. To the facts of his hero's life collected by Tegrimi, and perhaps also supplemented by gleanings from Villani and Biondo, Machiavelli added incidents and personal characteristics derived from his reading of ancient authors, especially Diogenes Laertius and Dionysius of Halicarnassus. His friends accepted this work as a sample of the method and style of his prospective history. Buondelmonti, replying to Machiavelli on September 6, 1520, submitted some criticisms on the aphorisms attributed to Castruccio from other sources, but declared himself pleased with this *"modello della storia."* He particularly praised the style of Castruccio's deathbed oration and urged Machiavelli to proceed to his history.

The pages which Buondelmonti praised for their style are likewise of particular interest as an exposition of the characteristics which Machiavelli had desired to emphasize in the portrait of his hero. They are interestingly different from those which Machiavelli had previously attributed to the figures who represented his political ideals. In spite of the fact that Castruccio is a man of spirit, vigor, and ambition like the heroes of antiquity, he is represented by Machiavelli as confessing in his dying speech that had he known he would be cut off by fortune in the full course of his career, he would have been content with Pisa and Lucca, and would not have stirred up the enmity of Pistoia and Florence. Thus he would have left to his heirs a state smaller in size, but more secure and better established. These are not the words of Cesare Borgia, nor are they the counsels of *The Prince*. It is probable, as Franco Gaeta has suggested,[8] that Machiavelli's presentation of Castruccio was much influenced by the problems which he had expounded in the *Arte della guerra*. The occasion of writing a specimen of historical interpretation offered also a concrete opportunity to present a picture of the kind of man who would be the restorer of Italy. Fabrizio Colonna at the end of the *Arte della guerra* had complained that he was now too old, but in Castruccio we have perhaps a portrait of what he might have been in his youth in more favorable circumstances when he would have been able to demonstrate *"in brevissimo tempo . . . quanto gli antichi ordini vagliono."* The suggestion of Castruccio's dying speech is that such an ideal hero would not be an aggressor and would thus leave to posterity a more stable inheritance. In this way the *Vita di Castruccio* combined a demonstration of the style in which history should be written with a reaffirmation of some of Machiavelli's earlier conclusions on its lessons.

Before he began serious work on the history mentioned in the contract of November 1520, he was requested by the Cardinal to draw up a recommendation for the Pope on the future government of Florence. The death of Lorenzo of Urbino had left no direct male heirs of the old line of the Medici family, and therefore the Pope was now more prepared to consider constitutional changes. To the essay he wrote in response to this request, Machiavelli gave a Latin title: *Discursus Florentinarum rerum post mortem iunioris Laurentii Medicis.*[9] In it he summarized what seemed to him to be the salient features of

---

[8] Machiavelli, *La Vita di Castruccio Castracani di Lucca* in *Storie Fiorentine,* Franco Gaeta, ed. (Milan, 1962), Preface, p. 5.

[9] This is probably to be dated in the last months of 1520. See Ridolfi, *Machiavelli,* p. 308, n. 28.

the political and social history of Florence which ought to be taken into account in making any new regulations for the government. Proposing rather sweeping reforms, including the abolition of most of the existing magistracies, Machiavelli urged upon the Pope the necessity of establishing a republic. His argument was based on one of his favorite themes which he was to take up at length in the history, that is, the political consequences of social equality. He declared to the Pope, "Your Holiness must understand that in all cities where there is a great degree of equality among citizens, a monarchy can only be created with the utmost difficulty, and in cities where there is great inequality among citizens, a republic cannot be set up." He was particularly impressed with the social hierarchy in France, where he felt that the king could not rule without the nobility and the nobility in turn depended on the landed gentry who ruled the people. For these reasons he urged the establishment of a republican government which he hoped would ensure the continuance on a stable basis of the great heritage of civic liberty in Florence. He closed the essay with a moving appeal to the Pope, declaring that the greatest honor a man can have is to serve his native land. After those who have been gods, the most worthy of praise are those who have reformed republics and kingdoms. It was Machiavelli's hope that the Pope would so provide for the government of Florence that its inhabitants would become citizens and not subjects.

The commission to write the history of Florence gave Machiavelli an opportunity to develop the same themes at length. The initial plan was limited to the history of the period from the rise to power of Cosimo de' Medici in 1434 down to Machiavelli's own time. In his *proemio* (preface) Machiavelli tells us himself why he extended the scope. He declares, not quite ingenuously, that when he came to read the histories of his predecessors, Poggio and Bruni, he found that they had neglected civil discords and internal dissensions. Reflecting on the importance of these for understanding the historical development, he determined to go back to the origins of the city.

As Ridolfi has pointed out, "It is difficult and not very rewarding to attempt to distinguish stages in the book's composition."[10] The plan which finally emerged was based on a division into eight books. The first surveyed the history of Italy from the fall of the Roman Empire, and was largely based on Flavio Biondo. The next three books analyzed the internal development of Florence and her relations with other powers up to the triumphant return of Cosimo from exile in 1434. These were intended to supply what Machiavelli maintained were the omissions in Bruni and Poggio. Books V, VI, and VII dealt with the Medici rule in Florence in both foreign and domestic aspects. The final section, Book VIII, carried the story of Florence under Lorenzo de' Medici from the Pazzi Conspiracy to the death of Lorenzo in 1492.

It is clear that in writing about the Medici, Machiavelli felt some sense of conflict between what his patrons might want and what he himself believed. He wrote to his friend Guicciardini on August 30, 1524, "I am now coming to certain particulars where I need to know from you whether I will offend too much either by exaggerating or diminishing certain affairs, but I shall take counsel with myself and be ingenious enough to be able to tell the truth and at the same time give no one cause for complaint."

The solution adopted by Machiavelli to solve his dilemma is suggested in a letter written in 1533 by Donato Giannotti to a friend in Venice. Giannotti had been a close friend of Machiavelli and had himself served as secretary to the Ten in the last Florentine Republic from 1527 to 1530. When in 1533 a question had been raised about the accuracy of the edition of Machiavelli's history, Giannotti wrote to his correspondent in Venice:

The History of Machiavelli has been faithfully printed and I can vouch for the fact since I read it

---

[10] However, the autograph drafts of some sections of the *Storie* conserved in the Biblioteca Nazionale in Florence, of which two recently discovered fragments were published by Doctoressa Eugenia Levi (*Bibliofilia*, vol. LXIX, 1969, pp. 309–323) provide interesting data on Machiavelli's method of working.

many years ago and showed to Messer Marco Foscari the original manuscript written in Machiavelli's hand and he also read it all. And I used to see it while Machiavelli was composing it, since, because of the close relationship between us, he imparted to me everything that was on his mind. And on the subject of his sincerity he said to me these very words:

"I cannot write this history from the time when Cosimo came to power to the death of Lorenzo as I would write it if I were in all respects free; the actions will be true and I shall omit nothing only I shall leave in the background the discussions of the general causes of things; for example, I shall describe the events and the happenings that followed Cosimo's taking the state, but I shall leave in the background the discussion of how and by what means and cleverness a single individual came to such a height. Let him who would like really to understand me note well what I make his opponents say; what I would be unwilling to say as coming from myself I shall put into the mouths of the opponents."

Machiavelli had already used direct discourse in the manner of Livy in his *Vita di Castruccio* and, in general, the methods he followed in *The History of Florence* were those already demonstrated to his Florentine friends in the biography. It is hardly necessary to say that Machiavelli had no conception of historical research in the modern sense of the critical study and comparison of sources and the discovery of hitherto unknown documents. His sources, Biondo, Villani, Poggio, Bruni Marchionne di Coppo Stefani, and others gave the well-known facts. Machiavelli's task was to illuminate their significance, to bring men to that *"vera cognizione della storia"* of which he had spoken in the *Discorsi*. It is often said that he applied to his presentation of Florentine history arbitrary principles of interpretation and presuppositions, but it is often forgotten that these very principles and presuppositions were the result of his own historical experience. He interpreted the earlier history of his native city in the light of what he had learned in the stormy period that had begun with the French invasion of 1494.

The second and third books of *The History of Florence* have generally been regarded as Machiavelli's most distinguished historical work. Pasquale Villari considered the second book "one of the masterpieces of our historical literature," and the Swiss scholar Eduard Fueter agreed with this high estimate of that part of Machiavelli's work which described the internal history of Florence from the origins to 1420.[11]

In these books Machiavelli analyzed the political life of the city with particular attention to the importance of factions. One of the themes to which he returned again and again was the contrast between the creative effects of the existence of faction in ancient Rome and its destructive results in Florence. He presented the decline of communal institutions as the result of the fatal tendency to oscillate between tyranny and license.

One of the dramatic episodes in this struggle in the fourteenth-century history of Florence provides a good example of the application of Machiavelli's ideas on how history should be written. In September 1342, a combination of disaffected magnates, bankers, and artisans called in a foreign prince, Walter of Brienne, Duke of Athens, and made him *Signore*, that is, chief executive magistrate, for life. This regime lasted, however, less than a year and, in July 1343, the Duke was expelled by a united effort of all classes and within a few months a more democratic regime excluding the magnates was installed in his place. The principal source available to Machiavelli for the events of this period was the contemporary chronicle of Giovanni Villani, although he may have depended more directly on the versions given in the humanist historians Poggio and Bruni, whose accounts in turn had been based also on Villani.

_____

[11] P. Villari, *Niccolò Machiavelli e suoi tempi illustrati con nuovi documenti*, 4th ed., M. Scherillo, ed. (Milan, 1927), Vol. II, p. 180; E. Fueter, *Geschichte der neueren Historiographie* (Munich, 1938), p. 57.

Machiavelli organized and condensed the story of these months, eliminating much of Villani's colorful but unrelated material, but preserving the essentials of what Villani had to say on the composition of the various factions and the activities of their leaders. In Machiavelli's narrative there are, however, significant additions.

On the occasion of the Duke's being named *Signore* for life, Villani has a description of the stages by which the coup was realized, and he describes how, on the evening of September 7, 1342, the priors and their colleagues went to Santa Croce to make representations to the Duke. He gives no detail of what was said, except that they urged that the traditional liberties of the commune should be maintained. This is enough for Machiavelli, who makes this the occasion of one of the most eloquent of the speeches in direct discourse inserted in the whole of his history.

> We come to you, my Lord, . . . [not] to oppose your plans with force, but only to show you what a heavy load you are taking upon yourself and what a dangerous decision you are making. . . . You are trying to enslave a city which has always been free. . . . Have you considered how important and how strong the name of liberty is in a city like this? No power can overcome it, no period of time can consume it, no other advantage can compensate for it. Think, my Lord, of the troops that are needed to keep such a town in bondage. Foreign ones that you can always command are not enough. . . . It is quite certain that time cannot extinguish the desire for liberty. . . . You must believe then that you have either to hold this town, using the maximum force . . . or to be content with the authority we have given you. We . . . remind you that the only lasting government is one based on the people's will. . . . Do not put yourself into a position where you cannot stay still or go any higher and are therefore forced to fall.

After this great speech, Machiavelli continues by reporting that the arguments of the priors did not in the least soften the obdurate mind of the Duke, who pointed out that he was not robbing the city of liberty but restoring it to her, because those cities alone are in slavery which are disunited while the united are free. Florence, by the operation of faction, had deprived herself of liberty, and he would restore it by uniting all the citizens under one rule.

The priors' speech, for which there is no documentary evidence, is a consequence of Machiavelli's reflection on the real and permanent significance of the events described by Villani. Almost three hundred years later, a famous American turned to Florentine history in search of lessons that might be applied to the newly founded Republic. John Adams wrote his long, rambling *Defense of the Constitution of the Government of the United States* in 1787. The second volume of this extensive inquiry into historical precedents was devoted to the experience of the Italian republics at the end of the Middle Ages and in the Renaissance. Adams depended for his account on the histories of Machiavelli, Guicciardini, Nerli, Nardi, and others, and incorporated large sections from their works without being scrupulous in the use of quotation marks. His method was in this respect very like that of Machiavelli, who had made a similar use of his predecessors.

Adams regarded fourteenth-century Florence as a particularly instructive example of a struggle for liberty, and he was also obviously fascinated by Machiavelli's general remarks on why faction had been a healthy condition in the Roman republic and yet fatal to the cause of liberty when it appeared in Florence.

On the merits of the regime established after the expulsion of the Duke of Athens, Adams took issue with Machiavelli. The latter, describing the measures adopted after the fall of the Duke, had remarked that if only the nobility had been content to be moderate, the republic would have been established on a firm basis. And he had further declared that it seemed after the new constitution had been put into effect that all causes of dissension had ceased.

Adams commented:

> It is impossible to read these reflections with any
> patience. It would be as wise to say that the nations
> would be quiet and happy under a despot if the
> despot would be moderate. . . . Machiavelli is as
> clear and full for a mixed government as any writer;
> but the noble invention of the negative of an execu-
> tive upon a legislature in two branches which is the
> only remedy in contests between nobles and com-
> mons seems never to have entered his thoughts; and
> nothing is more entertaining than that mist which
> is perpetually before eyes so piercing, so capable of
> looking far through the hearts and deeds of men as
> his, for want of that thought. "There seemed to be
> no seeds of future dissensions left in Florence." No
> seeds! Not one seed had been eradicated. All the
> seeds that ever existed remained in full vigor. The
> seeds were in the human heart.

This brief excerpt from what might be called a dialogue between Adams and Machiavelli brings vividly
before us the fact that the language of historical interpretation not only in the Renaissance but also in the
eighteenth century was very different from that which
we use today. In spite of Adams' scolding criticism, our
first impulse is to say that he and Machiavelli share the
same view of the nature and function of history. For
what is Adams doing but applying or trying to apply the
very methods which Machiavelli had recommended at
the beginning of the *Discorsi*? There is the same emphasis on systematization and on generalization from the
examples provided by history. There is the same view
of an unchanging human nature. There is the same
search for the secret of a polity which will guarantee
liberty and restrain license, which will provide security
against the degenerative forces of human nature. The
path which Machiavelli felt had been followed by no one
has become a broad highway.

Yet if Machiavelli can be considered from one point of
view as one of the founders of the historiography of the

Enlightenment, there is in his interpretation of the history of Florence evidence of a broader vision, more reflective and less concerned with the immediate application of lessons of the past. This deeper understanding of the process of historical development was in part the product of Machiavelli's progressive disillusionment. The hopes which he had still cherished in 1515 had given way to the despair, irony, and doubt which are reflected in some of the letters of the later period. Although he could still write the eloquent appeal to liberty put into the mouth of the orator of the Signoria addressing the Duke, he had no longer much hope that any constitutional provisions could ensure the maintenance of a liberty which had died in the hearts of men. On the rare occasions when liberty is secured for a brief period, it may be that the result is obtained without striving for it.

The perpetual mist which Adams thought clouded the clear vision of Machiavelli may be in reality a heightened perception of the ambiguities and ironies in the affairs of men and the realization that there were areas of political life beyond human control or prediction, as there were historical situations not susceptible of any single explanation. All Machiavelli's skill in avoiding explicit judgment on the Medicean regime cannot conceal a retrospective sense of tragedy. In the splendid conclusion to the last book, the death of Lorenzo the Magnificent and the consequences which follow are presented as if they were outside the usual course of nature, like the bolt of lightning that destroyed the highest pinnacle on the dome of the cathedral.

Machiavelli's search for the true savor of history in the past experience of Florence had therefore in the end brought him to a view very different from that which he had proclaimed at the beginning of *The Prince* and the *Discorsi*. There is now less emphasis on an impassioned plea for a "science of history" comparable to the sciences of medicine and jurisprudence. Although we still have many of the features of the "true use of history"—speeches which give us what ought to have been said, lessons which are universally applicable, sometimes on slender evidence—the whole panorama of Florentine history as Machiavelli gives it to us shows that he has become more aware that history is less a weapon for altering the present and controlling the future than it is a means of understanding how the present came to be what it is.

Note on the Selection of Texts

Machiavelli's ideas on the nature of history and its educational value are most fully expressed in *The Prince* and in the *Discourses on the First Ten Books of Titus Livius*. These works are so generally available in many editions and in a number of English translations that no excerpts from them have been included in this volume.

The first two selections here included, the *Description of the Affairs of France* and the *Discourse on Florentine Affairs After the Death of Lorenzo*, show how Machiavelli applied historical analysis to the consideration of contemporary problems.

The Life of Castruccio Castracani of Lucca is a kind of literary exercise that Machiavelli dashed off in a hurry to show his friends an example of the method and style he proposed to follow in executing the major commission he had received from Cardinal Giulio and the Florentine *Studio* to write *The History of Florence*. Of this latter work, Machiavelli's historical masterpiece, too long to reproduce here in its entirety, I have chosen to include two considerable portions: Books II through IV, which trace the history of Florence in both internal and external aspects from its origin to the return of Cosimo de' Medici from Venice in 1434; Books VII and VIII, which deal with the later years of Cosimo, the brief five-year rule of Piero, and the government of Lorenzo the Magnificent, closing with the latter's death in 1492.

Bibliographical Note

The most useful critical edition of the works of Machiavelli is that published by Feltrinelli and edited by Sergio Bertelli and Franco Gaeta (8 volumes, Milan, 1960–65). It contains excellent introductions and bibliographies. The most recent English translation of most of the works is that of Allen Gilbert, *Machiavelli: The Chief Works and Others* (3 volumes, Durham, 1965).

The best biography is by Roberto Ridolfi, *Vita di Niccolò Machiavelli* (Rome, 1954), English translation by Cecil Grayson (Chicago, 1963).

On Machiavelli's thought, see Federico Chabod, *Machiavelli and the Renaissance* (London, 1958); Felix Gilbert, *Machiavelli and Guicciardini: Politics and History in Sixteenth Century Florence* (Princeton, 1965); J. H. Whitfield, *Machiavelli* (Oxford, 1947); Felix Raab, *The English Face of Machiavelli: A Changing Interpretation* (London, 1964). A very satisfactory short account is provided by J. R. Hale, *Machiavelli and Renaissance Italy* (New York, 1960).

Chronology

May 1469	Niccolò Machiavelli born in Florence. In December of the same year, Lorenzo de' Medici succeeds his father as first citizen.
April 1478	Pazzi Conspiracy against the Medici.
April 1492	Death of Lorenzo de' Medici.
September 1494	Charles VIII of France invades Italy.
November 1494	Piero de' Medici exiled from Florence.
May 1498	Execution of Savonarola.
1498–1512	Machiavelli Second Chancellor of the Florentine Republic and Secretary of the Ten. Missions to Cesare Borgia, Rome, France, and the Empire.
1503–1513	Julius II Pope.
September 1512	Restoration of the Medici. Machiavelli deprived of office.
July–December 1513	Machiavelli writes *The Prince*.
1513–1521	Leo X (Medici) Pope.
1516–1519 (*ca.*)	Composition of the *Discorsi*.
1519	The dialogue, *Arte della guerra*.
1520	*Vita di Castruccio* and contract to write *The History of Florence*.
August 1521	*Arte della guerra* published in Florence.
1522–1523	Adrian VI Pope.
1523–1534	Clement VII (Medici) Pope.
May 1527	Sack of Rome by Imperial troops. The Medici again expelled from Florence. Formation of the last Florentine Republic.

June 1527	Death of Machiavelli at Florence.
1531	First edition of the *Discorsi* (Blado, Rome).
1532	First edition of *The Prince* and *The History of Florence* (Blado, Rome).

Description of the
Affairs of France

The kings and the Crown of France are stronger, richer, and more powerful today than ever before, for the following reasons.

The Crown has become rich as it is passed on according to heredity. If the king has no children and has nobody of his own line to suceed him, his substance, estates, and personal property are all left to the Crown. Since this has happened to a number of kings, the Crown has grown rich because of the numerous states which have accrued to it, like the Duchy of Anjou, and as in the case of the present king who has no male heirs, the Duchy of Orléans and the state of Milan, both of which will go to the Crown. The result is that today all the good fiefs in France belong to the Crown and not to individual barons.

Another very important reason for the king's strength is that in the past France was not united, owing to powerful barons, who had the audacity and courage to take sides against the king, such men as the Duke of Guyenne, the Duke of Bourbon, and the like, all of whom are very submissive today. This makes the king stronger.

Another reason is that all the neighboring princes felt encouraged to attack the kingdom of France, because there was always a Duke of Guyenne, Burgundy, or Flanders to give them a helping hand, allow them passage, and give them shelter: as happened when the English were at war with France. They always kept the king busy with the help of the Dukes of Brittany, and the Dukes of Burgundy did likewise with the Dukes of Bourbon, and the like. Now that Brittany, Guyenne, the Bourbonnais, and most of Burgundy are entirely subject to

1

France, not only are the princes deprived of this means of harrying the kingdom of France, but these states are their enemies. The king, too, is all the stronger for possessing these states, and his enemy weaker.

Yet another reason is that the richest and most powerful barons in France today are of royal blood and lineage. The Crown could come to one of them if those nearer in line were to die. So each one keeps close links with the Crown, hoping that either he or his children will reach that position. Rebellion or enmity would do more harm than good. This nearly happened to the present king when he was captured at the battle of Brittany, where he had gone to help the Duke against the French. There was controversy after King Charles' death as to whether, because of his dereliction and defection from the Crown, he should have lost the right to succeed. He was a wealthy man, however, because of his economies, and able to spend money, and so forth. Besides, the only one who could have been king if he was passed over was a little boy, Monseigneur of Angoulême in fact, so for the above reasons and because he had some supporters he was made king.

The last reason is this: The estates of the barons of France are not divided up among the heirs as happens in Germany and in most of Italy, but they all go to the firstborn, who is the real heir. The other brothers allow this, and with the help of their eldest brother, take up a military career in the hope of reaching a rank and status in that profession that will enable them to buy an estate. They live for this ambition. The result is that today the French men at arms are the best in the world, because they are noblemen and sons of lords, and their aim is to reach that rank.

The infantry trained in France cannot be very good, as they have not fought for a long time, and have no experience at all. In the provinces they are all common professional soldiers, and they are so submissive to the nobles, who control all their movements, that they are cowards. That is why the king does not use them in war, because they put up a poor fight, although there are the Gascons, whom the king does use, and who are a little

2

better than the rest. This is because they come from the Spanish border and have something of the Spaniard about them. But from what we have seen for many years now, they have proved to be thieves rather than brave men. Yet they give a good account of themselves in siege warfare, although they are poor in open country. This makes them the opposite of the Germans and Swiss who are unequalled in open country but useless in siege warfare. I think this is because they cannot keep the same dispositions in this type of fighting that they maintain in the field; and so the king of France always uses either Swiss or German troops, because his men at arms do not trust the Gascons when faced with the enemy. If the infantry were of the same standard as the French men at arms, there is no doubt that they would have the confidence to defend themselves against any prince.

By nature, the French are fierce rather than strong and quick. Anyone who can stand up to the violence of their first onslaught finds that they collapse, lose heart, and become as timid as women. They cannot bear discomfort and soon neglect things, so that they are easily surprised and beaten. We have often seen proof of this in the Kingdom of Naples, most recently on the Garigliano, where they outnumbered the Spaniards by half, and everyone expected them to swallow the Spaniards up at any moment. And yet because it was the beginning of winter the rains were very heavy, and the French began to go off one by one into the neighboring towns to more comfortable surroundings. The camp was left undermanned and undisciplined, and against all logic the Spaniards won. The same thing would have happened to the Venetians, who would not have lost the battle of Vailà if they had played along with the French for at least ten days. But Bartolomeo d'Alviano's impetuosity was countered by an even greater violence. The same thing happened to the Spaniards at Ravenna. If they had not gone near the French, they would have unsettled them because of the lack of organization in the French camp and the shortage of food supplies, held up by the Venetians near Ferrara. Other supplies from Bologna would have been blocked by the Spaniards. Because one side had little good advice

3

and the other even less judgment, the French army was victorious, though it was a bloody victory. It was a bitter struggle and would have been more so if each army had relied on the same kind of troops for its mainstay. But the chief fighting power in the French army lay with the men at arms, and in the Spanish army with the infantry. This meant that the slaughter was not so heavy. Anyone who wants to beat the French must beware of their first onslaught, and by keeping them waiting he will conquer them for the reasons already mentioned. That is why Caesar said the French were more than men to begin with and less than women at the end.

France is rich and affluent because of her size and the usefulness of her great rivers. And yet produce and manual labor are worth little or nothing because of the shortage of money among the people. They can hardly get together enough to pay the dues to their lord, although these are very small. The reason for this is that they have no market for their produce, because each man harvests the same crop. If someone wanted to sell a bushel of corn in a town he would not find a buyer, because everyone would be trying to sell. The gentry spend none of the money they take from their dependents except on clothing. They have enough cattle for their own needs, huge flocks of poultry, and lakes and reserves stocked with all kinds of game; and this is true of all the provinces. All the money goes to the nobility, and today they have a great deal of it; whereas the people think themselves rich if they have a florin.

The French prelates receive two-fifths of the kingdom's revenue, because many bishoprics have both temporal and spiritual power. Then as they can live on their own produce, the sums of money that come into their hands never leave them again, prelates and clergy being miserly by nature. The money that goes to the chapters and colleges of churches is spent on silver, jewels, and rich ornaments for the churches. So the churches' own property, together with the prelates' private possessions, both in money and plate, is worth a vast fortune.

Prelates always play the major part in deliberations and in the management of the affairs of the French

4

Crown and state. The other lords take no interest, knowing they will be called on to put the proposals into practice. In this way both are happy, some making plans, others carrying them out. Some old men do take part in the government, however, old soldiers who can advise the prelates, who have no experience of war, when such things have to be discussed.

In France benefices are granted by the colleges, according to an ordinance they obtained a long time ago from the popes. When their archbishop or bishop dies, the canons meet and confer the benefice on the person among them who seems to deserve it. Often there are quarrels, because there is always someone who presses his candidacy with money, while another does so by his virtues and good works. The monks appoint abbots in the same way. Other small livings are granted by the bishops in charge of them. And if at some time the king wants to contravene this ordinance and elect a bishop of his own choice, he has to use force, because they deny possession. If force is used, once the king is dead they withdraw possession from the prelate and grant it to the man of their own choice.

It is a characteristic of the French to want what belongs to other people; then they are generous with their own and other people's possessions. A Frenchman will steal anything to enjoy it, spoil it, and share it with the person he has stolen it from; quite different from the Spaniard who never lets you see anything he has stolen from you.

France is very frightened of the English because of their invasions and the harm they did to the kingdom some time ago. The English name is still feared by the people, as they do not realize that French conditions have now changed. France is now armed, well prepared and united, and controls those states that the English used as bases, such as the Duchies of Brittany and Burgundy. The English on the other hand are out of training. It is a long time since they were at war; no Englishman alive today has ever looked an enemy in the face. Then there is no one left to challenge them on land, except for the Archduke.

The French might fear the wisdom and vigilance of the Spaniards, but if the Spanish king wants to attack France, he comes up against great difficulties. The route from his own state to the passes over the Pyrenees into France is so long and goes through such barren country, that if the French sent their troops to the passes leading to Perpignan and Guyenne, the Spanish army could be broken up, if not because of lack of help, at least owing to lack of supplies, since they have to come so far. The country they would have behind them is so barren it is almost deserted, and where it is inhabited, it hardly produces enough to feed the local population. Hence, the French have little fear of a Spanish threat from the Pyrenees.

The French have nothing to fear from the Flemish. The Flemish do not produce enough to feed themselves because of their cold climate. This applies particularly to grain and wine, which they must import from Burgundy, Picardy, and other French states. Then the people of Flanders live by manufactures, and these goods and commodities are sold at the French fairs at Lyons and Paris. There is no market for them along the sea boundary, nor in Germany where production is even greater. If their trade with France ended, they would have nowhere to send their goods, and they would be left without food and without a market for their manufactures. So the Flemish will never make war on France unless they are forced into it.

France is afraid of the Swiss because of their proximity and the sudden attacks they can make; these cannot be prevented in time because they are so swift. The Swiss confine themselves to pillaging and raiding. The nearest French towns are well fortified, and the Swiss cannot advance very far, as they have no artillery or cavalry. Then they are naturally more suited to campaigning in open country than to siege warfare. The French dislike coming to grips with them in that area because their infantry is not good enough to stand up to the Swiss, and men at arms are of no use without infantry. Again the terrain is not one where lancers and men on horseback can maneuver easily; and the Swiss dislike crossing their boundaries to go down into the plain. They pay no attention to the big, fortified towns, as I have said. They are afraid, quite rightly, that their supplies would be cut off and that if they went down into the plain, they would not be able to get back again.

The French are not afraid of any threat from the direction of Italy because of the Apennines and the large towns they possess at their feet. If anyone wanted to attack the French state successfully with such barren country behind him, he would either have to starve, or avoid the big towns (which would be mad), or start laying siege to them. So the French have no fears about Italy. Besides, there is no prince in Italy capable of attacking them, and Italy is not united as it was at the time of the Romans.

France has no fears for her southern borders, as they are bounded by the sea. In the harbors there are always plenty of ships—some belonging to the king, others belonging to his subjects—to defend that area from an unexpected attack. There is time to take precautions against a premeditated attack, because it takes time to organize and plan, and everybody gets to know about it. France usually keeps garrisons of men at arms in these provinces in order to play safe.

Little is spent on policing towns because the subjects are very well behaved, and it is unusual for fortresses to be kept garrisoned inside the kingdom. On the frontiers where more might be spent, as this is where the men at arms are stationed, nothing is spent in fact, because there is time to prepare for a heavy attack, which itself takes time to plan and launch.

The French people are humble and very submissive, and they hold their king in great awe. They live very cheaply because food is so plentiful, and each one has some property of his own. They wear coarse clothes of cheap cloth; and neither the men nor the women ever dress in silk of any kind because they would be criticized by the gentry.

According to the latest calculations, there are one hundred and six bishoprics in the French kingdom, including the eighteen archbishoprics. There are one million, seven hundred parishes, including seven hundred and forty abbeys. The priories are not included.

I have been unable to find out the ordinary and extraordinary revenue of the Crown. I asked a number of people, and they all replied that it was as much as the king wanted. However, some say that part of the ordinary revenue known as the king's ready money is derived from *gabelles* (on bread, wine, meat, and such) amounting to one million, seven hundred thousand *scudi*. Any extra revenue needed comes from *tailles*, and these are increased or lowered as the king pleases. But if this is not enough, loans are instituted, which are seldom paid back. They are requested in royal letters in these terms: "Our lord the king commends himself to you, and because he is short of money, begs you to lend him the amount mentioned in the letter." This is paid straight to the local tax gatherer. There is one in each town who collects everything that comes in from *gabelles, tailles*, and loans alike.

Where money and dues are concerned, the lands subject to the Crown observe no other law but the king's, as has been explained.

The barons' authority over their subjects is complete. Their revenue is bread, wine, meat, as has been said, and so much every year per hearth, but not more than six or eight *soldi* per hearth every three months. *Tailles* and loans cannot be imposed without the consent of the king, and this is seldom granted.

The Crown exacts no contribution from them except for the salt tax, and the king never subjects them to the *taille* unless he is very hard pressed.

The king's practice as regards extraordinary expenditure, for wars or other things, is to command the *trésoriers* to pay the soldiers. This is done through the men who inspect the troops. Gentlemen and those in receipt of a pension go to the *généraux* and are given a voucher —that is, a bill for their payment—every month. These gentlemen and pensioners then go every three months to the tax collector for the province where they live and are paid immediately. There are two hundred of the king's gentlemen. They are paid twenty *scudi* a month in the way described above. There is a commander in charge of each hundred. These used to be Ravel and Vidames.

There is no record of the number of pensioners. They receive as much or as little as the king likes. Their incentive is the hope of reaching a higher rank, so there is no clear system.

The duty of the *généraux* of France is to collect so much per hearth and so much for the *taille*, with the king's consent, and to see that the ordinary and extraordinary expenses—that is, the vouchers mentioned above —are paid at the right time.

The *trésoriers* hold the money and pay it out according to the orders and vouchers of the *généraux*.

The Grand Chancellor's office carries *Merum imperium*. He can reprieve and condemn as he likes, even in the case of capital charges, without the king's consent. He can defer legal proceedings for defaulting litigants and confer benefices by royal consent. Because reprieves are granted by royal decree sealed with the great royal seal, it is he who keeps the great royal seal. He has a salary of ten thousand francs a year, with two thousand francs for entertaining. Entertaining means giving lunch and dinner to those members of the Council who are in the Grand Chancellor's train, lawyers and other gentlemen of his suite, who want to eat with him, as very often happens.

The annual payment that the king of France used to make to the king of England was fifty thousand francs, and it was compensation for expenses incurred by the present king of England's father in the Duchy of Brittany. This has now ceased and is no longer paid.

There is only one Grand Seneschal in France at the moment. But when there are several seneschals (not Grand Seneschals, as there is only one) they are in charge of the regular and special men at arms, who are obliged to obey them because of their high office.

There are as many governors of provinces as the king wishes, and they are paid as he likes. Their appointments are yearly or for life, according to the king's pleasure. The other governors, down to the lieutenants of small cities, are all appointed by the king. I should point out that all the offices in the kingdom are either given or sold by the king and no one else.

The Estates are summoned every year, sometimes in August, sometimes in October or January, as the king wishes. The expenditure and regular income for that year is accounted for by the *généraux;* then the revenue is apportioned according to the expenditure. And pensions and the number of pensioners are raised or cut, as the king sees fit.

There is no record of the number of payments made to gentlemen and pensioners. The *Chambre des Comptes* does not have to give its approval; the authorization of the king is all that is needed.

It is the business of the *Chambre des Comptes* to check the accounts of everyone who deals with the Crown finances, such as the *généraux,* the *trésoriers,* and the tax collectors.

The University of Paris is financed out of the incomes of the college foundations, small though these are.

There are five *Parlements:* Paris, Rouen, Toulouse, Bordeaux, and Dauphiné, and there is no right of appeal from any of them.

There are four main universities: Paris, Orléans, Bourges, and Poitiers. Then there are Tours and Angers, but they are not much good.

The garrisons are stationed where the king wants them, and there are as many as he likes, both as regards artillery and men. All the same, every city has some pieces of artillery among its equipment. And during the last two years, quite a number of pieces have been made in many different parts of the kingdom at the expense of the towns, where taxes have been put up a penny per animal or per measure. Usually, when the kingdom is not afraid of an attack, there are four garrisons: in Guyenne, Picardy, Burgundy, and Provence. Then they are changed and built up more in some places than in others, depending on the threat.

I have made careful inquiries about the king's yearly allowance, and I find that he is given as much as he asks for his own household and personal expenses.

There are four hundred archers appointed to guard the king's person. Among these are one hundred Scottish bowmen. Each man gets three hundred francs a year and a cloak in the king's livery. There are twenty-four members of the king's bodyguard, who are always at his side, and they each receive four hundred francs a year. Their commander is Monseigneur d'Aubigny Cursores, and their captain is Gabriel.

The footguards are German, and one hundred of them are paid twelve francs a month. At one time there were as many as three hundred with a wage of ten francs; they each received two uniforms every year, one for summer and one for winter—that is, the livery doublet and hose. And the hundred men of the bodyguard had silk doublets. This was in the time of King Charles.

The quartermasters are the men who have the job of finding lodgings for the court. There are thirty-two of them, and they receive three hundred francs a year and a cloak in livery. They have four marshals who receive six hundred francs each. This is the way they find lodgings: They divide into four groups. One group stays in the place the court has just left, with a marshal or with his deputy if he is not at court, to see that the landlords are duly rewarded. One group travels with the king. The other group goes on ahead of him to prepare lodgings for the court. The fourth group goes on to the place the king will reach the day after. And they are so wonderfully organized that everybody has a room when they arrive, even the whores.

The *prévôt de l'hôtel* is a man who always follows the king's person, and he has supreme power. Wherever the court goes, his bench is always the chief one. And the people of the town where he is can be taxed by him as if by their own lieutenant. Those who are imprisoned on criminal charges by him may not appeal to the *Parlements*. His normal salary is six thousand francs. He has two civil judges, each paid six hundred francs a year by the king, and a lieutenant in criminal law who has thirty archers paid as above. He hears both civil and criminal cases, and once the plaintiff has met the defendant in his presence the case can be settled.

11

There are eight stewards of the royal household, but their salary is not fixed, some of them getting a thousand francs, some more, some less, as the king wishes. The chief steward, who succeeded Monseigneur de Chaumont, is Monseigneur de la Palisse, whose father once held the same office. He gets two thousand francs, and his only duty is to supervise the other stewards.

The Admiral of France commands all the fleets and is responsible for them and for all the harbors in the kingdom. He can commandeer and build ships for the navy as he pleases. Préjan is Admiral at present, with a salary of ten thousand francs.

There is no fixed number of knights of the order since there are as many as the king wants. When they are knighted, they swear to defend the Crown and never to attack it, and they can never be deprived of their knighthood except by death. Most of them receive four thousand francs a year, but some receive less. Not everybody is given the same rank.

The Chamberlains' duty is to converse with the king, to have access to his chamber, and to advise him; in fact, they have the highest status in the kingdom. They receive a big salary: six, eight, ten thousand francs. Some are unpaid because the king sometimes makes a man a Chamberlain as an honor, even foreigners. But they have the privilege of exemption from taxes in the kingdom. At court they eat at the Chamberlains' table, which is second only to the king's.

The *Grand Ecuyer* is always with the king. His job is to supervise the king's twelve grooms, just as the Grand Seneschal, the Chief Steward, and the Lord Chamberlain have charge of their own men. He is responsible for the king's horses, sees him mount and dismount, takes care of his accoutrements, and carries his sword before him.

The gentlemen of the *Conseil du roi* all have a salary of between six and eight thousand francs, as the king pleases. They are Monseigneur de Paris, Monseigneur de Boucicaut, the *Bailli* of Amiens, Monseigneur de Bussy, and the Grand Chancellor. In practice, Robertet and Monseigneur de Paris decide everything.

Nobody keeps a table now since the Cardinal of Rouen

died. Since there is no Grand Chancellor, the Bishop of Paris has taken over those duties.

The reason why the king of France is laying claim to the State of Milan is that his grandfather married a daughter of the Duke of Milan who died without male heirs. Duke Gian Galeazzo had two daughters and I do not know how many sons. One of the daughters was called Valentina, and she was married to Duke Louis of Orléans, grandfather of this King Louis, who is also descended from the line of Pépin. When Duke Giovan Galeazzo died, his son, Duke Philip, succeeded him, and he died without legitimate heirs, leaving only an illegitimate daughter. Then the state was usurped by the Sforzas, illegally as they say. And for this reason, they maintain that the state should pass to the successors and heirs of the Lady Valentina. And the day the Orléans family was allied by marriage to the Milanese, a serpent was added to the three lilies on their coat of arms, as is still seen today.

In each French parish there is a man who is paid a good wage by the parish, and he is known as the *franc archer*. It is his duty to keep a good horse and to be well armed in order to meet any request of the king. If the king is out of the kingdom engaged in a war, or for other reasons, they must ride to the provinces where the kingdom is being attacked, or where there is fear of attack. They number one million, seven hundred, according to the parishes.

The quartermasters are obliged to find lodgings for everyone who follows the court. Usually every respectable man in a town will give hospitality to courtiers. The court has fixed charges which everyone observes, so that no one should have cause to complain, neither the host nor the guest. The charges are one *soldo* per day for a room with a bed and a bunk, to be changed at least once a week; two *denari* each per day for linen, that is, tablecloths and napkins, vinegar and verjuice. The linen should be changed at least twice a week, but depending on the quantity the town possesses, it is changed more or less frequently as the guest himself asks. It is also the host's duty to wash up, sweep, and make the beds.

13

Two *denari* per day are paid for each horse's stabling. There is no obligation to feed the horses, all they must do is clean out the stable. Many people pay less, out of the goodness of their own hearts or their hosts', but this is the usual court charge.

I have looked into the more recent reasons for the English claim to the French throne and find them to be as follows. Charles, King of France, the sixth of that name, married Catherine, his natural and legitimate daughter, to Henry, natural and legitimate son of Henry, King of England. In the contract, without making any mention of Charles VII, later King of France, he made Henry, his son-in-law and Catherine's husband, heir to the kingdom of France after his death (that is, Charles' VI's death), besides giving Catherine a dowry. And should Henry die before his father-in-law, Charles VI, leaving legitimate and natural sons of his own, then these heirs should also succeed Charles VI. This was not put into effect because Charles VII had been passed over by his father, which is against the law. The English, on the other hand, say that Charles VII was born of an incestuous alliance.

There are two archbishoprics in England, twenty bishoprics, and fifty-two thousand parishes.

Discourse on Florentine Affairs
After the Death of Lorenzo

The reason why Florence has always changed her forms of government frequently is that she has never had a thoroughgoing republic or monarchy. You cannot say that a monarchy is stable when policies are carried out according to the will of one man and agreed on with the consent of many. Nor can you believe a republic will last if it does not satisfy those aspirations which generally need satisfying if a republic is to survive. The truth of this can be seen if one considers the regimes the city has had since 1393. To begin with the reform made at that time by Maso degli Albizzi, it will be seen that the aim was to give the city the constitution of a republic governed by aristocrats, but the constitution had so many faults it did not last forty years; it would have lasted even less had it not been for the Visconti wars which kept the city united. One of the faults was the length of the intervals between the holding of electoral scrutinies, where rigging was easy and the choice might be a bad one. Men change easily and the good become wicked, and moreover citizens were eligible for office for a long period of time, so it could well happen that the initial choice was good but the actual draw bad. Besides this there was no built-in check against the nobles creating their own followings, which are the ruin of a state. Again the Signoria had too little standing and too much power, since it could dispose of the lives and property of citizens without appeal and could call the people to an assembly. Whenever a respected citizen could dominate or manipulate the Signoria it came to be not the defender of the regime but the means of bringing it down. Moreover as we have said, the Signoria had a bad reputation: It was

15

often made up of base young men; it lasted for a short time; and as it did no serious business, it could earn no respect.

There was another defect of no small importance in that regime, and this was that private citizens could be found advising on public matters. This kept up the reputation of the private citizens and undermined that of the public officials. It did away with the magistrates' authority and prestige, which is against all public order. Added to these irregularities was another which affected everything, and this was that the people had no part in the government. All these things together caused endless trouble, and as I have said, if the foreign wars had not kept the city stable, the regime would have collapsed sooner than it did. After this, Cosimo's regime was set up, which tended more toward a monarchy than a republic. If it lasted longer than the other, there were two reasons: one was that it had been set up with the people's support, and the other that it was ruled by two men of great wisdom, Cosimo and his grandson, Lorenzo. Yet it was so weakened by Cosimo's policy having to be debated by the many that he was in danger of losing it several times. This was the reason for the frequent assemblies and exiles that took place during that regime. Then it finally fell when King Charles passed through the city. After this, the city wanted to adopt a republican constitution, but it did not make up its mind to stand by it so that it would last, because that system did not satisfy the aspirations of all the citizens, and yet the city could not punish them. It was so unsatisfactory and so far from being a real republic, that a life gonfalonier could easily make himself ruler if he was clever and unscrupulous; while if he was good and weak, he could easily be got rid of, and the whole government be overthrown.

It would take a long time to put forward all the reasons for this, so I will only mention one. The gonfalonier had no one near him who could defend him if he was good, or restrain and correct him if he was bad. The reason why all these governments were failures is that the reforms they underwent were carried out not for the public good but in order to strengthen the party. Yet the security of the party was never achieved, because one wing was always dissatisfied, and this could be put to very good use by anyone who wanted change.

We should now discuss the kind of government there was from 1512 to the present day, with its strengths and weaknesses. But I will not do so because it is so recent and everyone knows about it. Since it has come to an end with the Duke's death, new kinds of government must be discussed, and I feel that it cannot be wrong to say what occurs to me, in order to show my allegiance to your Holiness. First I will give the opinion of many other people, as I think I have heard it expressed; then I will add my own opinion, and if I am mistaken in this, your Holiness must excuse me for being more loving than wise.

Some people think that no more stable government could be set up than the one that existed in the time of Cosimo and Lorenzo. Others would like it to be broader. Those who want a government like Cosimo's say that things easily return to their origins, and since it is natural for the citizens of Florence to honor your house, to enjoy the benefits they received from it, to love the things it loved, and since this has become a habit over the last sixty years, they could not fail to experience the same feelings, if they were treated in the same way again. They believe that there are very few who think differently because of a contrary habit and that these could easily be silenced. They add to these arguments the argument of necessity, saying that Florence cannot do without a ruler. If it must have a ruler, it is much better for him to come from the house they are used to honoring, than from somewhere else with less reputation, which would mean that everyone was less satisfied.

The reply to this view is that a regime of this kind is dangerous, if only because it is weak. If Cosimo's regime had so many weaknesses in his time as have been alleged above, they would be doubled in a similar regime today, because the city, the citizens, and the conditions are different from what they were then. In short, it is im-

17

possible to set up a regime in Florence that will last and yet be similar to that one.

First of all that regime had the goodwill of the people, and this one has not. At that time the citizens had never known a government in Florence that seemed more democratic than that one. Now they have found one which they feel is more just and under which they are happier. Then there were no armies or powers in Italy that the Florentines could not resist with their own arms, even on their own; now that Spain and France are here, they must be allied to one or the other. If their ally loses, they are immediately at the mercy of the victor, which did not happen before. The citizens were used to paying fairly heavy taxes; now they have lost the habit, either because it became impossible or because it had fallen into abeyance, and to try to accustom them to it again would be dangerous and would arouse their hatred. The Medici in power then had been brought up and educated with the citizens and behaved with so much familiarity that they had their goodwill; now they have grown so grand that they have lost all sense of their common citizenship and the same intimacy can no longer exist, nor, consequently, can goodwill. Considering these differences in conditions and personalities, there can be no greater mistake than to think that such dissimilar material can be molded in the same way as before. And if, as we said above, the old regime was in danger of collapsing every ten years, now it would actually collapse. It is wrong to believe that men easily go back to living in the old accustomed ways. This is true when they like the old ways better than the new; but when they do not, they only go back to them if they are forced to, and only for as long as the pressure lasts.

Besides this, although it is true that Florence must have a ruler, and that if the choice lies between leaders who are private citizens, then she would prefer one from the House of Medici rather than another house; nevertheless if the choice is between a private citizen and a public official, then she will always prefer a public official, wherever he might come from.

Some think that the regime could not fall without an

attack from outside, and they believe they would always be in time to make friends with their assailants. They are very much mistaken. Most often alliances are not made with the people who have most power, but with those who have most opportunity to harm you, or with those whom your mind and fancy persuade you to like. Then it may easily happen that your ally loses and finds himself at the mercy of the conqueror. The latter might not want to come to an agreement with you, either because you have no time to ask him, or because he has conceived a hatred of you because of your alliance with his enemies.

Lodovico, Duke of Milan, would have come to an agreement with King Louis XII of France if he had been able to. King Federigo would have made one with him, too, if he could. They each lost their countries because there was no agreement. Thousands of reasons arise to stop one from being made. So when all is said, one cannot call such a state secure or stable when it has so many reasons for instability, and it cannot possibly appeal to your Holiness and your friends.

As for those people who would like a broader government than this, I would say that if it is not broadened so as to become a well-ordered republic, its breadth would be more likely to make it fall sooner. If they would give details of the structure they would like, then I would answer them in detail, but while they confine themselves to general terms I can only reply in the same way. This reply must suffice. As for my rejection of Cosimo's regime, and my view that no stable government can be set up that is not either a true monarchy or a true republic, because all forms of government in between are defective, the reason is perfectly clear: A monarchy has only one way in which to evolve, which is downwards to a republic; similarly, a republic can only rise toward a monarchy. Intermediate forms of government can go either way, up toward a monarchy or down toward a republic. This is the reason for their instability.

If your Holiness wants to set up a stable government in Florence to your own glory and for the safety of your friends, your Holiness can only create a true monarchy or a properly organized republic. Everything else is use-less and shortlived. I will not go into the details of a monarchy, because of the difficulties that would arise in setting one up and because the instrument is lacking. Your Holiness must understand that in all cities where there is a great degree of equality among citizens, a monarchy can only be created with the utmost difficulty, and in cities where there is great inequality among citizens a republic cannot be set up. If one wanted to set up a republic in Milan, where there is great inequality, one would have to do away with all the nobility and reduce them to the level of the rest. They are so unruly that laws are not enough to control them, and they need a live voice and royal authority to keep them in order. On the other hand, in order to create a monarchy in Florence, where there is a great sense of equality, one would first have to introduce inequality and create nobles with castles and villas, who would join the prince in suppressing the city and the whole province with their armies and their factions. A prince alone, without the nobles, cannot bear the weight of a monarchy. There must be something between him and the people to help him bear that weight. This can be seen in all monar-chical regimes, particularly in the kingdom of France. The gentry rule the people, the princes the gentry, and the king the princes. However, as it is difficult, inhuman, and unworthy for anyone who wants to be thought good and merciful to set up a monarchy where a republic is what is wanted, or a republic where a monarchy is required, I will stop discussing monar-chies and turn to republics, both because Florence is very well suited to this form of government and because it is rumored that your Holiness is very well disposed toward it. It is believed that you are only postponing setting one up, because you want to find a system whereby you would still have great power in Florence and your friends would be secure. As I think I have found one, I want your Holiness to know my ideas, so that you can use them if they are any good, and they will be a token of my devotion to you. You will see that in this republic of mine your power is not only maintained but increased, your friends are honored and secure, and the rest of the people have obvious reasons for satisfaction.

I respectfully beg your Holiness not to criticize or praise this discourse before having read it all. And again I beg you not to be frightened by some changes in administrative structure, because when things are not well organized, the less there remains of the old, the less there remains that is bad.

Anyone setting up a republic must allow for the three different classes of men who exist in every city: the upper, the middle, and the lower. Although there is that equality in Florence that I mentioned above, nevertheless there are in the town some superior people who feel that they should have precedence over the others. They must be satisfied within the republican structure. The last regime fell for no other reason than that it did not meet these aspirations.

These people can only be satisfied if the chief offices in the republic are clothed in majesty, and this majesty is vested in their own persons.

This majesty cannot be given to the chief ranks in the Florentine government if the Signoria and the Colleges are maintained in their former state. Since serious men of good reputation can rarely be members, because of the way these bodies are created, the majesty of the state must either devolve on some subordinate body or be deflected to private citizens, which is against all good government. So this system must be put right, and at the same time the highest ambitions in the city must be met. This is the way it must be done.

Do away with the Signoria, the *Otto della pratica,* and the twelve *Buoni Uomini.* To give majesty to the government choose, in place of these, sixty-five citizens of over forty-five years of age, fifty-three from the Greater and twelve from the Lesser Guilds, who will be life members of the government in the following way.

Appoint a Gonfalonier of Justice for two or three years, if it does not seem right to appoint him for life. The sixty-four citizens remaining should be divided into two groups of thirty-two. One group should rule with the

Gonfalonier for a year and the other half the next year, and they should alternate in this way, maintaining the system described, and all together they should be called the Signoria.

The thirty-two should be divided into four groups, of eight each, and each group should reside with the Gonfalonier in the palace for three months. They should take office with the usual ceremonies, and carry out the business that the Signoria does by itself today, and with the rest of the thirty-two they should have all the power and do all the business that is done today by the Signoria, the *Otto della pratica,* and the Colleges that we propose to do away with. And as I have said, they should be the chief head and chief member of the state. If this system is considered carefully, it will be seen that majesty and reputation are given back to the head of state and that responsible men with authority would always hold the chief ranks. It would not be necessary to consult with advisory commissions of private citizens, which as I said above is harmful in a republic, because the thirty-two who were not in office that year would be there for consultation and advice. And your Holiness could place all your friends and trusted supporters in this first elected body, as I will explain below. But now we come to the second branch of the government.

I think that since there are three classes of men, as I mentioned above, there should also be three bodies in a republican government, and no more. I think it would be wise to do away with the mixture of Councils that existed at one time in your city. They were set up not because they were necessary for the public good, but to benefit a larger number of citizens. The latter were in fact benefiting from something that made no contribution to the general well-being of the city, because all the Councils could be corrupted through factions.

As I want to set up a republic with only three bodies, then I would dispense with the Seventy, the Hundred, and the Council of the People and of the Commune. In their place, I would set up a Council of two hundred, forty from the Lesser and one hundred and sixty from the Greater Guilds, all over forty years old. None of them would be able to belong to the sixty-five; and they would be appointed for life. The council would be called the Council of the Elect. This Council, together with the sixty-five already mentioned, should take over all the duties and authority of the Councils that I suggested earlier should be abolished in its favor. This would be the second body of the government, and all its members would be chosen by your Holiness. To do this and to maintain and supervise the arrangements I have described and those I will outline below, and to safeguard your power and the security of your friends, your Holiness and the reverend Cardinal de' Medici should receive from the *Balìa* during both your lifetimes as much power as the whole people of Florence possesses.

The officers of the *Otto di Guardia e Balìa* should be appointed from time to time on your Holiness's authority.

Again, for the greater security of the state and your Holiness's friends, the infantry command should be split into two companies. And your Holiness should appoint two commissioners each year, one for each company, on your own authority.

From what we have said, it can be seen that two classes of men have been attended to, and your power and that of your friends has been strengthened in the city. The army and criminal justice are in your hands, the laws in your keeping, and the government leaders are all your men.

It now remains to satisfy the third and last class of men, which is made up of the main body of citizens. They will never be satisfied (anyone who believes otherwise is ingenuous) if they are not given, or promised, power. But if you gave it back all at once, you would forfeit the safety of your friends and your Holiness's own power. It must be partly given back and partly promised, so that they feel quite certain of getting it back. For this reason I think that the Hall of the Council of the Thousand, or at least that of the six hundred citizens must be reopened, and they should appoint all the officials and magistrates, as they once did, except the sixty-five, the two hundred, and *Otto di Balìa* mentioned above, which during your Holiness's and the Cardinal's lifetimes should be appointed by you. To make certain that your friends got their names into the election bags when the Council was voting upon them, your Holiness should appoint eight *accoppiatori* who could secretly qualify anyone they wanted, but not disqualify anyone. To get the people to believe that the names of those they voted for were actually placed in the election bags, the Council should be allowed to send two specially elected citizens to witness the making up of the bags.

No stable republic was ever set up that did not satisfy the people. And the main body of Florentine citizens will never be satisfied if the Hall of the Great Council is not reopened. If you want to set up a republic in Florence, this Hall must be opened again, and the appointment of officials must be left to the people again. Your Holiness must realize that if anyone plans to oust you from power, the first thing he will think of is to reopen it. The best thing is for you to open it with limits and safeguards, and so deny your enemies the chance of reopening it, giving you trouble, and causing the downfall of your friends.

With the state organized along these lines, it would be unnecessary to worry about anything else if your Holiness and the reverend monsignor were going to live forever. But since you must die, and you want the republic to remain perfect and be supported by all parties, and you want everyone to see and understand that it must stay like that, there must be further provisions to keep the people happy (both with what they are given and with what they are promised).

The sixteen Gonfaloniers of the People's Companies should be appointed in the same way and for the same period as before, by your Holiness or by the Council, as you like. But the number of prohibitions should be increased so that they are better distributed through the city, and it should be arranged that none of the sixty-five citizens is eligible. Once they are appointed, four of them should be chosen to act for a month, so that at the end of their time they all will have held office. Of these four, one should be chosen to reside for a week in the palace with the nine Signori, so that all four will have been in residence by the end of the month. The Signori in residence in the palace would not be able to do anything if he was absent, and he would not have to make a decision, just witness their actions. He could hold up their proceedings, discuss a case, and ask the opinion of the whole thirty-two together. In the same way the thirty-two could not decide anything without the presence of two of these officers, and the latter would have no other power than to agree to a decision they had debated and refer it to the Council of the Elect. The Council of the Two Hundred could do nothing without at least six of the sixteen with the two officers. And they would only have power to take a case out of the jurisdiction of that Council and place it before the Great Council, if three of them were in agreement. The Great Council could not be called without twelve of the gonfaloniers, including at least three in office, and there they would have a vote like the other citizens.

This kind of arrangement of the Colleges is necessary after the death of your Holiness and the reverend Cardinal for two reasons. The first is to ensure that if the Signoria or the other Council does not come to a decision about something because of a split, or if they do something against the public good out of malice, there will be someone to deprive them of authority and place it in other hands. It is not right for one type of official or Council to be able to obstruct an action without there being someone else to take care of it. Similarly it is not right for citizens who have control of the state to have no one to keep an eye on them and make them refrain from evil actions by taking away their power if they abuse it. The other reason is that after the Signoria as it exists today has been abolished, and the people have lost the chance of belonging to it, they must be given a rank that resembles the one they are losing; and this rank is in fact greater, more useful to the republic, and carries more prestige. For the present, these gonfaloniers should be appointed to accustom the city to the system, but they should not be allowed to carry out their functions without your Holiness's permission. You

25

could make use of them to get reports of the actions of these bodies on your behalf.

Apart from this, to make sure that the republic is complete in every part after the deaths of your Holiness and the reverend Cardinal, a court of appeal for the *Otto di Guardia e Balìa* should be set up, consisting of thirty citizens to be drawn from the bag of the two hundred and the sixty-five together. This court could summon the plaintiff and the defendant within a certain time. During your lifetime, you would not allow the court to be used without your permission.

There must be this chance of appeal in a republic, because a few citizens together do not have the courage to punish important men. There must be a large number of citizens for this so that individual opinions are not noticed and everyone can deny responsibility. During your lifetime, this court would be useful in making the *Otto* speed up their cases and administer justice, because they would judge more fairly in case you did not allow an appeal. To prevent appeals over every single thing, it could be laid down that there may be no appeal in cases of fraud where less than fifty ducats were involved, nor in cases of violence where no bones had been broken, or blood shed, or where the damage done did not amount to fifty ducats.

When I consider this structure as a republic without your authority, I feel that it needs nothing more, as I have argued and explained at length above. But seen during the lifetimes of your Holiness and the Cardinal, it is a monarchy. You control the army and the judges of the criminal courts, and the laws are in your keeping. I can think of nothing else that anyone could wish for in a city. Your friends who are good and want to live on their income seem to have nothing to fear while your Holiness has so much power, and they can sit in the first ranks of the government. We cannot see how the people can be anything but contented, since some of the offices have been given to them to allot, and they can see that the others will fall, one by one, into their hands. Your Holiness could sometimes allow the Council to appoint some of the sixty-five if they were missing, and the same for the two hundred. And you could appoint some yourself, depending on conditions. I am certain that in a short time, thanks to the authority of your Holiness, who would control everything, the present state would be amalgamated with a republican regime, gradually, so that they would become one and the same thing, and that this would bring peace to the city and perpetual fame to your Holiness, because with your authority you could always take care of any shortcomings there might be.

I believe the greatest honor men can receive is one that is given voluntarily by their country. And I believe the greatest good one can do, and the most acceptable to God, is the good one does to one's country. Apart from this, no man is as ennobled in any of his actions as those who have reformed republics and kingdoms with laws and institutions. They are the first to be praised after those who have become gods. Because only a few have had the chance to do it, and very few had the ability, only a very small number have actually done it. This achievement has been so much admired by men who were never interested in anything but glory that if they could not create a republic in fact, they created one in writing: like Aristotle, Plato, and many others, who wanted to show the world that if they could not found a society like Solon and Lycurgus, it was not because of their ignorance, but because they were powerless to bring it into being.

Heaven cannot give a man a greater gift than this or point him a more glorious way. Amid all the happiness that God has given your house and your Holiness personally, this is the greatest: the gift of the power and the occasion to make yourself immortal and far outdo the fame of your father and your ancestors. Your Holiness must first consider that by keeping the city of Florence in its present condition, there are any number of risks if trouble comes. And before it comes, your Holiness must put up with any number of annoyances that anyone would find unbearable. His reverence, the Cardinal, will bear witness to this, having been in Florence during the past months. They arise partly because many citizens are presumptuous and overbearing in their demands, partly because many others do not feel safe as they are at present, and do nothing but call for the government to be put right. Some say that it should be broadened, others say that it should be restricted, and nobody will commit himself to details of how it should be restricted or broadened because they are completely confused. They do not feel safe the way they are living now, they do not know how to put things right, and they have no faith in the people who do know. And in their confused state, they are apt to unbalance anyone with a clear mind.

There are only two ways of avoiding these annoyances: either by limiting yourself to audiences and not encouraging people to ask for things even in the ordinary way, or to speak unless they are asked, which is what the Duke, of illustrious memory, did; or by organizing the state so that it runs itself, and your Holiness need only keep half an eye on it. The second of these ways sets you free from dangers and annoyances, the other only from the annoyances. To return to risks that you run by leaving things as they are, I want to make a prophecy, that if something goes wrong and the city is not reorganized in some other way, one of two things will happen, or both at once: either a revolutionary leader will be chosen suddenly, who will defend the state with arms and violence, or one party will run to open the Hall of the Council and will attack the other party. Whichever of these happens (which God forbid), let your Holiness think how many deaths, exiles, and extortions would result, enough to make even the cruellest of men die of sorrow, let alone your Holiness who is most merciful. There is no other way of avoiding these evils but to see that the city's constitution can stand up on its own. It will always stand firm when everyone has a hand in it, when everyone knows what he must do and whom he can trust, and when fear or ambition is not prompting any class of citizen to look for changes.

The Life of
Castruccio Castracani of Lucca

Written by Niccolò Machiavelli and sent to his friends Zanobi Buondelmonti and Luigi Alamanni.

Those who consider the matter, dear Zanobi and Luigi, find it remarkable that all, or nearly all, of those who have achieved things of very great importance in this world, and have outshone all their contemporaries, have had humble and obscure origins, or have been extraordinarily dogged by ill fortune in their early lives. They were all either exposed to wild beasts or had a father of such low birth that they were ashamed of him and pretended to be sons of Jove or of some other God. The reader would find it boring and tedious if I repeated who they were. Many are known to everyone, so we will omit this as superfluous. In my opinion, the reason is that Fortune, wanting to prove to the world that it is she and not prudence who makes men great, begins to show her power before prudence can take its part, so that she can have credit for everything.

Castruccio Castracani of Lucca was one of these. His achievements were very great, considering the times he lived in and the city where he was born. He was of no more fortunate or famous stock than the rest, as will be seen from the story of his life. This story seemed to me worth recording, for I felt that I had found in it many excellent examples of both *virtù* and fortune. I thought I would dedicate it to you, since you, more than anyone else I know, delight in deeds of *virtù*.

The Castracani family is numbered among the noble families of the city of Lucca, although, being subject to the laws of all earthly things, it no longer exists. Of this family there was born one Antonio, who became a priest and was made canon of San Michele in Lucca. As a mark of respect, he was called Messer Antonio. He had no brothers, and only one sister, whom he married to Buonaccorso Cennami. When Buonaccorso died, his widow came back to live with her brother, not intending to marry again.

Antonio had a vineyard behind the house he lived in, which could be easily entered on several sides since it was bordered by a number of gardens. Dianora (as Antonio's sister was called) was walking in the vineyard one morning shortly after sunrise, picking herbs for seasonings as women do, when she heard a rustling among the leaves under a vine, and looking in that direction, she heard a sound of crying. She went toward the noise and discovered the hands and face of a child, who was covered in leaves, and who seemed to be asking her help. Half amazed and half afraid, but full of pity and wonder, she picked it up, took it home, washed it, dressed it in the usual white clothes, and showed it to Antonio on his return home. When he had heard the story and had seen the baby, he was no less amazed and moved than she had been. They discussed what they ought to do and decided to bring him up themselves, since Antonio was a priest and she was childless. They engaged a nurse and cared for him as if he had been their own son; and when they had him christened, they called him after their father, Castruccio.

Castruccio grew more and more good-looking with the years and was always clever and wise. He learned quickly everything that Antonio set him to, according to his age. Antonio planned to make him a priest and to hand over the canonry and various other benefices to him eventually, and he was educating him accordingly. But he was dealing with someone entirely unsuited to the priestly way of life; for as soon as Castruccio reached the age of fourteen and began to rebel a little against Antonio, and to have no fear at all of Dianora, he put his ecclesiastical books to one side and began to practice arms. His one delight was to drill, or to run, jump, wrestle, and practice similar sports with his friends. In this he showed great *virtù* in mind and body and far outstripped all the others of his own age. If he did sometimes read, he liked nothing but stories about wars or deeds done by great men. This caused immeasurable sorrow and grief to Antonio.

In the city of Lucca, there was a gentleman of the Guinigi family, called Francesco, who far surpassed all the other people of Lucca in wealth, looks, and *virtù*. His profession was war, and he had fought for a long time under the Visconti of Milan. Since he was a Ghibelline, he was respected above all the others of that party in Lucca. On one occasion when he was in Lucca meeting other citizens morning and evening under the Podestà's loggia, which is at the top of the Piazza di San Michele, the main square in Lucca, he saw Castruccio several times, playing those games I mentioned earlier with the other boys of his district. Francesco felt that, as well as outstripping them, Castruccio had complete authority over them, and that they loved and respected him. Francesco grew particularly anxious to find out who Castruccio was. When some bystanders told Francesco, he conceived an even greater desire to have Castruccio with him. One day he called Castruccio over and asked him whether he would rather be in the house of a gentleman, who would teach him to ride and bear arms, or in the house of a priest, where he would hear nothing but services and Masses. Francesco realized how happy Castruccio was to hear talk of horses and arms: although Castruccio was a little shy, Francesco encouraged him to speak, and he replied that if his guardian agreed, nothing would please him more than to stop studying for the priesthood and to take up a military career. Francesco was very pleased with this reply, and in a very few days he arranged things so that Antonio let him have his way. Antonio was persuaded more by the boy's nature than anything else, as he felt he would be unable to keep him under control for very much longer.

Castruccio passed from the house of Antonio Castracani, the canon, to that of Francesco Guinigi, the soldier of fortune, and it is extraordinary to think how short a time he took to acquire all those qualities and manners that are expected in a real gentleman. To begin with, he

31

turned himself into an excellent horseman and managed even the wildest horses with superb skill; and in jousts and tournaments, although he was still young, he was more respected than anyone else. In every feat of strength or skill, he found no man to beat him. To this were added good manners and particularly a very great modesty. He was never seen to do or say anything unkind; he was respectful to his betters, modest with his equals, and friendly toward inferiors. All this resulted in his being loved not only by all the Guinigi family but by the whole city of Lucca as well.

When Castruccio was eighteen, the Ghibellines were expelled from Pavia by the Guelphs, and Francesco Guinigi was sent by the Visconti of Milan to give the Ghibellines support. Castruccio went with him in charge of his whole company. On this expedition Castruccio gave so many proofs of his foresight and courage that no one who took part in the engagement acquired as much prestige as he did. His name was famous and honored not only in Pavia but throughout Lombardy.

Castruccio returned to Lucca far more highly respected than he had been when he left. He set about making as many friends as possible, using every means necessary to win men over. Then Francesco Guinigi died, leaving a son called Pagolo, aged thirteen. Francesco made Castruccio guardian and trustee of his property, having sent for him before he died and begged him to agree to bring up his son with the same concern with which Castruccio himself had been educated, and to repay the son the debt of gratitude he had been unable to pay the father. After Francesco Guinigi died and Castruccio was left as Pagolo's trustee and guardian, his reputation and power grew so fast that the goodwill he had once enjoyed in Lucca turned partly to envy. In fact many people openly criticized him as a dangerous man with despotic ambitions. Chief among his detractors was Giorgio degli Opizi, leader of the Guelph party. He had hoped to become ruler of Lucca after Francesco's death, and he felt that Castruccio, who had won control because of the support his good qualities brought him, had put an end to his chances. So he fostered rumors that would undermine that support. At first Castruccio was annoyed by this, and he soon became afraid as well, because he thought Giorgio would not rest until he had ruined Castruccio's reputation with King Robert of Naples' lieutenant, who would have him banished from Lucca.

The Lord of Pisa at that time was Uguccione della Faggiuola of Arezzo, who had first been chosen by the Pisans as their captain and had then made himself their Lord. There were some Ghibelline outlaws from Lucca with Uguccione, and Castruccio agreed to reinstate them with Uguccione's help. He communicated this plan to his friends inside Lucca who could not tolerate the rule of the Opizi. When he had arranged what they should do, Castruccio secretly fortified the tower of the Onesti and filled it with ammunition and a great deal of food, so that, if necessary, he could hold out in it for some days. On the night he had agreed on with Uguccione, he gave a signal, and Uguccione, who had come down with a large army onto the plain between Lucca and the hills, advanced on Porta a San Pietro and set fire to the entrance. Meanwhile Castruccio roused the people, calling them to arms, and forced the gate from inside. Uguccione and his troops came in and overran the city, killed Giorgio and all the members of his household and many of his friends and supporters, and expelled the governor. The city's constitution was reformed according to Uguccione's wishes. Lucca suffered greatly, because the records show that more than a hundred families were expelled from the city at that time. Of those who fled, some went to Florence and some to Pistoia; these cities were in the hands of the Guelph party and therefore came to be enemies of Uguccione and the people of Lucca.

The Florentines and the other Guelphs felt that the Ghibelline party had too much power in Tuscany, and they agreed together to reinstate the Lucchese outlaws. They collected a large army, entered the Nievole Valley and occupied Montecatini, and from there they set up camp at Montecarlo in order to have free access to Lucca. When Uguccione had collected quite a number of men from Pisa and Lucca, as well as a great deal of German cavalry from Lombardy, he went in search of the Florentine camp. This had moved from Montecarlo at the approach of the enemy and was pitched between Montecatini and Pescia. Uguccione took up a position below Montecarlo, two miles from the enemy. For a few days there was some light skirmishing between the cavalry of the two armies because, as Uguccione was ill, the Pisans and Lucchese were avoiding a pitched battle with their enemies.

However, Uguccione's illness grew more serious and he withdrew to Montecarlo for treatment, leaving Castruccio in charge of the army. This caused the downfall of the Guelphs; for they took heart thinking that the enemy army was leaderless. Castruccio was aware of this, and waited several days to strengthen this idea, pretending to be afraid and allowing no one outside the fortifications. The Guelphs became more aggressive the more they noticed this fear, and each day, in battle array, they offered themselves to Castruccio's army. When Castruccio felt that he had bolstered up their courage and had got to know their dispositions, he decided to fight. First he made a speech encouraging his own soldiers and telling them that victory was certain if they obeyed his orders.

Castruccio had observed how the enemy had put all their strength in the center of their attack and their weaker men on the wings. Consequently he did the opposite and placed the bravest men he had on the wings of his army and the less formidable in the center. He left camp with his army drawn up in this way, and when he first sighted the enemy army, which had come out in search of him as usual, he ordered the units in the center to go slowly and those on the wings to move fast. This meant that when battle was joined with the enemy, only the wings of both armies were fighting while the center ranks were doing nothing; because the men in the center of Castruccio's army had stayed so far behind that the enemy's center ranks did not reach them. In this way Castruccio's finest soldiers came up against the weakest of the enemy, and the enemy's best troops rested without being able to come to blows with their opposite numbers or give any help to their companions. So it did not take much to turn both the enemy wings. The men in the center, seeing their flanks exposed, fled without having been able to show their *virtù*. The rout and the slaughter were very great; more than ten thousand men were killed, among them many commanders and great knights of the Guelph party from all over Tuscany, and also a number of rulers who had come in their support, such as Piero, brother of King Robert, and Carlo, his nephew, and Filippo, Lord of Taranto. On Castruccio's side there were less than three hundred dead. Among them was Uguccione's son, Francesco, a spirited young man, who was killed in the first clash.

This rout crowned Castruccio's fame; while Uguccione grew so jealous and suspicious of Castruccio's position that he thought of nothing but how to get rid of him. Uguccione felt that he had lost power rather than gaining it by the victory. He was obsessed with this thought and was only waiting for a decent pretext to act upon it, when Pier Agnolo Micheli, a man of distinguished reputation, was killed in Lucca, and his murderer took refuge at Castruccio's house. When the captain's sergeants went to arrest him, they were held off by Castruccio, while he helped the murderer to escape. Uguccione was at Pisa at the time and when he heard this, he felt he had just cause to punish Castruccio. He called his son, Neri, to whom he had already given the control of Lucca, and told him to take Castruccio prisoner and have him put to death, using an invitation to dine as a bait. Castruccio went unsuspecting to the ruler's palace and was first entertained at dinner by Neri and then taken prisoner. But Neri feared the people might be angry if he put Castruccio to death without a good reason, so he kept him alive until he had further instructions from Uguccione. The latter was annoyed by his son's slowness and cowardice and left Pisa for Lucca with four hundred horse to finish off the affair. But he had not arrived at the Bagni when the Pisans took up arms, killed Uguccione's deputy and the rest of his household who had stayed in Pisa, and made Count Gaddo della Gherardesca their ruler. Uguccione heard the news from Pisa before he reached Lucca, but decided against turning back in case the people of Lucca followed the Pisans' example and shut their gates in his face, too. But when the Lucchese heard of events in Pisa, even though Uguccione had come to Lucca, they seized the opportunity of Castruccio's imprisonment and began first of all to murmur discontentedly in groups in the squares, then to hold demonstrations, and finally they armed and demanded Castruccio's liberation. This made Uguccione let him out of prison for fear of worse. Castruccio immediately gathered his friends together and with the support of the people made an attack on Uguccione. Uguccione saw that the game was up, and he fled with his friends to Lombardy to the della Scala family, where he died in poverty.

Castruccio, however, from being a prisoner, had almost become Lord of Lucca, and using his friends and the new-found favor of the people, he managed to be made captain of their army for a year. When he had achieved this, he planned to win back for Lucca many of the towns that had rebelled after Uguccione's departure, in order to win himself a reputation as a soldier. With the support of the Pisans, with whom he had made an alliance, he set up his camp before Sarzana. To capture it, he built a fort above it, which has since been walled around by the Florentines and is now called Serezanello; and he took the town in two months. Afterwards, with this to his credit, he occupied Massa, Carrara, and Lavenza, and in a very short time he took the whole of Lunigiana. To close the pass that leads from Lombardy into Lunigiana, he seized Pontriemoli and ousted its Lord, Anastagio Palavisini. On his return to Lucca, with this victory to his name, he was met by the whole populace. Castruccio felt there was no time to lose before making himself ruler, and so with the help of Pazzino dal Poggio, Puccinello dal Portico, Francesco Boccansacchi, and Cecco Guinigi, who were greatly respected in Lucca at that time and whom he bribed, he became its Lord and was formally elected as ruler by deliberation of the people.

Frederick of Bavaria, king of the Romans, had come

to Italy at this time to take the imperial Crown. Castruccio made a friend of him and went to see him with five hundred horse, leaving Pagolo Guinigi as his lieutenant in Lucca. Because of Pagolo's father's memory, Castruccio felt like a father toward him. Castruccio was received by Frederick with great honor, given many privileges, and made his lieutenant in Tuscany. And since the Pisans had expelled Gaddo della Gherardesca, and for fear of him had turned to Frederick for help, Frederick made Castruccio Lord of Pisa. The Pisans accepted him for fear of the Guelphs, especially the Florentines.

When Frederick had gone back to Germany, leaving a governor in Rome, all the Tuscan and Lombard Ghibellines who were on the Emperor's side turned to Castruccio, and each one promised him control of their home town if he helped them to return there. Among them were Matteo Guidi, Nardo Scolari, Lapo Uberti, Gerozzo Nardi, and Piero Buonaccorsi, all Florentine Ghibelline exiles. Castruccio was planning to become master of all Tuscany, relying on their aid and his own strength. To gain more prestige, he made an alliance with Matteo Visconti, ruler of Milan, and armed the whole city and its neighborhood. As Lucca had five gates, he divided the *contado* into five parts, which he armed, giving each its own commanders and banners. In this way he collected twenty thousand men all at once, not counting those who could come to his aid from Pisa. When Castruccio had surrounded himself with these forces and allies, Matteo Visconti was attacked by the Guelphs of Piacenza. They had banished the Ghibellines with the help of armies sent by the Florentines and King Robert. So Matteo asked Castruccio to attack the Florentines, forcing them to call their troops back from Lombardy to defend their own homes. Castruccio attacked the Arno Valley with a large force and took Fucecchio and San Miniato, doing a great deal of damage; and the Florentines had to bring their soldiers back. They had hardly returned to Tuscany, however, before Castruccio was himself forced to go back to Lucca.

The Poggio family was important there because they were responsible not only for Castruccio's advancement but also for his coming to power. But they felt that they had not received their due reward, and they plotted with some other families in Lucca to stir up the city and expel Castruccio. They took their opportunity one morning and went armed to the deputy whom Castruccio had left to dispense justice, and killed him. They wanted to go on to organize a popular revolt, but Stefano di Poggio, a peaceable old man who had taken no part in the conspiracy, came forward, and with his authority forced his family to lay down their arms, offering to mediate between them and Castruccio and see that their wishes were carried out. They laid down their arms, no more wisely than they had taken them up; for when Castruccio heard the news from Lucca, he lost no time in coming back with part of his army, leaving Pagolo Guinigi in charge of the rest. He found the city much quieter than he had expected, and reckoning that he could therefore reestablish himself more easily, he put his own supporters, armed, in all the strategic places. Stefano di Poggio, thinking that Castruccio was under an obligation to him, paid him a visit and made no plea on his own account, as he thought there was no need, but did so for the rest of his family. He begged Castruccio to make allowances for youth and to remember their old friendship and the way Castruccio was beholden to their house. Castruccio answered him courteously and told him not to worry, saying that he was more pleased to find the riots over than he had been angry when they began. He asked Stefano to get them all to come to him, saying that he thanked God he had a chance to show his mercy and liberality. They came, trusting in Stefano's and Castruccio's word, and together with Stefano they were imprisoned and put to death.

Meanwhile the Florentines had retaken San Miniato; so Castruccio felt he ought to put a stop to the war, as he felt he could not leave home until he was quite sure of Lucca. He sounded the Florentines about a truce and found them well disposed, since they too were tired and were anxious to put an end to the expense. They made a two-year truce, agreeing that each should keep the territory they already possessed. No longer hampered by the war, Castruccio tried to avoid the risks he had run before, and used various pretexts to get rid of everyone in Lucca who might have aspirations to power. He spared no one, exiling them, confiscating their property, and taking their lives if he could lay hands on them. He said he had learned by experience that he could rely on none of them. And for his own greater security, he built a fortress in Lucca, using the towers of the men he had exiled and killed as building material.

While Castruccio was at peace with the Florentines and was putting up his fortifications in Lucca, he did everything he could to increase his power, short of resorting to open war. He particularly wanted to occupy Pistoia, as he felt that once in possession of that town he would have one foot inside Florence. He won the friendship of the whole mountain district in various ways and the trust of each of the factions in Pistoia. The city was divided at that time, as always, into Blacks and Whites. The leader of the Whites was Bastiano di Possente, and of the Blacks, Iacopo da Gia. Both of them had very close dealings with Castruccio, each wanting to drive the other out, with the result that, after much bad feeling, they resorted to force. They took up positions, Iacopo at the Florence gate, and Bastiano at the Lucca gate, and as each one trusted Castruccio more than the Florentines, judging him to be quicker off the mark when it came to war, they both sent to him secretly for help. Castruccio promised it to both of them, telling Iacopo that he would come himself and Bastiano that he would send Pagolo Guinigi, his ward. He gave them a strict timetable, and he sent Pagolo via Pescia and he himself went directly to Pistoia. At midnight, as Castruccio and Pagolo had arranged, they were both at Pistoia, and both were received as friends. Once they were inside, when Castruccio judged it was time, he gave Pagolo the signal; whereupon one of them killed Iacopo da Gia and the other Bastiano di Possente, and all the supporters of these men were either captured or killed. They overran Pistoia without meeting any further opposition. Castruccio forced the Signoria out of the palace and made the people submit to him, cancelling many of their old debts and making promises. He included all the *contado*, as a great many people had come in to see the new ruler. Everybody settled down hopefully, generally impressed by his powers.

At this time the people of Rome began to riot because of the high cost of living. They attributed it to the absence of the Pope, who was at Avignon, and blamed the German administration. Murders and other crimes occurred every day, and Henry, the Emperor's lieutenant, could do nothing about it. He began to be afraid that the Romans might call in King Robert of Naples and expel him from Rome, restoring the city to the Pope. As he had no friend whom he could turn to nearer than Castruccio, he sent to beg him not only to send help but to come to Rome himself. Castruccio realized there was no time to lose if he was to do the Emperor a service, and he felt that unless the Emperor was in Rome there was nothing else that could be done. So leaving Pagolo Guinigi at Lucca, he went off to Rome with six hundred horse and was received there with great honor by Henry. Very shortly his presence had brought so much credit to the imperial party that everything was settled without bloodshed or violence. Castruccio had quantities of wheat shipped from Pisa and so eliminated the cause of the trouble. Then partly by warning the Roman leaders, partly by punishing them, he brought them back under Henry's rule of their own accord. Castruccio was made a senator of Rome, and he received many other honors from the Roman people. Castruccio assumed this office with great pomp, putting on a brocade toga that had writing on the front which read: "God's will is done" and on the back: "God's will shall be done."

Meanwhile, the Florentines were annoyed that Castruccio had taken control of Pistoia during the truce and were plotting to make it rebel, which they believed would be easy while he was away. Among the Pistoian exiles in Florence were Baldo Cecchi and Iacopo Baldini, both men of authority, ready to take any risks. They contacted their friends inside Pistoia, then with the Florentines' help entered the city by night and drove out Castruccio's supporters and officers, killing some of them, and restoring the freedom of the city. The news of this made Castruccio very angry, and he took leave of Henry and came back posthaste to Lucca with his men. When they heard of Castruccio's return, the Florentines reckoned he would waste no time and so decided to forestall him by entering the Nievole Valley with their army before him. They judged that if they occupied the valley, they would cut off his route for retaking Pistoia. They assembled a large army of all their Guelph friends and entered Pistoian territory. Meanwhile, Castruccio reached Montecarlo with his army; and when he heard where the Florentine army was, he decided not to meet it in the plain of Pistoia, nor to wait for it in the plain of Pescia, but if he could, to meet it head on in the Serravalle gap. He considered that if this plan succeeded, he was certain of victory, because he had heard that the Florentines had thirty thousand men altogether, while he had chosen twelve thousand of his own. Although he had faith in his own skill and in their *virtù,* he was afraid that if battle was joined in an open space he might be surrounded by the enemy with their superior numbers.

Serravalle is a castle between Pescia and Pistoia, situated on a hill that shuts off the Nievole Valley, not right on the pass but about two bow shots above it. The place one has to pass through is narrow rather than steep, since it slopes gently up on either side; but it is so narrow, particularly on the hill where the waters divide, that twenty men shoulder to shoulder would span it. This was the place where Castruccio had planned to face the enemy, both to give his smaller army the advantage and to avoid sighting the enemy before the battle, as he was afraid that his own men might take fright when they saw the enemy's numbers. The lord of the castle was Manfredi, a German by birth, who had been installed in the castle before Castruccio took control of Pistoia. Neither town had had occasion to do him any harm and he had promised both to remain neutral and have no obligations to either side. Because of this and because of his strong position, he had been allowed to remain. But once these events had taken place, Castruccio grew impatient to occupy the castle. He had close relations with an inhabitant and arranged with him that he would let in four hundred of Castruccio's men the night before the battle took place and kill the lord of the castle.

Thus prepared, he did not move his army from Montecarlo in order to encourage the Florentines to go through the pass. Because they wanted to deflect the fighting away from Pistoia into the Nievole Valley, the Florentines camped under Serravalle with the idea of crossing the hill the next day. But having taken the castle without a disturbance during the night, Castruccio left Montecarlo at midnight, and with his men arrived silently in the morning at the foot of Serravalle. So both he and the Florentines began to climb the hill, each from their own side, at the same moment. Castruccio had sent his infantry by the usual road and had ordered a company of four hundred horsemen to make for the castle, keeping to the left. On the other side, the Florentines had sent ahead four hundred horse, then the infantry, and behind them the men at arms; and they did not dream they would find Castruccio at the top of the hill, because they did not know he had taken over the castle. So once they had climbed the hill, the Florentine cavalry came upon Castruccio's infantry unexpectedly, so near to them, that they hardly had time to do up their helmets. As it was a case of the unprepared being assailed by men who were prepared and well deployed, the latter attacked bravely and the others could barely stand up to them. Some of them did resist; but once the noise had reached the rest of the Florentine army, all was confusion. The cavalry was hampered by the infantry, and the infantry by the horses and wagons, the commanders could go neither forwards nor backwards because the place was so narrow; nobody knew what could or should be done in such a shambles. Meanwhile the cavalrymen who were fighting the enemy infantry were being killed and wounded without being able to defend themselves, because the difficulty of the ground gave them no scope. And yet they held their own more through need than *virtù*, since with the mountains on either side, their friends behind and their enemies in front, there was no way open to them for flight.

Meanwhile Castruccio saw that his men were not enough to force the enemy to retreat, and he sent a thousand foot soldiers along the road to the castle. He made them come down with the four hundred horse he had sent on ahead, and they attacked the enemy's flank with such force that the Florentine troops could not withstand their thrust and began to flee, beaten more by the terrain than by the enemy. The flight began with those who were at the back, toward Pistoia; they spread out over the plain, each one looking to his own safety as best he could.

It was a great and bloody rout. Many leaders were taken prisoner, among them Bandino de' Rossi, Francesco Brunelleschi, and Giovanni della Tosa, all Florentine noblemen, and with them many other Tuscans and men from the kingdom, who had been sent by King Robert in support of the Guelphs and who were campaigning with the Florentines.

When the Pistoians heard of the defeat, they immediately expelled the faction that favored the Guelphs and went over to Castruccio. Not content with this, Castruccio occupied Prato and all the castles on the plain on both sides of the Arno. And he camped with his men on the plain of Peretola, two miles from Florence. He stayed there for days, sharing plunder and celebrating victory, and to spite the Florentines he struck coins and organized races for horses, men, and whores. He did not omit to bribe some noble citizens to open the gates of Florence to him at night, but the plot was discovered and Tommaso Lupacci and Lambertuccio Frescobaldi were captured and beheaded.

The Florentines were frightened by the defeat and now saw no way of saving their liberty. To be more certain of his help, they sent ambassadors to Robert, King of Naples, to put the control of the city into his hands. The king accepted this, not so much because of the honor done him by the Florentines, but because he knew how important it was for his regime for the Guelph party to keep control of Tuscany. He agreed with the Florentines to receive two hundred thousand florins a year, and sent his son Charles to Florence with four thousand horse.

In the meantime, the Florentines had been relieved of Castruccio's army to some extent, because he had been forced to leave their territory and go to Pisa to put down a conspiracy against him that was planned by Benedetto Lanfranchi, one of the chief citizens of Pisa. This man could not tolerate the subjection of his home town to a man from Lucca, and he plotted against Castruccio, planning to occupy the citadel, throw out the guard, and kill Castruccio's supporters. But since in these affairs the number small enough to keep the secret is not sufficient to put it into effect, while he was trying to bring more men around to his view, he came across one who reported his plan to Castruccio. This disclosure also incriminated Bonifacio Cerchi and Giovanni Guidi of Florence, who were in exile at Pisa. So Castruccio arrested Benedetto, killed him, and sent all the rest of the family into exile, and he beheaded a number of other noble citizens. Feeling that Pistoia and Pisa were disloyal to him, he turned his attention to making sure of them, both by hard work and by force. This gave the Florentines time to recover their strength and wait for Charles' arrival. When he had come, they decided to waste no time and gathered a large army together, because they called nearly all the Guelphs in Italy to their aid and collected a vast force of more than thirty thousand foot and ten thousand horse. They discussed whether to attack Pistoia or Pisa first and decided it would be better to fight Pisa, as the enterprise was more likely to succeed, because of the recent conspiracy there, and to be more useful, because they judged that once they had Pisa, Pistoia would surrender of her own accord.

So the Florentines set out with this army at the beginning of May, 1328, occupied Lastra, Signa, Montelupo, and Empoli immediately, and came to San Miniato. When Castruccio heard of the great army the Florentines had brought against him, he was not in the least frightened and thought that this was the time when Fortune would give him control of Tuscany. He believed that the enemy would give no better account of themselves at Pisa than they had at Serravalle and that they had no hope of recovering as they had done then. He

44

collected twenty thousand of his foot soldiers and four thousand horse, encamped at Fucecchio, and sent Pagolo Guinigi to Pisa with five thousand infantrymen. Fucecchio is in a stronger position than any other castle in Pisan territory, as it is midway between the Gusciana and the Arno, fairly high above the plain. Once they were there, their enemies could not prevent supplies coming either from Lucca or Pisa, unless they split into two. They could not attack Castruccio or make toward Pisa without putting themselves at a disadvantage: if they went toward Pisa, they could be surrounded by Castruccio's troops and the ones from Pisa, but if they attacked, they had to cross the Arno, which was extremely dangerous with the enemy on top of them. To encourage them to take the decision to cross, Castruccio had not stationed his men along the bank of the Arno, but beside the walls of Fucecchio, and had left plenty of room between himself and the river.

After the Florentines had occupied San Miniato, they debated what to do: go to Pisa or engage Castruccio. They weighed the difficulties of both choices and decided to attack. The river Arno was so low that it could be forded, but not without the foot soldiers going in up to their shoulders and the horses up to their saddles. On the morning of the tenth of June, the Florentines, in battle array, got part of their cavalry and a company of ten thousand foot to begin the crossing. Castruccio was prepared and intent on his plan of campaign, and he fell on them with a force of five thousand foot and three thousand horse. He did not give all of them time to get out of the water before he struck, and he sent a thousand swift foot soldiers up the bank lower down the Arno, and a thousand farther up. The Florentine infantry were weighed down by the water and their arms, and not all of them had climbed up the river bank. After some of the horses had crossed, the riverbed was so broken up that the crossing became difficult for the rest. Many of the horses, finding the bottom pitted with holes, rolled over onto their riders, and many got so bogged down they could not be freed. The Florentine captains saw how difficult it was to cross at that point, and withdrew the cavalry to a place higher up the river, where they would find the bottom unspoiled and an easier slope on the other side. Waiting to oppose them were those foot soldiers whom Castruccio had sent up the bank; they were lightly armed with round shields and galley spears and struck the enemy in the face and chest, uttering loud cries. The horses were frightened by the blows and the cries, refused to go forward, and fell back one on top of the other. The fighting between Castruccio's men and those who had got across was fierce and bitter; many fell on both sides, and each tried as hard as they could to overwhelm the other. Castruccio's men wanted to plunge the enemy back into the river; the Florentines wanted to thrust them on in order to give the others room to climb out of the water and fight. The captains' exhortations added to this determination. Castruccio reminded his men that these were the same enemies they had conquered not long before at Serravalle; and the Florentines reproved their men for letting the few overcome the many. But when Castruccio saw that the engagement was dragging on, that his soldiers and their adversaries were already weary, and how many dead and wounded there were on either side, he sent in another contingent of five thousand foot. And when he had brought them around behind his own front line, he ordered the latter to break and to retreat half to the right and half to the left, as if they were withdrawing. This gave the Florentines room to advance and gain some ground. But once the fresh troops had come to grips with those who were already battle-worn, it did not take long for them to push the Florentines back into the river. So far, neither cavalry had the advantage of the other, for Castruccio, knowing his own to be inferior, had ordered the commanders simply to contain the enemy, as he was hoping to get the better of the infantry, and once he had done this, to be able to break up the cavalry more easily. And his plan in fact succeeded. When he saw that the enemy infantry had retreated into the river, he sent the rest of his foot soldiers to meet the enemy horse, and they forced them to turn tail, fighting with spears and arrows, while Castruccio's cavalry pressed down on them even harder. The

Florentine captains saw how difficult their horses were finding the crossing and tried to get the infantry across lower down the river in order to fight Castruccio's men on the flank. But as the banks were high and were held by his men, this was a vain attempt. So the Florentine army collapsed and the honor and glory went to Castruccio; and only a third of that vast army survived. Many of the leaders were captured, and Charles, King Robert's son, fled to Empoli with Michelagnolo Falconi and Taddeo degli Albizzi, the Florentine commissioners. There was a great deal of booty and the slaughter was very heavy, as was to be expected in such a struggle. There were twenty thousand, two hundred and thirty-one dead in the Florentine camp, and one thousand, five hundred and seventy in Castruccio's.

However, Fortune, who resented Castruccio's fame, took his life just when he needed more time and cut short the plans that he had long before dreamed of carrying out. Nothing but death could have stopped him. Castruccio had not spared himself in the battle all day, and when it was over he halted, weary and sweating, at the entry to Fucecchio to wait for his men to return from the victory, to welcome them and thank them personally. He also wanted to be ready to put things right if the enemy had rallied and were offering any new threat, as he judged it to be a good captain's duty to be the first to mount his horse and the last to dismount. He was exposed to a wind that very often blows up from the Arno at midday and is almost always unhealthy, and he got thoroughly chilled. He paid no attention, since he was used to such discomforts, but eventually it caused his death. The following night he had an attack of very high fever; his temperature went on rising, and as the illness was judged fatal by all the doctors, and Castruccio realized it, he called Pagolo Guinigi to him and said:

"My son, if I had known that Fortune was going to cut across my path when I was halfway to that fame which I looked forward to after so many successes, I would have striven less and left you a smaller state, but less envied and with fewer enemies. I would have been satisfied with the control of Lucca and Pisa and would not

47

have subjugated the Pistoians or angered the Florentines with so many insults. I would have made friends with both these peoples and certainly led a quieter life, if not a longer one. And I would have left you a safer and more stable state, even though a smaller one. But Fortune, who tries to be mistress of all human affairs, did not give me enough sense to recognize her beforehand; nor enough time to get the better of her. You have heard, for many people have told you and I have never denied it, how I came into your father's house as a boy without any of those ambitions that are bound to grip every noble mind, and how he brought me up and loved me more than if I had been his own flesh and blood, so that under his guidance I grew skilled in arms and fitted for the successful career which you yourself have seen and still see. Because he committed you and all his fortune into my keeping at the point of death, I have brought you up with the love, and added to that fortune with the care, that I promised. So that you should have not only what had been left you by your father, but also what I had won by my own fortune and *virtù*, I have never married, to avoid the love of children hindering me in any way from showing what I considered to be suitable gratitude toward your father's family. I am glad that I am leaving you a large state, but very sorry that I am leaving it to you weak and unstable. The city of Lucca is yours, but it will never be content to live under your government. Pisa is yours, where men are fickle and full of deceit: And although it has been used to bondage at different times, nevertheless it will always resent having a master from Lucca. Pistoia also is yours, disloyal because divided, and resentful against our family because of recent wrongs. As neighbors you have the Florentines, outraged and insulted in a thousand different ways, yet not beaten; they will be more pleased by the news of my death than they would be by winning the whole of Tuscany. You cannot trust the rulers of Milan nor the Emperor, for they are far away, slow, and their help comes too late. In fact, you should put your faith in nothing but your own efforts, the memory of my *virtù*, and the prestige that this victory will bring you: And if you can trade on this prudently, it will help you to come to an agreement with the Florentines. They will be frightened by this defeat and should willingly consent to an agreement. Whereas I wanted to make enemies of them, thinking that their enmity would bring me power and glory, you must try with all your might to make friends with them, because their friendship will bring you security and advantage. In this world it is very important to know oneself and to be able to measure the strength of one's mind and one's estate: A man who recognizes that he is not suited to war must try to rule by the arts of peace. If you take my advice, you will turn to them and contrive to enjoy the fruits of my labors and risks in this way. You should manage easily enough if you believe these maxims of mine to be true. And you will owe two things to me: one that I left you this realm and the other that I taught you to maintain it."

After he had summoned those citizens of Lucca, Pisa, and Pistoia who were fighting with him, he recommended Pagolo Guinigi to them and made them swear obedience to him; he died, and he left happy memories of himself with all those who had heard him mentioned. He was missed by his friends as much as any other prince who ever died. His funeral was celebrated with great pomp, and he was buried in San Francesco in Lucca. But *virtù* and Fortune were not as friendly to Pagolo Guinigi as they were to Castruccio; because, not long after, he lost Pistoia, and then Pisa, and only kept his hold on Lucca with difficulty. This remained in his family's hands down to Pagolo, his great-grandson.

As we have seen then, Castruccio was a rare man not only for his own times, but also for those that had gone before. Physically, he was taller than average and well proportioned; and he was very handsome, and he treated people with such charm that no one who spoke to him ever left his presence dissatisfied. His hair tended to red, and he wore it cut short above the ears; and he always went bareheaded whatever the weather, even in rain and snow.

He was generous to his friends, relentless with his enemies, just toward his subjects, and treacherous toward outsiders. If he could conquer by guile, he never tried to conquer by force, for he said that it was victory, not the method of victory, that brought glory.

No one was bolder when approaching danger or more careful when getting out of it. He used to say that men should attempt everything and be afraid of nothing, and that God loved strong men, because it was obvious that he always punished the weak with the powerful.

Again, he was admirable in repartee, sometimes sharp, sometimes urbane; and as he gave quarter to no one, he was not angry when he himself was the victim. There are records of many stinging remarks of his and many that were made at his expense.

When a friend was reproving him for having bought a partridge for a ducat, Castruccio said: "You would not have spent more than a *soldo* on it." When his friend agreed, he replied: "A ducat is worth much less to me."

When he was being pestered by a flatterer whom he had spat on out of scorn, the flatterer said: "Fishermen get themselves wet through in the sea to catch a little fish; I will allow myself to be wet by one gob of spit to catch a whale." Castruccio not only took this lying down but rewarded him.

When someone reproached him for living too luxuriously, Castruccio said: "If this were a vice, such sumptuous banquets would not be seen on saints' days."

When he was going down a street and saw a youth coming out of a whore's house and blushing because Castruccio had seen him, he said: "Do not be ashamed when you come out, but when you go in."

When a friend gave him a carefully tied knot to undo, he said: "Idiot, do you think I am going to untie something that gives me so much trouble even when it is tied up?"

When Castruccio said to a man who was a professional philosopher: "You are like dogs who are always hanging around those who can feed them best"; the other replied: "We are more like doctors who go to those who need them most."

Castruccio was going to sea from Pisa to Leghorn and was overtaken by a dangerous storm that frightened him badly. One of the men who were with Castruccio accused him of cowardice and said he was not afraid of anything. Castruccio replied that he was not surprised, for each person set the right value on his own soul.

When someone asked what he should do to be respected, Castruccio said: "See to it that when you are at a banquet one piece of wood is not sitting on another."[1]

When someone was boasting of having read a great deal, Castruccio said: "It would be better to boast of having remembered a lot."

When someone else boasted that he did not get drunk if he drank a lot, Castruccio said: "An ox does exactly the same."

Castruccio had a young girl who was living with him. When a friend criticized him for this, saying particularly that he was wrong to let himself be taken in by a woman: "You are mistaken," said Castruccio, "I have taken her, not she me."

When someone else criticized him for eating too delicate food, he said: "You would not spend as much on it as I do." When the other replied that that was true, he added: "So you are more miserly than I am greedy."

When he was invited to dinner with Taddeo Bernardi of Lucca, a very rich and lavish man, he arrived at the house and Taddeo showed him a room all decked with cloth and paved with fine stones in different colors, patterned to represent flowers and leaves and other greenery. Castruccio gathered some saliva in his mouth and spat it all in Taddeo's face. When the latter remonstrated, Castruccio said: "I did not know where I could spit that would offend you less."

On being asked how Caesar died, he said: "Would to God I might die like him."

One night when he was at the house of one of his gentlemen and several women were invited to the party, he was dancing and enjoying himself rather more than became a man of his standing. When a friend reproved

---

[1] I.e., "When at a banquet, do not sit like a block of wood on your chair." This rude retort was obviously not meant to be immediately intelligible.

him, he said: "The man who is considered wise by day will never be thought a fool at night."

When someone came to ask him a favor and Castruccio pretended not to hear, the man fell to his knees. Castruccio upbraided him for this, but he replied: "You yourself are to blame, for your ears are in your feet." For this he received double the favor he was asking.

Castruccio used to say that the way to hell was easy since you went downwards, with your eyes closed.

When someone asked him a favor, using a lot of superfluous words, Castruccio said to him: "When you want anything else of me send another man."

When a similar person had bored him with a long speech and had ended by saying: "Perhaps I have tired you by talking too much"; "Not at all," he said, "because I did not hear a word you said."

He used to say of someone who had been a beautiful boy and then a handsome man, that he had done too much harm, since he had first taken the husbands away from their wives and now took the wives away from the husbands.

To an envious man who was laughing, he said: "Are you laughing because you are fortunate or because someone else is unfortunate?"

When he was still under the tutelage of Francesco Guinigi, and one of his companions said to him: "What would you like me to give you, in return for letting me slap you in the face?", Castruccio replied: "A helmet."

When he had put to death a citizen of Lucca who had helped him to power and someone told him that he had done wrong to kill one of his old friends, he replied that he was mistaken, because he had killed a new enemy.

Castruccio praised those who became engaged but did not marry, likewise those who said they wanted to go to sea and never went.

He used to say that he was amazed by men who when they buy an earthenware or glass vase make it ring first in order to see if it is a good one, but when they take a wife are content simply to see her.

When someone asked him, just before he died, how he wanted to be buried, he replied: "With my face downwards, because I know that when I am dead this country will be turned upside down."

When he was asked whether he had ever thought of becoming a monk in order to save his soul, he replied that he had not, because it seemed strange to him that Fra Lazzero should go to heaven while Uguccione della Faggiuola went to hell.

Asked when it was right to eat in order to keep healthy, he replied: "If you are rich, when you are hungry; if you are poor, when you can."

Seeing one of his gentlemen getting a servant to lace him up, he said: "I hope to God they spoon-feed you too."

Seeing that someone had written a Latin text over their house, asking God to protect it from evildoers, he said: "He will have to keep out himself."

Going down a street where there was a small house with a large door, he said: "That house will escape through its own door."

When he was told that a foreigner had corrupted a young boy, he said: "He must be from Perugia."

When he asked which city was famous for cheats and swindlers, the reply was "Lucca," because everybody there was a cheat by nature, except Buontura.

When Castruccio was arguing with an ambassador of the King of Naples about exiles' property, he grew somewhat angry, and the ambassador said: "Are you not afraid of the King then?" Castruccio replied: "Is this King of yours good or bad?" When the other answered that he was good, Castruccio retorted: "Then why do you imagine that I should be afraid of good men?"

One could go on relating any number of other things he said, in all of which his wit and good sense would be seen; but these must suffice as evidence of his great qualities.

He lived forty-four years and ruled through all kinds of fortune. As there are several memorials to his good fortune, he also wanted there to be some record of his evil days; so the handcuffs with which he was chained in prison can still be seen today fixed to the tower of his house, where he placed them to commemorate his adversity. And because when he was alive he was not a lesser man than either Philip of Macedon, Alexander's father, or Scipio of Rome, he died at the same age as they did: And he would certainly have outdone them both if instead of Lucca he had had Macedon or Rome as his homeland.

The History of Florence

BOOK II

The republics and monarchies of antiquity had among their great noteworthy institutions, now no longer maintained, one which provided for numbers of new towns and cities to be built at any time. Nothing befits a good prince or a well-governed republic more than the creation of new towns, where men can go to defend themselves or to cultivate the land. The ancients could easily do this, as it was their custom to send new inhabitants, called colonists, into countries that had been conquered or that were empty. This provision not only created new towns but it meant that a conquered country was more firmly in the grip of the conqueror, empty spaces were filled with settlers, and the population was evenly distributed throughout the province. The result was that when life was more comfortable in a province, the population increased and the men were more eager to attack an enemy and were more reliable in the defense of their country. Today, republics and rulers have allowed this custom to lapse through neglect, and this has meant the collapse of the provinces. For this policy alone makes empires more secure and keeps the country's population up, as has been said. It produces stability, because a colony planted by a ruler in a newly occupied country is like a fortress or a watchdog that keeps the others loyal. A province cannot be kept fully inhabited, nor can the population be kept evenly distributed if this practice is dropped. Not all the places in a province are productive or healthy, consequently some are highly populated and others underpopulated. If there is no way of taking men from the highly populated to the underpopulated areas, the province will decline very quickly, because one part of it will eventually be deserted, and another will become impoverished through overpopulation. Nature cannot rectify this imbalance, so ingenuity must. Unhealthy countries can become healthy if a vast number of men occupies them suddenly, cultivating the soil to improve it and clearing the air with fires, which nature could never do. The city of Venice is a good example. It was founded in a marshy, unhealthy place, yet the number of settlers who gathered there suddenly turned it into a healthy place. Pisa, too, was never fully inhabited because of its bad climate until Genoa and its coastline were raided by the Saracens. Such great numbers of refugees gathered there suddenly that they made Pisa a powerful, crowded city. Since the system of planting colonies has lapsed, it is more difficult to keep conquered territories, empty spaces are not filled, and overpopulated areas are not relieved. As a result, many parts of the world are deserted in comparison with ancient times, and particularly in Italy. All this has come about and still continues because rulers have no desire for true glory, and republics have no institutions worthy of praise. But in ancient times, colonization meant either that new cities were founded frequently or that those already begun were helped to grow. Among these was the city of Florence, which owed its foundation to Fiesole and its growth to colonization.

II

It is quite certain, as Dante and Giovanni Villani show, that the city of Fiesole, set on the top of a hill, arranged that its markets should be situated not on the hill but in the plain, between the foot of the hill and the river Arno, so that they would be better patronized and more convenient for those who wanted to bring their merchandise. I believe that these markets were the reason for the first buildings being put up there. The merchants wanted to have shelters where they could take their goods easily, and in time these became proper buildings. Then when the Romans conquered the Carthaginians and made Italy safe from foreign wars, their number greatly increased. Men do not persevere in difficult circumstances if they are not forced to by some necessity. If the fear of war makes them live willingly in rough, barren country, once the fear has ceased they much prefer to live in the comfort of flat, cultivated places. The sense of security that arose in Italy because of the reputation of the Roman Republic caused the number of houses, already begun as has been described, to increase so much thát they formed a town that was at first called "Villa Arnina." Then the civil wars broke out in Rome, first between Marius and Sulla, then between Caesar and Pompey, and later between Caesar's murderers and the men who wanted to avenge his death. Settlers were sent to Fiesole, first by Sulla, then by those three Roman citizens who divided the Empire among themselves after they had avenged Caesar. Part or all of these settlers built their houses in the plain near the city that had already been founded. And the place became so built-up, so densely populated, and so well organized, because of these additions, that it could count as one of the cities of Italy. There are various opinions about the derivation of the name *Florence*. Some think it was called after Florinus, one of the chiefs of the colony; others think it was first called not Florentia but Fluentia, because it was situated near the river Arno, and they quote Pliny who says: "The Fluentines are near the flowing Arno." This could be wrong, however, because Pliny in his text shows where the Florentines were, not what they were called; and that word *Fluentines* must be corrupt, because Frontinus and Cornelius Tacitus, who wrote almost at the same time as Pliny, say *Florence* and *Florentines*. Already in Tiberius' time they were governed in the same way as other Italian cities, and Cornelius reports that Florentine ambassadors came to the Emperor to beg that the waters of the Chiana should not be diverted onto their territory, and it is unlikely that the city had two names at the same time. Therefore I believe it was always called Florence, whatever the

57

reason; and furthermore, whatever the cause of its foundation, it was founded under the Roman Empire and began to be mentioned by writers at the time of the first emperors. When the Empire was attacked by the barbarians, Florence was laid waste by Totila, King of the Ostrogoths, and was rebuilt two hundred and fifty years later by Charlemagne. From that time until A.D 1215, it depended on the fortunes of the men who ruled in Italy. To begin with, the rulers were Charlemagne's descendants, then the Berengars, and last of all the German emperors, as we explained in our survey of world history. During this time, the Florentines could not increase their power or achieve anything memorable, because of the might of the rulers to whom they owed allegiance. Nevertheless, in 1010, on the day of St. Romulus, a feast day in Fiesole, they took Fiesole and destroyed it. They did this either with the Emperor's consent, or at a time between the death of one Emperor and the creation of another, when everyone had more freedom. But since the popes gained more power in Italy and the German emperors grew weaker, all the states in the province behaved with less reverence toward the prince. In fact, in 1080, in Henry III's time, Italy was openly divided between him and the Church. Despite this the Florentines remained united until 1215, obeying the victors, and seeking nothing for themselves apart from their own preservation. But just as in our own bodies the later an illness strikes, the more dangerous and mortal it is, so the later Florence chose to become involved in Italian factions, the more troubled she was by them. The reason for the first quarrel is very well known, as it has been made famous by Dante and other writers; still I feel it should be recounted briefly.

III

The most powerful families in Florence were the Buondelmonti and the Uberti, and after them the Amidei and the Donati. There was a rich widow of the Donati family who had a very beautiful daughter. This widow had planned in her own mind to marry her daughter to Buondelmonte, a young knight and head of the Buondelmonti family. Through carelessness or because she thought there was plenty of time, she had not divulged this plan to anyone, when Buondelmonte became engaged to a girl from the Amidei family. The widow was extremely annoyed, and hoped to put a stop to the wedding before it was celebrated, with the aid of her daughter's beauty. One day when she saw Buondelmonte coming toward her house alone, she went downstairs, leading her daughter behind her. As he passed by, she went up to him saying: "I do congratulate you on your engagement, although I had been keeping this daughter of mine for you"; and pushing the door open, she let him see her. When he saw the girl's extraordinary beauty and thought of her family and her dowry, which was no less than his fiancée's, he was so anxious to possess her that he forgot about the promise he had given, the harm he would do by breaking it, and all the evil that might follow. He said: "Since you had kept her for me, it would be ungrateful of me to refuse her while there was still time"; and the wedding was celebrated without any time being wasted. When this affair was known, it infuriated the Amidei family and the Uberti, who were related to them. At a meeting with several other relations, they decided that this insult could not be tolerated honorably and that there could be no other revenge than Buondelmonte's death. Some did mention the trouble that might follow, but Mosca Lamberti said that people who think of different things never achieve any of them and quoted that famous old saying: "What's done can't be undone." They gave the responsibility for the murder to Mosca, Stiatta Uberti, Lambertuccio Amidei, and Oderigo Fifanti. On the morning of Easter Sunday, they shut themselves up in the Amidei's houses between the Ponte Vecchio and Santo Stefano, and as Buondelmonte was crossing the river on a white horse, thinking it was as easy to forget an insult as it was to break off an engagement, he was attacked and killed by them at the foot of the bridge, beneath the statue of Mars. This murder divided the city; one party rallied around the

Buondelmonti, the other around the Uberti. These families were well provided with houses, towers, and men, and so they fought for a long time without either expelling the other. Although their quarrels did not end in peace, truces were agreed upon. This meant that the feuds petered out or flared up according to events.

IV

Florence was beset by these troubles until the time of Frederick II. Because he was King of Naples, he believed that he could increase his power and make a stand against the Church. To strengthen his command in Tuscany, he favored the Uberti and their followers. With his backing, they expelled the Buondelmonti; so our city was split between Guelphs and Ghibellines, just as the rest of Italy had been for some time. I do not think it would be superfluous to record the names of the families who joined the two parties. Those who belonged to the Guelph faction were: the Buondelmonti, Nerli, Rossi, Frescobaldi, Mozzi, Bardi, Pulci, Gherardini, Foraboschi, Bagnesi, Guidalotti, Sacchetti, Manieri, Lucardesi, Chiaramontesi, Compiobbesi, Cavalcanti, Giandonati, Gianfigliazzi, Scali, Gualterotti, Importuni, Bostichi, Tornaquinci, Vecchietti, Tosinghi, Arrigucci, Agli, Sizi, Adimari, Visdomini, Donati, Pazzi, Della Bella, Ardinghi, Tedaldi, and the Cerchi. Those on the Ghibelline side were: the Uberti, Mannegli, Ubriachi, Fifanti, Amidei, Infangati, Malespini, Scolari, Guidi, Galli, Cappiardi, Lamberti, Soldanieri, Cipriani, Toschi, Amieri, Palermini, Migliorelli, Pigli, Barucci, Cattani, Agolanti, Brunelleschi, Caponsacchi, Elisei, Abati, Tedaldini, Giuochi, and the Galigai. Besides them, many families from among the people joined with the nobles on both sides; almost all the city was infected by the feud. The exiled Guelphs went to the towns of the upper Arno valley, where most of their castles were, and where they could best defend themselves against the enemy forces. But when Frederick died, those in Florence who followed a middle course, and had most prestige among the people, thought it would be better to reunite the city than to harm it by keeping it divided. They managed to get the Guelphs to forget their grievances and return, and the Ghibellines to set aside their fears and receive them. Once they were united, they felt it was time to decide on a form of democratic government and a defense policy before the new Emperor became powerful.

V

They divided the city into six parts and elected twelve citizens to govern it, two for each sixth. They were to be called *Anziani* and appointed yearly. To do away with quarrels arising out of the passing of judgments, they made provision for two foreign judges, one called the Captain of the People, and the other the Podestà. They were to judge civil and criminal cases as they occurred among the citizens. Since no form of government is stable without proper provision for defense, they set up twenty standards in the city and seventy-six in the *contado*, and enrolled all the young men under them. They ordered everyone to be ready, armed, and under his standard when called on by the Captain or by the *Anziani;* they altered the device on the flags according to the men's arms: The crossbowmen had a different flag from the shield bearers. Every year, on Whitsunday, they handed the colors to the new men at a great ceremony and appointed the new heads for the whole organization. To lend their armies distinction and also to give everyone a place to run to and make a stand against the enemy if hard pressed in battle, they had a large chariot built. It was drawn by two oxen decked in red and on top was a red and white standard. When they wanted to call the army out, they took this chariot to the New Market and handed it over to the leaders of the people with great solemnity. To add dignity to their expeditions, they also had a bell called "Martinella," which used to ring continuously for a month before the armies were led out of the city, in order to give the enemy time to defend themselves. Then men were so full of *virtù* and

behaved so generously that, whereas today it is thought
noble and prudent to attack the enemy suddenly, then
it was considered shameful and treacherous. The army
used to take this bell with them, and used it to give orders to the guards and other sectors in battle.

VI

The Florentines laid the foundations of their liberty
with these civil and military institutions. It is unbeliev-
able how much power and authority Florence gained
in a short time, not only becoming the chief city in Tuscany but being numbered among the most important
cities in Italy. She would have risen to greater heights
if she had not been frequently troubled by fresh disputes.
The Florentines lived under this government for ten
years, and during that time they forced Pistoia, Arezzo,
and Siena to make alliances with them. Coming back
with their army from Siena, they took Volterra, destroyed
some castles, and brought their occupants to Florence.
These operations were all carried out on the advice of the
Guelphs, who were much more powerful than the Ghibellines. This was because the people hated the Ghibellines
for their arrogant behavior when they had been in power
in Frederick's time, and because the Church party was
more popular than the Emperor's. The people hoped
to keep their freedom with the help of the Church, and
were afraid of losing it under the Emperor. Consequently,
the Ghibellines could not rest, seeing their authority
waning, and they were waiting for a chance to resume
power. They felt that this chance had come when they
saw that Manfred, Frederick's son, had assumed control
of the kingdom of Naples and had dealt the Church a
heavy blow. They entered into secret negotiations with
him to regain power, but did not manage to keep these
negotiations hidden from the *Anziani*. The *Anziani* summoned the Uberti, who not only disobeyed, but armed
and barricaded themselves in their houses. The people
were annoyed by this, took up arms, and with the
Guelphs' help, forced the Uberti to leave Florence and

go to Siena with the entire Ghibelline party. From there the Ghibellines asked Manfred, King of Naples, for help. Through the initiative of Farinata degli Uberti, the Guelphs were defeated by the king's troops at the river Arbia, with so much bloodshed that those who did survive took refuge not in Florence but in Lucca, because they believed their own city to be lost.

VII

Manfred had sent Count Giordano to the Ghibellines as commander of his troops. He was a man with a great reputation as a soldier in those days. After the victory he went to Florence with the Ghibellines and forced the whole city into subjection to Manfred, abolishing the magistracies and all other established institutions in which some form of her liberty appeared. This outrage, carried out rather imprudently, aroused the bitter hatred of the people and confirmed them in their anti-Ghibelline sympathies. This was the cause of the eventual downfall of the Ghibellines. When Count Giordano had to return to Naples because of his duties in the kingdom, he left Count Guido Novello, Lord of the Casentino, as the king's vicar in Florence. The latter called a council of Ghibellines at Empoli, where they all decided that if the Ghibelline party was to retain power in Tuscany, Florence must be destroyed, since she was the only city that could restore the strength of the Church parties, because the people were Guelphs. There was no citizen or friend who opposed this cruel sentence passed against such a noble city except Farinata degli Uberti. He defended Florence openly and unashamedly, saying that he had only taken up the struggle and run so many risks in order to live in his own home town. He was not going to give up what he had been working for, nor refuse what Fortune had given him. He would be no less opposed to those who thought otherwise than he had been to the Guelphs. If any of them feared his home town, let them destroy it, because he would defend it with the same spirit as he had routed the Guelphs. Farinata was

63

a man of great courage, a superb fighter, a leader of the Ghibellines, and highly esteemed by Manfred. His authority put an end to that discussion, and they decided on other ways of maintaining their control.

VIII

The Guelphs who had taken refuge in Lucca were told to leave by the Lucchese because of threats from the Count, and they went to Bologna. They were called in from there by the Guelphs of Parma against the Ghibellines, and when they had beaten the enemy by their *virtù*, all the enemy's property was made over to them, and so their wealth and honors greatly increased. Knowing that Pope Clement had called in Charles of Anjou to take the kingdom from Manfred, they sent ambassadors to the Pope, offering him their forces. The Pope not only received them as friends, but gave them his standard, which was always borne in battle by the Guelphs afterwards, and is the one still used in Florence. Then Manfred was deprived of the kingdom and killed by Charles. Since the Guelphs of Florence had taken part in the campaign, their party became stronger and the Ghibellines' weaker. Those who were ruling Florence with Count Guido Novello thought it best to propitiate the people on whom they had previously heaped all kinds of injustice. But measures that would have been of some use had they been taken earlier before the need arose were not only useless but hastened the Ghibellines' fall, because they were taken late and with a bad grace. They thought they could gain the people's friendship and support if they gave back some of the honors and authority they had taken away. They elected thirty-six *popolani* who, with two knights brought in from Bologna, were to reform the city's constitution. At their first meeting they divided the whole city into Guilds and put an official in charge of each Guild to dispense justice to its members. Besides this, they gave a flag to each Guild so that all the men would muster beneath it whenever the city required it. To begin with, there were twelve Guilds, seven greater and five lesser. Later the lesser Guilds grew to fourteen, so that there were twenty-one altogether as at present. The thirty-six reformers acted in other matters also for the common good.

IX

Count Guido ordered the citizens to pay a tax for the upkeep of his soldiers; but he had so much trouble that he did not dare enforce the demand. Feeling that he had lost control, he withdrew with the Ghibelline leaders, and they decided to take back by force what they had imprudently granted to the people. When they seemed to be suitably armed, and the thirty-six were assembled, they began to create a disturbance. The reformers were frightened and withdrew to their homes, and immediately the flags of the Guilds came out with large armed followings. When they heard that Count Guido and his party were at San Giovanni, they gathered at Santa Trinita and made Giovanni Soldanieri their leader. The Count, hearing where the people were, left to find them. The people did not try to avoid a fight; they went to meet the enemy, and they clashed where the Tornaquinci loggia is today. The Count was repulsed and suffered a number of casualties; he was dismayed and afraid that the enemy would attack him at night, find his men beaten and disheartened, and would kill him. He was so obsessed by this fear that without thinking of any other remedy he decided to save himself by flight rather than by fighting, and he went to Prato with all his men, against the advice of the party leaders. But as soon as he lost his fear, once he was in safety, he recognized his mistake. Hoping to correct it, when it was light in the morning, he came back to Florence with his troops to force an entry into the city he had given up through cowardice. But his plan did not succeed because the people who would have had difficulty in expelling him had no trouble keeping him out. So he went off into the Casentino, sad and humiliated, and the Ghibellines withdrew to their villages. The people

65

were the winners, and on the advice of those who had the good of the republic at heart, it was decided to reunite the city and recall all the exiled citizens, Guelph and Ghibelline alike. So the Guelphs came back six years after they had been expelled, and the Ghibellines were again forgiven the more recent wrongs and brought back home. Nevertheless, they were very much hated by the Guelphs and the people. The former could not entirely forget their exile, and the latter had too vivid a memory of the tyranny of the Ghibelline government they had lived under. This meant that neither party was happy. While life went on in Florence in this way, news spread that Conradin, Manfred's grandson, was coming from Germany with an army to take Naples. The Ghibellines were very hopeful of coming back to power, and the Guelphs were planning how to defend themselves against their enemies. They asked King Charles for help against Conradin if he passed through Florence. Because Charles' troops were coming, the Guelphs became aggressive, and the Ghibellines were so afraid, that two days before the troops' arrival they fled of their own accord.

X

When the Ghibellines had left, the Florentines reorganized the city's constitution. They elected twelve men to sit in office for two months. They did not call them *Anziani* but *Buoni Uomini*. Besides these there was a council of eighty citizens, called the *Credenza*. After these came one hundred and eighty *popolani*, thirty per sixth of the city, who together with the *Credenza* and the twelve *Buoni Uomini* were called the General Council. They also set up another council of one hundred and twenty citizens, *popolani* and nobles, whose duty it was to approve proposals debated in the other councils, as well as to allot the offices of the republic. Once this government had been established, they also strengthened the Guelph party with magistracies and other institutions so that they could defend themselves better against the Ghibellines. They divided the latter's possessions into three parts, confiscated one part, gave another to the ruling body of the party called the Captains, and the third to the Guelphs as compensation for damages received. To keep Tuscany Guelph, the Pope made King Charles Vicar Imperial of Tuscany. When the Pope died, the Florentines were maintaining their reputation with laws at home and arms abroad. After a long dispute, Gregory X was elected two years later. He had been in Syria for a long time and was still there at the time of his election. He was out of touch with the feelings of the parties and did not respect the parties as much as his predecessors had done. When he was in Florence on his way to France, he felt it was the duty of a good pastor to reunite the city. Owing to his mediation, the Florentines agreed to receive the Ghibelline syndics in Florence to negotiate their return. Although an agreement was reached, the Ghibellines were so afraid that they did not want to go back. The Pope blamed this on the city, and he was so angry that he excommunicated it. Florence remained in a state of contumacy during the Pope's lifetime, but after his death it was rehallowed by Pope Innocent V. Then came the pontificate of Nicholas III, born of the Orsini family. Because the Popes always feared anyone who had become powerful in Italy, even though this had happened because of the favors of the Church, and because the Popes tried to decrease this power, frequent disorders and changes followed there. The fear of one powerful man made a weak man grow strong, and once he was powerful he was feared, and once he was feared there were attempts to bring him down. This was why the kingdom was taken from Manfred and given to Charles, and later this was why Charles was feared and his downfall was looked for. For these reasons, Nicholas III arranged, through the Emperor, that Charles would lose Tuscany, and he sent Latino, his legate, to the province in the name of the Emperor.

XI

At that time Florence was in rather a bad state. The Guelph nobility had grown unruly and had no respect for the magistrates. Every day there were several murders and other acts of violence that went unpunished, as the culprits were favored by one noble or another. The people's leaders thought that it would be wise to readmit the exiles to curb this arrogance. This gave the legate a chance to reunite the city, and the Ghibellines came back. In place of the twelve rulers they had fourteen, seven from each party, who would rule for a year and be elected by the Pope. Florence kept this form of government for two years, until Pope Martin became Pope. He was French by birth and he gave to King Charles all the authority that Nicholas had taken from him. The parties immediately came to life again in Tuscany, because the Florentines took up arms against the imperial governor, and to keep the Ghibellines out of power and to keep a check on those in power, they set up a new form of government.

It was 1282, and the Guilds were very highly thought of since they had been given their officials and standards. On their own authority these officers laid it down that three citizens were to be appointed instead of the fourteen. They were to be called Priors and were to remain in charge of the government of the republic for two months. They could be *popolani* or nobles as long as they were merchants or members of a Guild. After the first magistracy the number was altered to six, so that there was one from each sixth, and this number was kept until 1342 when the city was divided into quarters, and there were eight Priors, although at that time they occasionally elected twelve for some particular reason. As it turned out, this office brought about the downfall of the nobility, because they were excluded from it by the people for various reasons, and later beaten unmercifully. To begin with, the nobles consented because they were not agreed among themselves. They all lost control of the state because each one wanted to take it from the other. A palace was granted to the magistracy where it could reside permanently. Before it had been customary for officials and councils to meet in churches. They were also allowed sergeants and other necessary functionaries. To begin with, they were only called Priors, but later the name Signori was added for greater prestige. Peace was maintained at home for some time while the Florentines made war on the Aretines who had expelled the Guelphs, and they beat them at Campaldino. The city was increasing in population and wealth, so it seemed wise to add to its walls, and they increased their span to what it is today. Earlier their diameter was only the distance from the Ponte Vecchio to San Lorenzo.

XII

War abroad and peace at home had put an end to Guelph and Ghibelline party strife in Florence. There only remained smoldering feelings, which naturally exist in all towns between the rulers and the people. The people want to live according to the laws, and the rulers want to control the laws, and the two cannot possibly agree. This discontent did not reveal itself while they were afraid of the Ghibellines; but as soon as the Ghibellines were restrained, it asserted itself. Every day some man of the people was abused, and the laws and the officials were not sufficient to avenge him because every noble could defend himself against the power of the Priors and the Captain with the help of his relatives and friends. The leaders of the Guilds, wanting to remedy this, provided that every Signoria should appoint a *popolano* as Gonfalonier of Jusice at the beginning of its term of office, and they gave him a thousand men enrolled under twenty banners. He was to be ready with his standard and his armed men to uphold justice whenever he was called on by the leaders of the Guilds or by the Captain. The first one elected was Ubaldo Ruffoli. He brought out the banner and destroyed the Galletti's houses, because one of the family had killed a *popolano* in France.

The Guilds could easily make this provision because of the bitter enmities that reigned among the nobility. The nobles had hardly thought of the provisions made against them, when they saw the harshness with which they were put into practice. At first they were rather afraid, but they soon became aggressive again, because one of them was always a member of the Signoria, and they could easily stop the Gonfalonier from doing his duty. Besides this, when someone received an injury, he needed witnesses before he could bring an action, and no one could be found to witness against the nobles. So in a short while, Florence had the same troubles all over again, and the people suffered the same injustices from the nobles, because judgments were late and sentences were not carried out.

XIII

The *popolani* did not know what to do. Giano della Bella, a man of very noble birth who yet loved the city's liberty, encouraged the heads of the Guilds to reform the constitution. On his advice it was decreed that the Gonfalonier should reside with the Priors and have four thousand men under his command. They also deprived the nobles of the privilege of being made Signori. They forced the relatives of a guilty man to share the same punishment, and they made common reputation enough to judge a man. These laws, which were called the Ordinances of Justice, meant that the people were greatly respected and Giano della Bella was very much hated. The powerful had a very poor opinion of him, as he had destroyed their power, and the rich *popolani* envied him because they felt that he had too much authority, which was soon shown to be the case. Fate brought about the death of a *popolano* in a fight in which several noblemen were involved, among them Corso Donati. As he was the boldest, he was blamed for it. He was arrested by the Captain of the People, but for some reason he was freed, either because he was not guilty or because the Captain was afraid to condemn him. The people were so annoyed by his being set free that they armed and went to Giano della Bella's house to beg him to see that the laws he had invented were observed. Giano, who wanted Corso to be punished, did not get them to put down their arms, as many thought he should have done. He advised the people to go to the Signori to complain and ask them to see to it. The people were very angry. They felt that the Captain had wronged them and Giano had let them down, and they went not to the Signori but to the Captain's palace, took it, and sacked it. This act annoyed all the citizens, and those who were hoping Giano would fall laid all the blame on him. As there were some of his enemies among the next Signori, he was cited before the Captain as a rabble-rouser. While his case was being considered, the people armed and went to his house, offering to defend him against the Signori and his enemies. Giano did not want to put the favors of the people to the test, nor to trust his life to the officials, fearing the instability of the former and the ill will of the latter. To avoid his enemies wronging him and his friends harming his country, he decided to leave, thus surrendering to envy and freeing the citizens from the fear they had of him. He chose voluntary exile and left the city, which on his own initiative and at his own risk, he had freed from servitude to the aristocracy.

XIV

After his departure the nobility grew hopeful of getting their privileges back. Believing that their troubles were the result of their disunity, the nobles met and sent two of their members to the Signoria, which they judged to be favorable to them, to ask for the laws against them to be made a little less harsh. The *popolani* were upset when this request was discovered, because they feared the Signori might grant it. With the nobles' ambition on one side and the people's fear on the other, they resorted to arms. The nobles were concentrated in three places:

at San Giovanni, in the New Market, and at the Piazza de' Mozzi, and under three leaders: Forese Adimari, Vanni de' Mozzi, and Geri Spini. The *popolani* gathered in great numbers at the Signori's palace, which was near San Brocolo at that time. Because the people were suspicious of that Signoria, they deputed six citizens to rule with them. While both parties were preparing to fight, some men, both *popolani* and nobles, together with some clergy of good reputation, intervened to mediate. They reminded the nobles that their pride and bad government had been the reason for their loss of privileges and the laws against them, and that taking up arms and trying to get back by force what they had allowed to be taken away through their disunity and evil ways would lead to nothing but the ruin of their country and a worsening of their conditions. They told them to remember that the people surpassed them in number, wealth, and hatred and that their nobility, which they thought set them above others, could not fight; and when it came to action, it was only an empty name which was not enough to defend them against so many. On the other hand, they reminded the people that it was not prudent always to want the last word, that it was never wise to make men desperate, because a man who does not hope for good will not fear evil, and that they ought to remember that the nobility was the same that had brought honor to the city in the wars, so that it was neither good nor just to persecute the nobles with so much hatred. They pointed out that the nobles could easily bear to lose the possibility of enjoying the chief magistracy, but that they could not tolerate everybody having the power to banish them from their country under the new laws. So it would be wise to temper the laws, and in order to do this, to arrange for everyone to disarm. They should not wait to see the outcome of the fight, putting their trust in numbers, because the many had often been known to be overcome by the few. The people had different views. Many wanted to fight, believing that it was bound to come to that one day, and it was better to get it over now than to wait until the enemy was more powerful; they felt that if it was thought that the aristocracy would rest content if the laws were modified, then it would be right to modify them, but that the nobles' pride was so great that they would never give in until forced to. Others, wiser and more peacefully inclined, felt that altering the laws did not matter very much, while open warfare did. Their opinion prevailed, and they decreed that witnesses were necessary for accusations against noblemen.

XV

After they had disarmed, both sides were still very fearful, and they built up their defenses with arms and towers. The people reorganized the government and restricted its numbers because the former Signori had favored the nobles. The leaders were the Mancini, Magalotti, Altoviti, Peruzzi, and Cerretani. Once the government had been stabilized, they laid the foundations of the palace of the Signori in 1298, to give them greater prestige and more security, and they made room for it by demolishing the Uberti's houses. At the same time, they also began the public prisons, both of which buildings were finished in a few years. Our city was never in a better or happier state than in those times. It was full of people and wealth, and its reputation stood high. Citizens capable of bearing arms amounted to thirty thousand, and those in the *contado* amounted to seventy thousand. All Tuscany owed allegiance to Florence, either as a subject or as an ally. Although anger and fear were felt by the nobles and the people, they resulted in no evil deeds, and everyone lived in unity and peace. This peace would have had nothing to fear from enemies outside, if it had not been disturbed by enemies from within. The city had reached the point where it no longer feared the Empire or its own exiles, and it could have stood up to all the states of Italy with its own forces. But the harm that outside forces could not do was done by others from inside.

XVI

In Florence there were two families, the Cerchi and the Donati, who were very powerful because of their wealth, nobility, and manpower. There had been some disagreement between them because they were neighbors in Florence and in the *contado*, but it was not serious enough to lead to violence. Perhaps nothing very much would have come of it if new reasons had not added to the bad feeling. Among the leading families of Pistoia were the Cancellieri. It happened that Lore, son of Guglielmo, and Geri, son of Bertacca, both of that family, were gambling. There was a quarrel, and Geri was slightly wounded by Lore. Guglielmo was annoyed, and hoping to put an end to the affair by courtesy he made matters worse, because he ordered his son to go to the house of the wounded man's father and ask his pardon. Lore obeyed his father. But this courteous action did not soften Bertacca's hard heart at all. He had Lore captured by his servants and, as a greater insult, had his hand cut off on a manger, and said to him: "Go back to your father and tell him that wounds are treated with steel and not with words." The cruelty of this action annoyed Guglielmo so much that he armed his men for revenge. Bertacca also armed to defend himself, and not only the family but the whole of Pistoia took sides. Since the Cancellieri were descended from Cancelliere who had had two wives, one of whom was called Bianca, one of the parties was called White after those who were descended from her, and the other one, taking the opposite name, was called Black. There followed a period of fighting in which several men were killed and houses were destroyed. They could come to no agreement, and weary of the strife, wanting either to put an end to their quarrels or to add to them by embroiling others, they came to Florence. The Blacks were favored by the Donati because of their friendship with Corso, the head of the family, so the Whites sought a powerful support against the Blacks in Veri de' Cerchi, a man in no way inferior to Corso.

XVII

The strife which had come from Pistoia added to the old enmity between the Cerchi and the Donati. It was already very obvious that the Priors and other good citizens were afraid that fighting might break out between them at any time, and this would lead to the whole city's being divided. So they turned to the Pope and asked him to use his authority to impose the remedy for these troubles, which they could not do by themselves. The Pope sent for Veri and charged him to make peace with the Donati. But Veri appeared to be amazed and said that he had no quarrel with them, and since peace presupposed war, he did not know why peace was necessary because they were not at war. Veri returned from Rome without anything having been concluded. The differences grew so that the slightest accident could have been the last straw, as in fact happened.

It was May, at which time there is public merrymaking on holidays in Florence. Some young men of the Donati family, riding with their friends, stopped near Santa Trinita to watch some women dancing. Some of the Cerchi also arrived accompanied by a number of noblemen. They did not know the Donati who were in front, and also wanting to watch, they pushed their horses in among them and jostled them. The Donati considered this an insult and grasped their weapons; the Cerchi replied boldly, and after many wounds had been inflicted on both sides they parted. This disturbance was the source of a great deal of trouble, because the whole city took sides, the people as well as the aristocracy, and the sides took their names from the Whites and the Blacks.

The Cerchi were the leaders of the White party, and they were joined by the Adimari, the Abati, some of the Tosinghi, Bardi, Rossi, Frescobaldi, Nerli, Mannelli, and all the Mozzi, Scali, Gherardini, Cavalcanti, Malespini, Bostichi, Giandonati, Vecchietti, and Arrigucci. Added to these were many *popolano* families and all the Ghibellines in Florence; and because of the large size of their

75

following, they almost controlled the government of the town. The Donati, on the other hand, were the leaders of the Black party, and sided with them were those parts of the families mentioned above who had not joined the Whites, together with all the Pazzi, Bisdomini, Manieri, Bagnesi, Tornaquinci, Spini, Buondelmonti, Gianfigliazzi, and Brunelleschi. The quarrel did not only involve the city but spread to the whole *contado*. The party leaders and everybody who favored the Guelphs and the republic were very afraid that this new feud might undermine the city and cause the revival of the Ghibelline party. They sent to Pope Boniface again, asking him to think of a solution unless he wanted the city that had always been a shield to the Church to fall or become Ghibelline. The Pope sent Matteo d'Acquasparta, Cardinal of Porto, as legate to Florence. Because he had difficulty with the White party, which seemed to him more powerful and less afraid, he left Florence in an angry mood and laid an interdict on it. So the city was left in a greater state of confusion than before his arrival.

XVIII

At the time when everybody's feelings were roused, many of the Cerchi and Donati happened to be at a funeral together. They started quarrelling and soon came to blows, which for the moment only gave rise to riots. Everyone went back home, and the Cerchi decided to attack the Donati and went to look for them with a large following. But they were defeated by Corso's *virtù*, and many of them were wounded. The whole town was up in arms. The Signori and the laws were overcome by the fury of the aristocracy, and the wisest and best citizens lived in fear. The Donati and their party were most afraid because they had least power; and to look after their interests, Corso met the other Black leaders and party chiefs, and they agreed to ask the Pope to get someone of royal blood to reform Florence, thinking that they could get the better of the Whites in this way. The Priors were notified of this meeting and its decision, and

76

the opposing party condemned it as a conspiracy against the freedom of the city. As both parties were armed, the Signori, of whom Dante was one at that time, took heart because of Dante's prudence and good advice and armed the people, including a great many men from the *contado*. Then they forced the party leaders to disarm and exiled Corso Donati with many of the Black party. To show they were neutral in their judgment, they also exiled many of the White party, who came back soon after on various honorable pretexts.

XIX

Corso and his friends went to Rome because they thought the Pope favored their party. In his presence they were able to convince the Pope of what they had already written to him. At the Pope's court was Charles of Valois, the King of France's brother, who had been called to Italy by the King of Naples in order to invade Sicily. The Pope thought it would be a good thing to send him to Florence, as the Florentine exiles were pressing him to, until a suitable time for him to sail. So Charles came. Although the Whites who were in power were suspicious of him, they did not dare stop him from coming, since he was head of the Guelphs and sent by the Pope. To win his friendship, they gave him authority to do what he liked with the city. Once Charles had this authority, he armed all his friends and supporters. This made the people so afraid that he was trying to deprive them of their liberty that everyone armed himself and stayed in his own house in order to be ready in case Charles made a move.

The Cerchi and the leaders of the White party had come to be hated by the common people because they had ruled the republic for some time and had acted in a high-handed way. This encouraged Corso and the other Black exiles to come to Florence, especially since they knew that Charles and the party leaders were on their side. When the city was armed because of its fear of Charles, Corso entered Florence with the exiles and many others of his followers, without anybody trying to stop them. Although Veri de' Cerchi was urged to go out to meet him, he refused, saying that he wanted Corso to be punished by the people of Florence, whom he was attacking. But the opposite happened, because he was not punished but welcomed by them. Veri had to flee to save himself. Once Corso had forced the Porta a Pinti, he made his headquarters at San Piero Maggiore, which was near his houses. Many friends and other people who favored change gathered around him. The first thing he did was to free everybody who was in prison, whether for public or private reasons. He forced the Signori to go back to their homes as private citizens, and he elected new ones from the *popolani* and the Black party. For five days he plundered the men who had been chiefs of the White party. The Cerchi and the other leaders of their faction had left the city and retired to their castles, seeing that Charles and most of the people were against them. Where before they had never wanted to follow the Pope's advice, they were obliged to turn to him for help, pointing out to him that Charles had come to divide Florence, not to unite it. The Pope again sent Matteo d'Acquasparta as his legate, who arranged a peace between the Cerchi and the Donati and strengthened it with new marriage ties. He wanted the Whites to have a share of the offices again, but the Blacks, now in power, would not agree. So the legate did not depart any more satisfied or less angry than before, and he left the city under an interdict because of its disobedience.

XX

Both parties remained in Florence, both of them discontented. The Blacks, seeing the enemy party beside them, feared it would win back its old authority and cause their downfall. The Whites missed their authority and privileges. Then new insults were added to these tensions and natural fears. Niccolò de' Cerchi was going to his estate with several of his friends, and when he had reached the bridge over the Africo he was attacked by

Simone, Corso Donati's son. There was a big fight which ended tragically on both sides, because Niccolò was killed and Simone was so badly wounded that he died the next night. This affair upset the whole town again, and although the Black party was more to blame, it was still protected by the government. Before judgment was given, a conspiracy was discovered between the Whites and Piero Ferrante, one of Charles' barons, with whom the Whites had been negotiating to get back into power. This came to light through letters written to him by the Cerchi, although it was thought that the letters were forged and that they had been invented by the Donati to attract attention from the shame they had incurred by Niccolò's death.

The Cerchi were all banished with their White followers, among whom was the poet Dante. Their goods were confiscated and their homes destroyed. They dispersed to different places, with many Ghibellines who had been their allies, and sought a new future with new problems. Charles, having done what he came to Florence to do, left and went back to the Pope to carry on his Sicilian venture. In this he was no better or wiser than he had been in Florence, and he went home to France in disgrace with many of his men missing.

XXI

Life was fairly quiet in Florence after Charles' departure. Only Corso was restless, because he did not seem to command as much respect in the city as he felt he ought to. As it was a popular government, he saw the republic being administered by many people who were inferior to him. Spurred on by these feelings, he thought of a way of making his evil intentions appear good by means of a high-minded complaint. He accused a number of citizens who had administered public funds of using them for private purposes and said they should be found and punished. This accusation was taken up by others who had the same aims. Added to this was the ignorance of many others who believed that Corso was acting out of love of his country. On the other hand, the accused were defending themselves, and they had the support of the people. The disagreement went on for so long that when legal methods failed they turned to force. On one side were Corso and Lottieri, Bishop of Florence, with many aristocrats and some of the people, and on the other, the Signori and most of the people. There was fighting in several parts of the town. When the Signori saw the great danger they were in, they sent to Lucca for help, and all the people of Lucca came to Florence immediately. Under their direction the quarrels were patched up for the moment, the riots ceased, and the people retained their status and liberty without the disturbers of the peace being punished in any other way.

The Pope had heard about the disturbances in Florence, and he sent Niccolao da Prato as his legate to put a stop to them. He was a man of great reputation for rank, learning, and manners; and he immediately won so much confidence that he was given authority to set up what government he liked. Because he was born a Ghibelline, he meant to bring the exiles home. But he wanted to win the people over first, and to do this he revived the old Companies of the People. This provision increased their power very much and lessened that of the aristocrats. The legate felt that the masses were beholden to him, and he planned to let the exiles return. He tried various ways, but not only were none of them successful, but he became so suspect to the government that he was forced to leave. He went back to the Pope in a very angry mood, and he left Florence in a state of great confusion and under an interdict. The city was troubled by more than one dissension. There were the clashes between the people and the aristocrats, the Ghibellines and the Guelphs, and the Whites and the Blacks. So the whole town was up in arms; there were frequent scuffles because many people were annoyed by the legate's departure, since they wanted the exiles to return. The first to make trouble were the Medici and the Giugni, who had declared themselves to the legate as being in favor of the rebels. There was fighting in several parts of Florence.

On top of these troubles a fire broke out, first near

Orto San Michele in the Abati houses, and spread from there to the houses of the Capo in Sacchi. They were burned down and so were the houses of the Macci, Amieri, Toschi, Cipriani, Lamberti, and Cavalcanti, and all the New Market. From there the fire spread into Porta Santa Maria, burned it all; and going around by the Ponte Vecchio, it burned the houses of the Gherardini, Pulci, Amidei, and Lucardesi, and so many more with them that the number came to seventeen hundred or more. Many people thought that the fire had been started by chance during the heat of battle. Others say it was started by Neri Abati, prior of San Piero Scheraggio, a dissolute man who delighted in evil. When he saw people busy fighting, he thought he could do a wicked thing which no one would be able to stop because they would all be too busy. And to be more sure of success, he set fire to his family's house, where he had more opportunity. It was July 1304 when Florence was beset by fire and sword. Corso Donati was the only one who did not take up arms during the riots, because he thought he would more easily mediate between both parties when they were tired of fighting and turned to peacemaking. They laid down their arms more because they had had enough trouble than because any agreement had come about between them. The only result was that the rebels did not come back, and the party which supported them remained less powerful.

XXII

The legate was back in Rome when he heard of the new outrages that had taken place in Florence, and he persuaded the Pope that if he wanted to unite Florence he would have to get twelve of the leading citizens of the town to come to him. Then after having got rid of the fomentors of trouble, there was a good chance of putting an end to it. The Pope took this advice, and the citizens who were invited obeyed. Among them was Corso Donati. After they had left Florence, the legate let the exiles know that it was now time to return to Florence while she was without her leaders. So the exiles made their attack, reached Florence, and came in over the still unfinished walls right up to the Piazza San Giovanni.

It was remarkable that those who shortly before had striven for the return of the exiles when they were unarmed and begging to be allowed back to their country, now, when they saw them armed and trying to take the city by force, took up arms against them (they respected public good so much more than private friendship) and together with all the people, forced the exiles to go back where they had come from. The exiles lost the battle because they left some of their troops at Lastra and did not wait for Tolosetto Uberti, who was to have come from Pistoia with three hundred horse. This was because they believed that speed rather than numbers would bring them victory. It often happens in such attempts that slowness robs you of the opportunity and speed of the numbers. Once the rebels had gone, Florence returned to her old feuds. To take away the power of the Cavalcanti family, the people forced them to give up the Stinche, a castle in the Greve Valley which used to belong to them. And because the men who were captured in it were the first to be put in the newly built prisons, they were named after the place they came from, and they are still called the Stinche.

The leaders of the republic also renewed the Companies of the People and gave them standards. Before they had been used to gathering under those of the Guilds. The commanders were called Gonfaloniers of the Companies and Colleges of the Signori, and they were meant to help the Signoria with their weapons during disturbances and with their counsel in peacetime. An executor was added to the two existing magistrates, who with the gonfaloniers was to put a check on the disorderliness of the nobles.

Meanwhile the Pope had died, and Corso and the other citizens had come back from Rome. Life would have been quiet if the city had not been upset again by Corso's restlessness. He had always held the opposite opinion from the most powerful in order to attract attention. He would lend his authority to whatever he saw was fancied by the people, in order to win more approval from them. He backed all the faultfinders and people with new ideas, and everyone who wanted to obtain some extraordinary favor looked to him. Many respected citizens hated him, and this hatred grew until the Black party was openly divided, because Corso made use of his private strength and authority while his adversaries used that of the state. But he carried so much authority in his own person that everyone was afraid of him. Nevertheless, they spread it about that he wanted to set up a dictatorship, in order to deprive him of popular support, which can easily be done in this way. The idea was easy enough to put over, as his style of living exceeded all reasonable bounds. Then the rumor spread faster after he had married a daughter of Uguccione della Faggiuola, chief of the Ghibelline and White party, and an extremely powerful man in Tuscany.

XXIII

When this match became known, it encouraged Corso's enemies and they took up arms against him. The people would not defend him for the same reasons; in fact most of them joined his opponents. His enemies' leaders were Rosso della Tosa, Pazzino de' Pazzi, Geri Spini, and Berto Brunelleschi. With their followers and most of the people, they mustered with their arms beneath the palace of the Signori, on whose orders Corso was accused before Piero Branca, captain of the people, of wanting to set himself up as a dictator with the help of Uguccione. After this he was cited and judged by default to be a rebel, and there was no more than two hours between the accusation and the sentence. Once the Signori had given this judgment they went to fetch Corso, with the Companies of the People bearing their standards. As for Corso himself, he was not frightened by his friends deserting him, or by the sentence, the power of the Signori, or the vast number of his enemies. He entrenched himself in his houses, hoping to be able to defend himself there until Uguccione, whom he had sent for, came to his aid. The houses and the streets around them had been barricaded by him and then fortified by his partisans. They were defending them so that the people, however numerous, could make no headway. There was heavy fighting, with dead and wounded on both sides. The people saw that they could not overcome him by attacking from the open, so they occupied the houses nearest to his; and breaking through them, they penetrated into his house through unguarded openings. Seeing himself surrounded by enemies and no longer trusting in Uguccione's help, Corso decided to see if he could find some way to save himself, since he now despaired of victory. He and Gherardo Bordoni rallied many of his strongest and most trusted friends. They made a dash against the enemy, opened them up so that they could pass through them fighting, and left the town by the Porta alla Croce. Yet they were followed by a lot of people, and Gherardo was killed by Boccaccio Cavicciuli on the Africo. Corso was overtaken and captured at Rovezzano by some Catalan horsemen in the pay of the Signoria. On the way back to Florence he let himself fall from his horse, so as not to look his enemies in the face and be tortured by them. When he was on the ground, his throat was cut by one of his guards. His body was taken up and buried, without any honors, by the monks of San Salvi. This was the end of Corso, to whom the country and the Black party owed much good and much evil. If he had had a quieter mind, his memory would have been happier. Nevertheless, he deserves to be numbered among the rare citizens of our town. True his restlessness made his country and his party forget the debts they owed him, and at the end he brought about his own death and a great deal of trouble to both country and party. Uguccione, on his way to help his son-in-law, heard at Remoli how Corso had been beaten by the people, and feeling that he could not be of any use, he turned back to avoid getting into trouble, without being able to help Corso.

XXIV

After Corso's death, which took place in 1308, the riots stopped. Things were quiet until it was heard that Henry, the Emperor, was coming to Italy with all the Florentine rebels whom he had promised to restore to their country. The leaders of the government felt it would be wise to decrease the number of exiles in order to have fewer enemies. They decided that all the rebels should be allowed back except those who were forbidden to return by name in the decree. Most of the Ghibellines were excluded, and some of the White party, among whom were Dante Alighieri and the sons of Veri de' Cerchi and Giano della Bella. Besides this they sent for help to Robert, King of Naples. They could not get his help as an ally, so they gave him the town for five years so that he would defend them as his subjects. The Emperor came by way of Pisa and went through the Maremma to Rome, where he took the crown in 1312. Then, having decided to tame the Florentines, he came by way of Perugia and Arezzo to Florence. He stayed with his army at the monastery of San Salvi, a mile from the town, for fifty days without achieving anything. He despaired of overthrowing the city's government, and left for Pisa, where he agreed with Frederick, King of Sicily, to make an attack on the Kingdom. He set off with his troops, and just when he was hoping for victory and King Robert was contemplating defeat, he died, while he was at Buonconvento.

XXV

Soon after this, Uguccione della Faggiuola became Lord of Pisa, and a little later of Lucca, too, where he was invited by the Ghibelline party. He inflicted serious damage on his neighbors with the help of these two cities. To protect themselves, the Florentines asked King Robert to send his brother Piero to command their armies.

Uguccione was still increasing his power; and using force and trickery, he had occupied a great many castles in the Arno and Nievole valleys. When he besieged Montecatini, the Florentines felt they must go to its aid, as they did not want that fire to burn up all their territory. They collected a large army and went into the Nievole valley, where they joined battle with Uguccione and were defeated after heavy fighting. Piero, the King's brother, died there, and his body was never found. More than two thousand men were killed with him. Nor was Uguccione's a happy victory, because one of his sons died there with many other army commanders.

After this defeat the Florentines fortified their towns all around, and King Robert sent the Count of Andria, called Count Novello, to be their captain. Either because of his behavior or because it is natural for Florentines to dislike all governments and to take sides over the slightest thing, the city divided into friends and enemies of the King, despite the war with Uguccione. The leaders of the King's enemies were Simone della Tosa, the Magalotti, and some other *popolani* who outnumbered the rest of the government. They had a mission sent to France and then to Germany to look for troops and commanders, so that when they arrived they could expel the Count, the King's governor, but as Fortune would have it they could find nobody. They did not give up their aim, however, and as they could not find anyone in France or Germany whom they could idolize, they got someone from Gubbio. First having driven the Count out, they got Lando d'Agobio to come as executor, or *bargello,* and gave him full powers over the citizens. He was a greedy, cruel man, and he would go through the city with numbers of armed men and take the lives of different people, according to the wishes of those who had elected him. He grew so overbearing that he struck a false coin under the Florentine stamp and no one dared to stand up to him. Florence's quarrels had brought him to such heights! Truly great and wretched city, which neither the memory of past feuds, nor the fear of Uguccione, nor a King's authority could keep under control! She was in a very bad way, attacked by Uguccione from the outside and plundered from the inside by Lando d'Agobio. The King's friends and the enemies of Lando and his followers were noble families and important *popolani,* all Guelphs. However, they could not reveal themselves without serious danger, as their enemies had control of the government. Nevertheless, they decided to get rid of this shameful tyranny and they wrote to King Robert in secret, asking him to make Count Guido da Battifolle his lieutenant in Florence. The King immediately commanded this to be done, and the enemy party did not dare oppose the Count, because of his good qualities, even though the Signori were opposed to the King. The Count did not have much authority, however, because the Signori and the Gonfaloniers of the Companies favored Lando and his party. While Florence was passing through these troubles, the daughter of King Albert of Germany came on her way to meet her husband, Charles, King Robert's son. She was much honored by the King's friends, and they complained to her about conditions in the city and the tyranny of Lando and his supporters. The result was that before she left, with her support and that of the King, the citizens joined together, deprived Lando of his authority, and sent him back to Gubbio laden with plunder and steeped in blood. When the government was reformed, the King was granted control for three years. Because there were seven Signori of Lando's party already elected, six more from the King's men were elected. There followed several administrations of thirteen men, but later they were reduced to seven, according to the old tradition.

XXVI

It was at this time that Uguccione was deprived of control of Lucca and Pisa. Castruccio Castracani, once a citizen of Lucca, became its Lord. Because he was young, bold and fierce, and fortunate in his exploits, he very soon became the leader of the Ghibellines in Tuscany. Their internal strife over, for several years the Florentines thought at first that Castruccio's power would not grow, then when it had grown, against their wishes, they had to think how to defend themselves against him. So that the Signori should be better advised in their deliberations, and be able to put them into effect with more authority, they set up a body of twelve citizens called the *Buoni Uomini*, without whose advice and consent the Signori could do nothing important. It was at this time that King Robert's period of rule came to an end, and the city, now a sovereign state, reorganized itself under its usual magistrates and officials. It was kept united by the great fear it had of Castruccio. After he had made several attacks on the Lords of Lunigiana, he fell upon Prato. The Florentines decided to help the town, and they shut up their shops and went in a body to Prato, twenty thousand on foot and one thousand, five hundred on horseback. To thin out Castruccio's forces and to add to their own, the Signori proclaimed that if any Guelph rebels came to the aid of Prato they would be readmitted to their country after the battle. More than four thousand rebels presented themselves. This large army, which had been brought to Prato so swiftly, frightened Castruccio so much that he went back toward Lucca without wanting to try his luck in battle. This caused a disagreement in the Florentine camp between the people and the nobles. The former wanted to follow Castruccio and fight him to the finish; the latter wanted to go back, and they said it was enough to have put Florence in danger to free Prato, which was all right when they were forced by necessity, but now that there was no need it was not right to tempt Fortune, since there was little to gain and much to lose. As they could not agree, they passed the decision on to the Signori, who found the same disagreements between the people and the aristocrats in the Councils. When this was known in the city, a number of people collected in the square and uttered threats against the nobles. So the nobles gave in out of fear. But because this decision was taken late, and unwillingly in many cases, it gave the enemy time to retreat safely to Lucca.

XXVII

This crisis made the people so annoyed with the nobles that the Signori did not want to keep the promise made to the exiles on the nobles' orders and recommendations. The exiles anticipated this and decided to make the first move. They placed themselves at the head of the army in order to be the first to enter the gates of Florence. But they did not succeed, because they were forestalled and repulsed by those who had stayed in Florence. To see if they could get by agreement what they had not been able to achieve by force, they sent eight men as ambassadors to remind the Signori of their promise and the risks they had run because of it, hoping for the reward they had been promised. The nobles did feel that they were under an obligation, as they had privately pledged what the Signori had promised, but although they worked hard on the exiles' behalf, they could achieve nothing because the people were angry that the victory over Castruccio had not been as great as it could have been. This brought blame and dishonor to the town. Many of the nobles were annoyed, and they tried to get by force what they had been denied on request. They agreed with the exiles that the latter should come to the town armed, while those inside would take up arms to help them. The plot was discovered before the day fixed, and the exiles found the city under arms and prepared to withstand an attack from outside, and to frighten those inside so that no one dared arm. So the exiles gave up the attempt without gaining anything. After they had left, it was felt that those who were guilty of getting the exiles to come should be punished. Although everyone knew who the culprits were, no one dared name them, much less accuse them. So to get at the unbiased truth, it was laid down that in the Councils everyone should write down the names of the criminals, and the papers would be handed secretly to the captain. The accused were Amerigo Donati, Teghiaio Frescobaldi, and Lotteringo Gherardini; their judge was more lenient than perhaps their crimes deserved, and they were sentenced to a fine.

XXVIII

The riots that broke out in Florence on the rebels' arrival at the gates showed that one commander was not enough for the people's companies. So it was laid down that in future each one should have three or four leaders. In addition to each gonfalonier, they appointed two or three men they called pennoniers, so that in cases where the whole company was not needed, part of it could be used under one leader. In all republics, after something has happened, some old laws are repealed and others are renewed. Where formerly the Signoria had been elected from time to time, the Signori and Colleges then in power were strong enough to arrange to be given the authority to appoint the Signori who would sit for the following forty months. They put the names of these men in a bag and drew them every two months. Before the forty months were over, new names were put into the bag, because many citizens were afraid that their names had not been included. This was the origin of the system of putting into a bag the names of all the magistrates for some time ahead, both at home and abroad. Before this, the Councils had elected the magistrates' successors at the end of their period of office. The making up of the bag was later called "a scrutiny." Because they were held every three, or at most every five, years, they seemed to spare the city trouble and do away with the reason for riots, which used to break out at the beginning of every new magistracy, because of the number of competitors. As they could not control these riots in any other way, they adopted this method, not seeing the faults which lay hidden beneath the slight convenience.

XXIX

It was 1325, and Castruccio had occupied Pistoia and gained so much power that the Florentines were afraid that it would increase. They decided to attack him and take Pistoia out of his hands before he had got it completely under his control. From among their citizens and friends they collected twenty thousand foot and three thousand horsemen, and they camped with this army at Altopascio to occupy it and thus stop him from aiding Pistoia. The Florentines succeeded in taking the place. Then they went toward Lucca, plundering the countryside, but they did not make much progress because of the captain's little prudence and less reliability.

The Florentines' captain was Ramondo di Cardona. He saw that they had formerly been generous with their liberty and had given it now to the King, now to the legate, now to men with lesser qualities, and he thought that if he got them into some difficult situation, they would easily make him their ruler. He did not fail to remind them of this often and asked for the authority that he had over the army to be extended to the town; otherwise he maintained that he could not command the obedience necessary to a captain. Because the Florentines would not allow this, he wasted time, which was to Castruccio's advantage, because he received the aid that had been promised him by the Visconti and the other dictators of Lombardy. Ramondo strengthened his troops, but just as he had not been able to win before, because of his unreliability, now he could not save himself because of his lack of prudence. As he was going along slowly with his army, he was attacked by Castruccio near Altopascio and was defeated after a big battle. Many citizens were captured and killed, and among them was Ramondo, who received from Fortune the punishment for his disloyalty and bad advice that he had deserved from the Florentines. The damage that Castruccio inflicted on the Florentines after the victory, by plundering, taking prisoners, destroying and burning, is impossible to relate. Without anyone to stop him, for several months he rode and pillaged where he wanted, and the Florentines were lucky to save the city after such a beating.

XXX

They were not too disheartened, however, to raise funds, hire troops, and send to their allies for help. But no measures were enough to restrain such an enemy, and they had to elect Charles, Duke of Calabria, King Robert's son, as their Lord, if they wanted him to come to their defense, because the King was so used to ruling Florence, he wanted her rather as a subject than as an ally. Charles was involved in the Sicilian wars and could not come to take over the government, so he sent Walter of Brienne, of French birth and Duke of Athens. He took possession of the city as the Lord's vicar and appointed officers as he thought fit. But his behavior was so unpretentious and out of character that everyone liked him.

When the Sicilian wars were over, Charles came to Florence with a thousand horsemen and made his entry in July 1326. His arrival meant that Castruccio could not plunder Florentine territory as he liked. However, the respect that the Duke won abroad he lost at home, and damage that had not been done by enemies had to be tolerated from friends. The Signori did nothing without the Duke's consent. Either he or his father imposed so many taxes every day that by the end of a year he had taken four hundred thousand florins from the city, even though it had been agreed that he was not to exceed two hundred thousand. Added to these inflictions were new fears and new enemies. The Ghibellines of Lombardy were so worried by Charles' arrival in Tuscany that Galeazzo Visconti and the other Lombard rulers enticed Ludwig of Bavaria into Italy with money and promises. He had been elected Emperor against the Pope's wishes. He came to Lombardy and then to Tuscany, and took Pisa with Castruccio's help. Having replenished his funds there, he left for Rome. This caused Charles to leave Florence, fearing for the kingdom, and he left Filippo da Saggineto as his vicar. After the Emperor had gone, Castruccio took control of Pisa, and the Florentines took Pistoia from him, following the treaty. Castruccio besieged it and kept up the siege with such *virtù* and obstinacy that the Florentines could not shake him either by force or persistence, although they attacked both his army and his territory and tried to relieve the town several times. Castruccio was so anxious to punish the Pistoians and disconcert the Florentines! And the Pistoians were forced to recognize him as their Lord. This meant a great deal of glory for him, but it also meant so much strain that when he returned to Lucca he died. Because Fortune rarely fails to link a good or an evil to another good or evil, Charles, Duke of Calabria and Lord of Florence, also died in Naples, and the Florentines were freed much quicker than they had imagined possible from the fear of one and the rule of the other. Once they were free they reformed the constitution, abolished the whole system of the old Councils, and established two new ones, one of three hundred *popolani* and the other of two hundred and fifty nobles and *popolani*. The first was called the Council of the People and the second, the Council of the Commune.

XXXI

When the Emperor arrived at Rome, he created an antipope and made many innovations detrimental to the Church; and he attempted unsuccessfully to make others. In the end he left dishonored and came to Pisa. There about eight hundred German knights rebelled against him, either out of anger or because they had not been paid, and they entrenched themselves at Montechiaro on the Ceruglio. When the Emperor had left Pisa for Lombardy, they occupied Lucca and expelled Francesco Castracani, whom the Emperor had left there. Hoping to draw some profit from their prize, they offered the city to the Florentines for eighty thousand florins. It was refused on the advice of Simone della Tosa. This decision would have been very valuable to the city if the Florentines had stuck to it. But it was disastrous because they changed their minds very shortly. If at that time they could have had Lucca by peaceful means and so cheaply and they did not want it, later they did not get it when they wanted it, although they offered a much higher price for it. This caused Florence to change her government several times, much to her disadvantage. Having been refused by the Florentines, Lucca was bought by Gherardino Spinoli of Genoa for thirty thousand florins. Since men are slower to take what they can have than they are to desire what they cannot reach, as soon as Gherardino's purchase was made known, even though they had valued Lucca so little, the people of Florence conceived an urgent desire to possess it, and blamed themselves and their advisers for its loss. In order to take it by force, since they had not wanted to buy it, they sent their troops to sack and plunder the Lucchese.

In the meantime, the Emperor had left Italy, and the antipope had been sent prisoner to France on the orders of the Pisans. From Castruccio's death until 1340 the Florentines were at peace at home. They only attended to foreign affairs and waged many wars in Lombardy because of the arrival of King John of Bohemia, and in Tuscany on account of Lucca. Also they decorated their town with new buildings. They built the tower of Santa Reparata according to the designs of Giotto, who was a very famous painter at that time. And in 1333 the waters of the Arno rose more than twelve yards in some places, owing to flooding, and destroyed some of the bridges and a great many buildings. A great deal of care and money was put into restoring the things that had been damaged.

XXXII

In the year 1340, there were new reasons for trouble. Powerful citizens had two ways of increasing or maintaining their power. One was to restrict the number of names that went into the bags for the election of officials, so that their own or their friends' names were always drawn. The other was to be in charge of the election of the chief magistrates, so that the latter would favor them in their judgments later on. They considered this second way to be so important that the ordinary magistrates were not enough for them, and they sometimes brought in a third. At this time they had brought Iacopo Gabrielli d'Agobio in specially as Captain of the guard and let him have complete authority over the citizens. He committed a number of abuses every day with the government's connivance. Among the injured parties were Piero de' Bardi and Bardo Frescobaldi. They were nobles, proud by nature, and could not bear a foreigner to wrong them with the connivance of a few powerful men. For revenge, they plotted against him and the government. In the conspiracy there were a great many noble families and some from the people who disliked the tyranny of those in power.

The plan was that everyone should collect numbers of armed men in their houses, and the morning after All Saints' Day, when everyone was in church praying for the dead, take up arms, kill the Captain and leaders of the government, and then reform the constitution with new Signori and new institutions. But because dangerous decisions are much less willingly taken the longer they are considered, it always happens that conspiracies which allow time to lapse before they are carried out are discovered. Andrea de' Bardi was one of the conspirators, and when he thought things over, the fear of punishment had more effect on him than the hope of revenge. He told his brother-in-law, Iacopo Alberti, everything. Iacopo told the Priors, and the Priors told the government. A great many citizens met in the palace because All Saints' Day was near and the matter was urgent. They thought it was dangerous to waste time, and they wanted the Signori to ring the bell to call the people to arms. Taldo Valori was Gonfalonier, and Francesco Salviati one of the Signori. As they were related to the Bardi, they did not want the bell to be rung; and they said it was wrong to arm the people for the slightest thing because unlimited authority given to the masses never did any good. It was easy to cause trouble but difficult to stop it; so it would be better first to hear the truth of the matter, and then to punish legally those responsible, than to act simply on hearsay and try to put things right by rioting, and cause the fall of Florence. These words went entirely unheard, and amid abuse and insults the Signori were forced to ring the bell. At the sound of it, all the people ran into the square armed. The Bardi and Frescobaldi, seeing that their plot had been discovered, took up arms to conquer with glory or die honorably. They hoped to be able to defend the part of the city over the river where they had their houses. They fortified the bridges, hoping for help from the nobles of the *contado* and other friends of theirs. This plan was foiled by the *popolani* who lived in that part of the city with them, and who took up arms on behalf of the Signori. So finding their numbers halved, they gave up the bridges and retreated to the street where the Bardi lived, as it was better protected than any others, and they defended it bravely. Iacopo d'Agobio, knowing that this whole plot had been directed against him, was frightened of being killed, and he remained paralyzed with fright among his armed soldiers near the palace of the Signori. But the others of the government who were less to blame had more courage, most of all the Podestà who was called Maffeo da Carradi. He appeared where the fighting was, and afraid of nothing, he crossed the Rubaconte bridge, went in among the Bardi swords, and signaled that he wanted to talk to them. The respect in which he was held, his behavior, and his other great qualities caused the battle to stop suddenly, and he was heard in silence. He spoke gently and seriously, condemning their conspiracy, showed them the danger they would be in if they did not yield to this popular uprising, and gave them hope that they would be heard later and judged mercifully, promising to see that their reasonable grievances would be considered favorably. Then he went back to the Signori and persuaded them not to conquer with the blood of their citizens, and not to judge them without a hearing. He was so successful that with the consent of the Signori the Bardi and the Frescobaldi left the city with their friends and returned without hindrance to their castles.

When they had left and the people had disarmed, the

Signori only proceeded against those in the families of the Bardi and the Frescobaldi who had armed; and to deprive them of power, they bought from the Bardi the castles of Mangona and Vernia, and they made it illegal for any citizen to own castles within twenty miles of Florence. A few months later Stiatta Frescobaldi was beheaded and many others of the family were declared rebels. It was not enough for those who were governing to have overcome and tamed the Bardi and the Frescobaldi. As is almost always the case, the more power men have the worse they use it and the more aggressive they become. Where before there had been one Captain of the guard who oppressed Florence, they elected another one in the *contado* and gave him very great powers to prevent men they suspected from living either in Florence or outside. The nobles were so provoked by him that they were ready to sell the city and themselves to have their revenge. They were only looking for the opportunity. It came in good time, and they made even better use of it.

XXXIII

Owing to the numerous upheavals there had been in Tuscany and Lombardy, Lucca had come under the rule of Mastino della Scala, Lord of Verona. Although it had been stipulated that he should hand Lucca over to the Florentines, he had not done so, because as Lord of Parma he thought he could keep it; and he did not care about the promise he had given. To be revenged, the Florentines made an alliance with the Venetians and waged such a bitter war on him that he was about to lose his state. However, they got nothing out of it but the slight satisfaction in having beaten Mastino, because the Venetians, like all those who make alliances with weaker people, made peace once they had won Treviso and Vicenza, without having any consideration for the Florentines. But since the Visconti, Lords of Milan, took Parma from Mastino shortly afterwards, he felt he could not keep Lucca any longer and decided to sell it. The Florentines and the Pisans both made offers; and as

97

negotiations drew to a close, the Pisans saw that the Florentines were going to get it because they were richer. So the Pisans resorted to force, and with the Visconti's help they laid siege to the city. The Florentines did not retire from the purchase because of this, but signed the treaty with Mastino, paid part of the money and gave hostages for the rest, and sent Naddo Rucellai, Giovanni di Bernardino de' Medici, and Rosso di Ricciardo de' Ricci to take possession. They forced an entry into Lucca, and the city was handed over to them by Mastino's soldiers. However, the Pisans continued to attack and tried all ways to capture it, while the Florentines were trying to raise the siege. After a long war the Florentines were driven out, having suffered great financial losses and having gained only dishonor. The Pisans became rulers of the city. As always happens in such cases, the loss of this town made the Florentine people angry with the government. And they criticized them publicly everywhere, all over the city, accusing them of greed and bad management.

At the beginning of this war, twenty citizens had been put in charge of operations. They had appointed Malatesta da Rimini as captain of the expedition. He had managed it with little courage and less prudence. They had sent to King Robert of Naples for help, and the King had sent Walter, Duke of Athens. As it pleased the heavens, who were preparing trouble for the future, he arrived in Florence just when the war over Lucca had been utterly lost. The Twenty, seeing that the people were angry, thought that they could give them new hope by electing a new captain, and by this appointment they hoped either to put a check on the people or to take away the reason for their criticisms. So that they would still have cause to fear, and so that the Duke of Athens would be able to defend them with better authority, they elected him first as *conservadore,* then as captain of their men at arms. The nobles were unsettled because of reasons already mentioned, and many of them had been acquainted with Walter when he had governed Florence before in the name of Charles, Duke of Calabria. They thought that the time had come to fulfil their ambitions with the collapse of the city. They felt there was no other way to control the people who had harried them but to place themselves under a prince, who when he saw the *virtù* of one side and the disorderliness of the other, would reward the former and curb the latter. Added to this was the hope of benefits they would deserve, if he was made ruler through their good offices. So they went to him several times in secret and persuaded him to take absolute control, and they offered him as much help as possible. Some families from among the people backed up their authority and advice, and they were the Peruzzi, Acciaiuoli, Antellesi, and Buonaccorsi. They were all badly in debt, and being unable to make good their debts with their own money, they hoped to do so with other people's money and to free themselves from slavery to their creditors by enslaving their country. Their arguments appealed to the Duke's ambition and gave him an even greater desire for power. To gain a reputation for severity and justice, and thus acquire favor with the people, he prosecuted those who had been in charge of the war for Lucca. He put Giovanni de' Medici, Naddo Rucellai, and Guglielmo Altoviti to death, sent many people into exile, and fined many others.

XXXIV

These executions frightened the middle classes a good deal. Only the nobles and the lower classes were pleased: The former because they were revenged for the many insults they had suffered from the people, and the latter because it is their nature to enjoy trouble. When the Duke went through the streets, he was praised out loud for his decisiveness, and everyone urged him to investigate cases of dishonesty among the citizens in public and to punish them. The period of office of the Twenty had come to an end; the Duke's reputation was great, and the fear of him even greater. Everyone had the Duke's arms painted on his house to show that he was friendly toward him. He was prince in all but name.

When he felt he could safely try to crown his achievement, he let the Signori know that he believed that for the city's sake he should be given a free hand and that he would like their consent, seeing that the whole town already agreed. Although they had foreseen their country's ruin long before, the Signori were very dismayed by this request, and even though they knew the danger they were in, they courageously refused to give their consent in order not to fail their country.

The Duke had chosen to live in the monastery of the Friars Minor at Santa Croce—to create the impression of having religious and kindly sentiments. With the aim of putting his evil desires into effect, he issued a decree that all the people should appear before him the next morning in the square in front of Santa Croce. The Signori were much more frightened by this decree than they had been earlier by his words. They had a meeting with the citizens they considered to be on the side of liberty and their country. Knowing the Duke's strength, they did not think they could do anything but ask and see whether, as their strength was insufficient, their appeals might be enough to make the Duke give up his attempt or make his rule less harsh. So some of the Signori went to see him, and one of them spoke to him in this way:

"We come to you, my Lord, first because of your requests, then because of the orders you have given for the people to assemble. We feel certain that you want to obtain by extraordinary means what we have not allowed you to have by ordinary methods. Nor is it our intention to oppose your plans by force, but only to show you what a heavy load you are taking upon yourself and what a dangerous decision you are making. This way you will always be able to remember our advice and the advice of those people who counsel you otherwise, not for your good but to pander to their own anger. You are trying to enslave a city which has always been free. The rule we granted the Kings of Naples was an alliance of equals, not servitude. Have you considered how important and how strong the name of liberty is in a city like this? No power can overcome it, no period of time can consume it, no other advantage can compensate for it. Think, my Lord, of the troops that are needed to keep such a town in bondage. Foreign ones that you can always command are not enough; you cannot trust troops from inside, because the men who are still friendly toward you and have advised you to take this step will try to do away with you and take power themselves, when they have beaten their enemies by using your authority. The lower classes whom you trust change their mind at the slightest thing, so that in a very short time you might have the whole city against you, which will bring about its ruin and your own. You will find no remedy, because rulers can only make their government secure if they have few enemies who can be easily done away with by death or exile. But if a ruler is universally hated, there can never be any security, because you do not know where trouble might come from. If you are afraid of everyone, you can be sure of no one. If you do try to trust some, you increase the dangers because those you pass over find fuel for their hatred and are more ready for revenge. It is quite certain that time cannot extinguish the desire for liberty, because you often hear of free government being adopted again in a city by people who never tasted it, but who loved it for the memory that their fathers had left behind, and when they get it back they hang on to it obstinately in spite of dangers. If their fathers have left no records of it, the public buildings, the government offices, and the arms of the free institutions recall it, and the citizens are bound to know of these things, which will increase their desire for them. What achievements of yours could counterbalance the sweetness of freedom, or make men lose their desire for their present conditions? Not even if you added the whole of Tuscany to this state and came back to the town triumphing over your enemies every day; because all that glory would belong to you and not to the city, and the citizens would not be getting subjects but fellow servants, who would only make their slavery seem more wretched. And even if your behavior was saintly, your dealings kindly, and your judgments fair, they would not be enough to

101

make you beloved. You would deceive yourself if you thought they would be enough, because to someone who is used to living free, every chain is heavy and every bond is too tight. You cannot find a police state with a good prince, because they are bound either to grow alike or to cause one another's downfall. You must believe then that you have either to hold this town, using the maximum force (for which citadels, guards, and friends from outside are often not enough), or to be content with the authority we have given you. We urge you to do this, and we remind you that the only lasting government is one based on the people's will. Just because you are blinded by a little ambition, do not put yourself into a position where you cannot stay still or go any higher and are therefore forced to fall, causing grave damage to yourself and to us."

XXXV

This speech did not move the Duke from his purpose at all, and he said it was not his intention to take the city's freedom away but to give it back, because only disunited cities were slaves, and united ones free. If Florence got rid of factions, private ambitions, and quarrels because of his reforms, her liberty would be restored, and not lost. He was prompted to take on this task not by his own ambition but by the requests of many of the citizens, so they would do well to give their consent to something that others had agreed to. He was not concerned with the dangers he might run, because it was a bad man who would give up a good cause for fear of evil, and a coward who would abandon a glorious enterprise in favor of a doubtful goal. He believed that his actions would soon lead them to recognize that they had trusted him too little and had feared him too much. Seeing they could do no good, the Signori agreed that the people should meet the next morning in their square, and with the people's authority sovereignty was given to the Duke for one year, on the same conditions as those made for Charles, Duke of Calabria.

It was the eighth of September 1342, when the Duke entered the square accompanied by Giovanni della Tosa and all his relations, and many other citizens. With the Signoria, he climbed up onto the rostrum, which is the name the Florentines give to the steps at the foot of the palace of the Signori. There the agreements made between the Signoria and the Duke were read to the people. And when they came to the part where he was given sovereignty for one year, the people cried out: "For life!" Francesco Rustichelli, one of the Signori, got up to speak and quiet the mob, but his words were interrupted by shouting. So with the people's consent, he was elected Lord, not for one year, but in perpetuity. He was taken and carried among the crowd who were shouting his name all over the square. It is the custom that whoever is appointed to guard the palace stays locked inside in the absence of the Signori. This office was held at the time by Rinieri di Giotto. He had been bribed by the Duke's men, and he allowed the Duke in without waiting for an attack. The Signori went to their homes frightened and disgraced, and the palace was sacked by the Duke's men, the people's standard torn up and the Duke's arms placed above the palace. Good men felt untold sorrow and anger at these events, but those who agreed to them either out of ignorance or malice were greatly pleased.

XXXVI

Once he had won power, the Duke forbade the Signori to meet in the palace and gave them a private house— in order to take authority away from those who had once been the defenders of liberty. He took the standards from the Gonfaloniers of the People's Companies, raised the legal bans against the nobles, freed prisoners, had the Bardi and the Frescobaldi return from exile, and forbade everyone to bear arms. To defend himself against those at home, he made friendships abroad. So he favored the Aretines and all the Florentines' other subjects. He made peace with Pisa, although he had been made prince in order to make war on that city. He canceled the allowances of the merchants who had lent the republic money during the war for Lucca. He increased the earlier taxes and made new ones and took all power away from the Signori. His ministers were Baglione da Perugia and Guglielmo d'Ascesi, and he took counsel with them and with Cerrettieri Bisdomini. The dues he imposed on the citizens were heavy, his judgments were unfair, and the modesty and kindliness that he had feigned were now turned into pride and cruelty. Many noble and middle-class citizens were condemned, killed, or tortured in new ways. So as not to behave better outside than in, he appointed six magistrates for the *contado* who robbed the peasants and beat them up. He was suspicious of the nobles, even though he had been favored by them and had brought many of them back to their country. He could not believe that the great hearts that are usually found among the nobility could be content to owe him allegiance. So he began to woo the lower classes, thinking that with their favors and with foreign troops he would be able to maintain his dictatorship. The month of May came, when the people usually celebrate, and he got the lowest classes and the *popolo minuto* to form several companies, honored them with splendid titles, and gave them standards and money. Part of them went through the city making merry, and the rest received the merrymakers with great pomp. As the fame of his new sovereignty spread abroad, many people of French birth came to visit him; and he gave honors to them all, as if they were his most trusted men. So Florence very soon became a slave not only to the French but also to their customs and fashions. Men and women imitated them shamelessly, without any respect for decent living. But what was most disliked was the violence he and his men did to women indiscriminately. The citizens were filled with indignation seeing the glory of their state brought low, its traditions broken, its laws annulled, decent living corrupted, and civilized modesty forgotten. Men who had not been used to seeing any regal pomp could not help feeling pain when they met the Duke surrounded by armed hangers-on on foot and on horseback. They saw their disgrace more clearly and were forced to honor the man they most hated. Added to this was fear, caused by the frequent deaths and the grinding taxes with which he never ceased to burden and drain the city. The Duke knew of, and was afraid of, this anger and fear; but he wanted to pretend to everyone that he believed he was liked. When Matteo di Morozzo, either to gain his favor or to protect himself, revealed to him that the Medici family and some others had plotted against him, the Duke not only failed to look into it, but had the informer put to death. By this decision he discouraged those who would have warned him about his safety and encouraged those who were trying to bring him down. He also had Bettone Cini's tongue cut out, with so much cruelty that he died of it, because Bettone had criticized the taxes imposed on the citizens. This added to the citizens' anger and their hatred of the Duke. The city had been used to doing anything and speaking about anything with complete freedom, and it could not bear to have its hands tied and its mouth gagged. This anger and hatred grew so much that not only the Florentines, who cannot keep freedom but who are unable to put up with slavery, but any subject people would have been provoked to win back their liberty. Many citizens of all classes resolved to lose their lives or regain their freedom. These conspiracies were started by three parties which were made up of three different kinds of citizens: nobles, *popolani,* and artisans. The causes, apart from the general reasons, were the nobles' feeling that they had not won back control of the state, the *popolani*'s feeling that they had lost it, and the artisans' worry over their loss of earnings.

Agnolo Acciaiuoli was Archbishop of Florence, and he had at one time praised the Duke's actions in his sermons, and won him popularity among the people. But when he saw the Duke made Lord, and witnessed his tyrannical behavior, he felt that he had deceived his country. He thought that there was no better way of making up for his mistake than to heal the wound with the hand that inflicted it. He made himself leader of the first and strongest group of conspirators, among whom were the Bardi, Rossi, Frescobaldi, Scali, Altoviti, Magalotti, Strozzi, and Mancini. The leaders of one of the other two were Manno and Corso Donati, and with them were the Pazzi, Cavicciuli, Cerchi, and Albizzi. The head of the third was Antonio Adimari, and with him were the Medici, Bordoni, Rucellai, and Aldobrandini. These last planned to kill the Duke in the Albizzi's house, where they expected him to go on St. John's Day to watch horse racing, but their plan failed because he did not go. They thought of attacking him while he was walking through the town, but they saw how difficult this was, because he always went well accompanied and armed, and he changed his routes so that he could not be expected with certainty anywhere. They discussed killing him in council, where they felt they would be at the mercy of his troops, even though he was dead. While these things were being planned by the conspirators, Antonio Adimari let some of his Sienese friends in on the secret in order to get men from them, and he told them the names of some of the conspirators and said that the whole city was prepared to liberate itself. One of them mentioned the affair to Francesco Brunelleschi, not in order to give it away, but because he thought Francesco was one of the conspirators. Francesco revealed everything to the Duke, either because he feared for himself or because of some personal hatred. Pagolo del Mazzeca and Simone da Monterappoli were arrested. They revealed the nature and number of the conspirators, which frightened the Duke. He was advised to send for them rather than to arrest them, because if they fled he could rid himself of them by exile without trouble. So the Duke summoned Antonio Adimari. He came immediately, as he had complete faith in his associates, and he was held prisoner. The Duke was advised by Francesco Brunelleschi and Uguccione Buondelmonti to ride armed through the city and kill those he captured. But he disagreed because he felt that he did not have enough men to take on so many enemies. He took another course which, if it had succeeded, would have taken care of his enemies and would have provided him with men. The Duke was in the habit of summoning citizens to advise him in case of need. Having sent outside for reinforcements, he made a list of three hundred citizens and had his sergeants summon them, pretending that he wanted to ask their advice. Once they were assembled, he planned to do away with them either by killing them or by imprisoning them. Antonio Adimari's capture and the request for reinforcements, which could not be made in secret, had frightened the citizens, particularly the guilty ones, and the bravest refused to obey. Because everyone had read the list and found each other's names there, people were encouraged to arm and to hope to die like men with their weapons in their hands, rather than like calves being led to the slaughter. So in a very few hours all three conspiracies were made known to one another. They agreed that on the following day, which was July 26, 1343, they would create a disturbance in the Old Market, and then arm and call the people to liberty.

XXXVII

The next day they armed according to orders when Nones was ringing. The people all armed at the cry of Liberty. People barricaded themselves in their own districts, under banners bearing the people's coats of arms, which the conspirators had made secretly. All the heads of families met, both nobles and *popolani*, and they swore to defend each other and to kill the Duke. The only exceptions were some of the Buondelmonti and the Cavalcanti and the four *popolano* families who had together been responsible for making the Duke Lord. They came out into the square in the Duke's favor with the butchers and others of the proletariat. At this uproar the Duke fortified the palace, and his men who were lodged in different places mounted their horses to ride to the square. And in many places on the way they were attacked and killed. However, about three hundred horsemen got through. The Duke was uncertain whether to come out and fight his enemies or to stay in and defend the palace. The Medici, Cavicciuli, Rucellai, and the other families whom he had wronged most, feared that if he came out many who had armed against him might turn out to be his friends. To give him no chance of coming out and finding reinforcements, they mustered and attacked the square. When they appeared, the *popolano* families who had come out for the Duke changed their minds now that they were openly attacked and saw that the Duke's fortune had changed, and they all went over to their fellow citizens. The exceptions were Uguccione Buondelmonti, who went into the palace, and Giannozzo Cavalcanti, who withdrew to the New Market with some of his associates, climbed onto a bench, and begged the people to go to the square armed in favor of the Duke. He made every effort to frighten them and threatened them all with death if they were obstinate enough to persist in their action against their Lord. Finding no one to follow him or to punish his arrogance, and seeing that he was wasting his time, he withdrew into his own houses to tempt Fortune no longer. Meanwhile, there was a big battle in the square between the people and the Duke's men, and despite the help the palace gave, the latter were beaten. Some of them placed themselves in their enemies' hands; the others left their horses and took refuge in the palace. While fighting was going on in the square, Corso and Amerigo Donati broke into the Stinche with some of the people, burned the records of the Podestà and the public chamber, sacked the magistrates' houses, and killed all the Duke's ministers they could lay their hands on. As for the Duke, he saw that he had lost the square, that the whole city was against him, and that there was no hope of help, so he tried to see if he could win the people over by some kindly deed. He had the prisoners brought before him and freed them with friendly, gracious words. He made Antonio Adimari a knight, much as he disliked it. He had his own arms taken down from the palace and put up those of the people. All these things done late and at the wrong time did him very little good, because they were forced upon him against his will. So he was uneasy, besieged in the palace, and he realized that he was going to lose everything because he had wanted too much. He was afraid of dying in a few days either of hunger or by the sword. The citizens met in Santa Reparata to draw up a constitution. They elected fourteen citizens, half nobles and half *popolani,* who would have absolute authority with the Bishop to reform the constitution of Florence. They also chose six others who would have the authority of the Podestà until the one who had been elected arrived. Many troops had come to Florence to help the people, among whom were some Sienese with six ambassadors, who were highly respected in their own country. They tried to negotiate a settlement between the people and the Duke. But the people refused to hear any talk of an agreement before Guglielmo d'Ascesi had been handed over to them with his son and Cerrettieri Bisdomini. The Duke did not want to agree, but he let himself be persuaded by the threats of those who were shut up with him. Indignation seems greater and injuries appear more serious when liberty is being won back than when it is being defended. Guglielmo and his son were let loose in the midst of thousands of their enemies; the boy was not eighteen; yet his age, figure, and innocence could not save him from the fury of the mob. Those who could not strike them while they were alive struck once they were dead; and as if it were not enough to hack them with steel, they tore at them with their hands and teeth. After they had heard their shrieks, seen their wounds, touched their torn flesh, in order to let all their senses enjoy their revenge, they still wanted taste to savor it, so that after all the external organs the internal ones should be satisfied, too. This mad fury was as useful to Cerrettieri as it was harmful to the other two. The mob was weary of its cruelty and it forgot about him. As he was not sent for again he stayed in the palace, and during the night he was taken to safety by some friends and relations. After the mob had vented its feelings on those two, an agreement was reached. The Duke was to leave with his men and possessions and was to renounce all the claims he had on Florence; then once outside the state, he would ratify this renunciation in the Casentino. After this agreement, he left Florence on the sixth of August accompanied by many citizens. When he arrived in the Casentino, he ratified the renunciation, although with bad grace; and he would not have kept faith if Count Simon had not threatened to take him back to Florence. This Duke was greedy and cruel, as his rule showed; he was difficult in audiences and proud in his replies; he wanted men's service, not their goodwill, and therefore he preferred to be feared rather than loved. His person was no less odious than his behavior, for he was short and dark, with a scant, long beard; so he deserved to be hated on all counts. His bad behavior lost him in ten months the sovereignty that the bad advice of others had given him.

XXXVIII

These events in the city encouraged all the towns ruled by the Florentines to return to their earlier independence. Arezzo, Castiglione, Pistoia, Volterra, Colle, San Gimignano, all rebelled; and Florence found herself suddenly without her dictator and her territory. By regaining her own liberty, she taught her subjects how they could win back theirs. After the Duke's expulsion and the loss of their territory, the fourteen citizens and the Bishop thought the best thing was to placate their subjects by peace, rather than to antagonize them by war, and to show themselves to be as happy about their subjects' liberty as they were about their own. They sent ambassadors to Arezzo to renounce their claims on that city and to come to an agreement so that Arezzo would think of itself as an ally of their town, since it could not think of itself as a subject. They made the best agreements they could with the other towns, the main purpose being to keep them friendly, so that while the Florentines were free they could help to maintain their liberty. This decision, prudently taken, had a very happy outcome. After a few years, Arezzo returned under Florentine rule, and the other cities returned to their former obedience in a few months. So it happens that one very often gets things more quickly, with less danger and expense, by avoiding them rather than by pursuing them with all one's might and main.

XXXIX

Once the trouble abroad had been settled, they turned to home affairs. After some disputes between the nobles and the *popolani,* they decided that the nobles should have a third of the places in the Signoria and half of the other offices. As we showed above, the city was divided into sixths, so that six Signori were always elected, one for each sixth, except that in some circumstances twelve or thirteen had sometimes been elected, but soon afterwards they had gone back to six. They felt that this part of the city's constitution should be reformed, both because the sixths were unevenly divided and because the number of Signori needed to be increased since the nobles were to have their share. So they divided the city into quarters and appointed three Signori for each. They left out the Gonfaloniers of Justice and the Gonfaloniers of the People's Companies, and instead of the twelve *Buoni Uomini* they had eight counselors, four of each kind. Once the government was set up along these lines, the city would have been quiet if the nobles had been content to live with the modesty required in a civilized community; but they acted in exactly the opposite way, because as private citizens they would admit no equals, and in the magistracies they wanted to be the rulers. Every day there occurred some instance of their insolence and pride. This annoyed the people, and they grumbled that in the place of one dictator who had been cut down a thousand more had sprung up. The arrogance on one side and the anger on the other grew so much that the leaders of the *popolani* complained to the Bishop about the nobles' bad faith and their lack of partnership with the people. They persuaded him to get the nobles to agree to have their share of the other offices and to leave just the office of the Signoria to the people.

The Bishop was good-natured but easily won over to one side or the other. This was the reason why he had first been influenced by his relatives to favor the Duke of Athens, and then had plotted against him on the advice of other citizens. Over the reform of the constitution he had favored the nobles, and now he felt like favoring the people because of the points these *popolani* reported to him. Thinking that he would find an instability similar to his own in others, he was convinced that he would reach an agreement. He called a meeting of the Fourteen, who had still not lost their authority, and did his best to persuade them to give up the office of the Signoria to the people, promising in return the peace of the city or else their own downfall and undoing. These words infuriated the nobles, and Ridolfo de' Bardi rebuked him harshly, calling him a man of little faith, and accusing him of thoughtlessness in his friendship for the Duke and of treachery over the Duke's expulsion. He ended by saying that the honors they had won at their own risk they would defend at their own risk. Ridolfo left with the others in an angry mood and told his relations and all the nobility. The *popolani* also made their views known to the others. While the nobles were organizing themselves with outside help to defend their Signori, the people decided not to wait until they were ready and ran armed to the palace, shouting that they wanted the nobles to give up the office. There was a great noise and tumult. The Signori found themselves deserted, because the nobles did not dare to take up arms when they saw all the people armed, and everyone stayed in his own house. The *popolani* among the Signori tried first to quiet the people, telling them that their colleagues were modest, good men, and when they did not succeed they made the best of a bad job and sent them home, though they had difficulty in getting there safely. Once the nobles had left the palace, the four noble counselors also lost their offices, and twelve *popolani* were appointed instead. The eight remaining Signori appointed a Gonfalonier of Justice and sixteen Gonfaloniers of the People's Companies, and they reformed the councils so that the whole government was in the hands of the people.

XL

When these events took place, there was a great famine in the city, and the nobles and the lower classes were
dissatisfied, the former because they had lost their honors, the latter because of hunger. This encouraged Andrea
Strozzi to think that he could usurp the freedom of the
city. He sold his grain at a lower price than the others,
and great crowds gathered at his house. One morning he
had the audacity to get on his horse and, followed by a
number of men, to call the people to arms. In a very
short time he collected more than four thousand men,
went with them to the Piazza de' Signori, and demanded
to have the palace opened to them. But the Signori
fended them off with threats and force, and then so
frightened them with proclamations of banishment that
one by one they all went home. Andrea was left alone
and barely managed to save himself from the officials by
flight. Although it was foolhardy and ended in the way
that such disturbances usually do, this attempt encouraged the nobles to hope that they could bring pressure
to bear on the *popolani,* seeing that the lowest classes
were at odds with them. Not to miss this opportunity,
they decided to provide themselves with every kind of aid
so that they could win back by force rightly what had
been taken by force unjustly. They grew so confident of
victory that they made no secret of getting arms, fortifying their houses, and sending for help from their
friends as far away as Lombardy. The people and the
Signori were also making their preparations, arming
themselves and asking help from the people of Perugia
and Siena. Help had arrived for both sides and the whole
city was up in arms. The nobles on this side of the Arno
were concentrated in three places: at the Cavicciuli's
houses near San Giovanni, at the Pazzi's and the Donati's
houses at San Piero Maggiore, and at the Cavalcanti's
houses in the New Market. Those beyond the Arno had
fortified the bridges and the streets near their houses;
the Nerli were defending the Ponte alla Carraia; the

113

Frescobaldi and the Mannegli, Santa Trinita; the Rossi and the Bardi, the Ponte Vecchio and the Rubaconte. The *popolani* for their part mustered beneath the standard of the Gonfalonier of Justice and the banners of the People's Companies.

XLI

When things had reached this point, the people felt that a clash should no longer be put off, and the first to move were the Medici and the Rondinegli. They attacked the Cavicciuli from the street that leads from Piazza San Giovanni to their houses. The fighting was very heavy here because they were pelted with stones from the towers and were shot at by crossbows from below. This battle lasted three hours, but the people went on growing in strength, and seeing themselves outnumbered by the mob, and without help, the Cavicciuli grew frightened and surrendered to the people. The latter saved their houses and property for them. They only took their arms and ordered them to split up unarmed and go to their friends and relatives among the people.

Once this first attack had been repulsed, the Donati and the Pazzi were fairly easily beaten because they were less powerful. On this side of the Arno, there only remained the Cavalcanti, who were strong both in their numbers and in their position. Nevertheless, seeing all the standards turned against them and knowing that the others had been beaten by only three of them, they gave in without much of a fight. Three parts of the city were already in the people's hands: only one remained in the nobles' control, but it was the most difficult, both because of the strength of its defenders and because it was guarded by the river Arno. The bridges had to be taken, and they were defended as has been described above. The Ponte Vecchio was the first attacked. It was strongly defended because the towers were fortified, the roads were barricaded, and the barricades were manned by very fierce fighters. The people were thrown back with heavy losses. When they realized that they were wasting their time there, they tried to cross the Rubaconte bridge. Finding the same resistance there, they left four companies to guard these two bridges and attacked the Ponte alla Carraia with the rest. Although the Nerli stood up to the attack manfully, they could not resist the people's onslaught, partly because the bridge was weaker (as it had no towers to defend it), and partly because they were attacked by the Capponi and other families of the people who were their neighbors. Because they were under attack from all sides, they left the barricades and let the people through. The people went on to beat the Rossi and the Frescobaldi, which meant that all the *popolani* beyond the Arno joined up with the victors. Now only the Bardi were left. They were not frightened by the collapse of the others, or by the people's alliance against them, or by the small hope of reinforcements. They preferred to fight and either die or see their houses burned and sacked rather than agree to submit to their enemies' wishes. They defended themselves so well that the people made several unsuccessful attacks on them from the Ponte Vecchio or from the Rubaconte bridge and were always thrown back with many dead and wounded. Some time before this, a road had been made which led from the Via Romana, through the Pitti's houses, to the walls on the top of the hill of San Giorgio. The people sent six companies along this road and gave them orders to attack from behind the Bardi's houses. This attack sapped the morale of the Bardi and won the battle for the people, because when the men who were manning the barricades heard that their houses were being attacked, they left the fighting and went to defend them. This meant that the barricade over the Ponte Vecchio was captured and the Bardi were put to flight on all sides; they were taken in by the Quaratesi, the Panzanesi, and the Mozzi. Meanwhile, the people, and particularly the lowest of them, were thirsting for booty, and they plundered and sacked all the Bardi's houses. They destroyed and burned their palaces and towers with such fury that even the Florentines' fiercest enemy would have been ashamed at the havoc wreaked.

115

XLII

Once the nobles were beaten, the people reformed the constitution. Because there were three classes of people, the powerful, the middle, and the lower, it was laid down that the upper class should have two Signori, and the middle and lower three each, and that the Gonfalonier should be taken from each alternately. Besides this, all the provisions against the nobles were readopted, and so as to make them weaker, many nobles were made to mingle with the common people. This defeat of the nobility was so final, and such a blow to their party, that they never dared take up arms against the people again, and they became tractable and humble. This caused Florence to lose not only her fighting men but also all fighting spirit. After the defeat the city remained quiet until 1353, during which period there occurred the historic plague so eloquently described by Giovanni Boccaccio, which caused the death of more than ninety-six thousand souls in Florence. The Florentines also waged the first war on the Visconti, caused by the ambition of the Archbishop, who was at that time ruler of Milan. As soon as this war was over, factions sprang up within the city again, and although the nobility had been overthrown, Fortune was not short of ways of stirring up new trouble with fresh conflicts.

BOOK III

The cause of all the evils that arise in cities is the bitter and natural enmity that lies between the common people and the nobility. The latter want to command and the former do not want to obey. Everything that disturbs the peace of a republic is fostered by this clash of interests. It kept Rome disunited; and, if one may liken small things to great, it has kept Florence divided, although it produced different effects in both cities. The early quarrels between the nobles and the people in Rome were settled by discussions, those in Florence by fighting. In Rome they ended with laws, in Florence with the exile and death of many citizens. In Rome they increased military *virtù*, in Florence they destroyed it altogether. In Rome they changed the state of equality among the citizens to a state of very great inequality, in Florence they led from inequality to a remarkable state of equality. These different results must have been determined by the difference in the aims of the two peoples. The people of Rome wanted to enjoy the chief honors with the nobles, the people of Florence fought to have the government to themselves without the participation of the nobility. Because the Roman people's desire was more reasonable, their attacks on the nobles were more tolerable, and the nobles gave in easily without resorting to violence; after some differences they agreed upon a law which satisfied the people and allowed the nobles to keep their privileges. On the other hand, the Florentine people's aim was unjust and abusive, and the nobility prepared to defend themselves more effectively. This led to bloodshed and exile. The laws that were made afterwards were not passed for the common good but in favor of the victor. This meant that with the people's victories the city of Rome became more noble. Since the common people could be put in charge of the administration, the

117

armies, and the dominions with the nobles, they acquired the same *virtù* as the nobles. As the city's *virtù* grew, so its power grew. In Florence, however, the nobles were deprived of office after the people were victorious, and if they wanted to regain office they had not only to be like the *popolani* in their behavior, in their opinions, and in their style of living, but they had to be seen to be so. This was the reason for the changes in coats of arms and the alteration of surnames, which the nobles made in order to seem to be of the people. The *virtù* in arms and the greatness of spirit, which were part of the nobility's makeup, died away and could not be rekindled in the common people because they had never possessed them, and Florence became more and more humble and base. Once the Roman citizens' *virtù* had turned into pride, Rome was reduced to such a state that she could not be held together without a prince. Florence has reached a stage where she could easily be reformed by a wise lawgiver and given any form of government. These conclusions can easily be drawn from a reading of the preceding book, which discussed the birth of Florence and the origins of her liberty, the reasons for her divisions, and how the rivalry between the nobles' and people's parties ended in the Duke of Athens' tyranny and in the collapse of the nobility. Now there remains to be told the story of the quarrels between the middle and the lower classes, and the different events brought about by them.

II

Once the nobles' power had been broken and the war with the Archbishop of Milan was over, there seemed to be no other reason for trouble left in Florence. But our city's ill fortune and its bad institutions brought about a quarrel between the Albizzi and the Ricci families which divided Florence as the quarrels first between the Buondelmonti and the Uberti and then between the Donati and the Cerchi had done. The Popes, who were then in France, and the Emperors, who were in Germany, had sent quantities of soldiers of different nationalities at different times to keep up their reputations in Italy. At this time English, German, and Breton troops were to be found there. After the wars were over they went unpaid, so they placed themselves under a private banner and were holding for ransom one prince after another. In 1353 one of these companies came to Tuscany, captained by Monreale of Provence, and his arrival frightened all the cities of the province. The Florentines not only made public provision for troops but many citizens armed for their own safety, and among them were the Albizzi and the Ricci.

These two families hated each other deeply, and both aimed at getting the better of the other and winning the leadership of the republic. They had not yet come to blows, but clashed in the magistracies and in the councils. When the whole city was armed, a quarrel chanced to break out in the Old Market and a crowd gathered, as usually happens on such occasions. As the news spread, it was reported to the Ricci that the Albizzi were attacking them, and to the Albizzi that the Ricci were coming for them. The whole city rose, and the officials just managed to restrain both families and stopped the fight that had been rumored by chance and in which neither family intervened. This accident, however trivial, inflamed them further, and they tried even harder to find supporters. Because the citizens had been in a state of such equality since the overthrow of the nobles that the officials were respected more than they had been in the past, they planned to get their way by orthodox means and not by private violence.

III

We have already told how the magistracy of the Guelph party was created after the victory of Charles I, and how it was given great power over the Ghibellines. But time, new events, and fresh quarrels had caused this power to be forgotten, and many people who were descended from Ghibellines were holding leading offices.

Uguccione de' Ricci, the head of his family, had the law against the Ghibellines renewed. Many people believed the Albizzi were of that party. They had been natives of Arezzo much earlier and had emigrated to Florence. Uguccione thought that by renewing this law he could bar the Albizzi from office, as it was laid down that anyone descended from a Ghibelline should be condemned if he held any office. This plan of Uguccione's was revealed to Piero di Filippo degli Albizzi, and he decided to come out in favor of it, reckoning that if he opposed it he would be declaring himself a Ghibelline. So this law, which was renewed because of the ambition of the Ricci, did not damage Piero degli Albizzi's reputation but increased it, and it brought about a great deal of trouble. No more dangerous law can be made for a republic than one which is retroactive. Since Piero had been in favor of the law, what had been invented by his enemies as a hindrance to him was instead the cause of his aggrandizement. He became chief supporter of this new regulation and acquired more and more power, as he was favored more than anyone else by the new Guelph faction. Because no official body could be found to sort out who the Ghibellines were, and the law was being allowed to lapse, he ordered authority to be given to the Captains to make known who the Ghibellines were, and then to inform and warn them that they should not hold any offices. If they did not obey this warning, they were to be condemned. This is the reason why all those in Florence who are ineligible for office are called *ammuniti*, or "warned." The Captains' boldness had increased with the years, and motivated by greed or ambition they warned indiscriminately not only those who deserved it but anyone they liked. From 1357, when this regulation came into force, to 1366 more than two hundred citizens had already been warned. The Captains and the Guelph faction had become very powerful. For fear of being warned, everybody honored them, particularly the party leaders, Piero degli Albizzi, Lapo da Castiglionchio, and Carlo Strozzi. Although many people were annoyed by this insolent procedure, the Ricci were the most dissatisfied of all, as they felt that they were the cause of this irregularity which they saw was harming the republic, while, contrary to their plans, their enemies the Albizzi had grown extremely powerful.

IV

When Uguccione de' Ricci was a member of the Signoria, he wanted to put an end to the evil that he and his friends had begun, and by a new law he laid it down that the six Captains of the party should be increased by three, of whom two must belong to the Lesser Guilds; and that those declared to be Ghibellines should be confirmed by twenty-four specially appointed Guelph citizens. This provision went a long way to tempering the power of the Captains for the time being, and the warnings stopped for the most part. If some people were still warned, they were very few. Nevertheless, the Albizzi and Ricci clans were on the lookout, and they opposed alliances, expeditions, and deliberations out of hatred for each other. Such troubles filled the years from 1366 to 1371, during which time the Guelph faction regained its strength.

In the Buondelmonti family there was a knight called Benchi, who had been made a *popolano* for services in a war against the Pisans, and so had become qualified to be made a member of the Signoria. When he was waiting to take up the office, a law was passed to stop any noble who had become a *popolano* from holding office. This greatly offended Benchi, and he plotted with Piero degli Albizzi to get the better of the lesser *popolani* by warning them, so that the two of them would remain in power alone. Because of the favor Benchi enjoyed with the old nobility, and Piero with the greater part of the powerful *popolani,* they strengthened the Guelph faction, and by new reforms within the party they arranged things so that they could do as they liked with the Captains and the twenty-four citizens. So they started warning again with more effrontery than ever, and as party leaders the house of the Albizzi grew more and more powerful. On

121

the other hand, the Ricci and their friends never stopped trying to hinder the Albizzi's plans. Everyone lived in great apprehension, fearing some kind of disaster.

V

Prompted by patriotism a great number of citizens met in San Piero Scheraggio, and after they had spoken at length about these irregularities, they went to the Signori, and one of the most influential made the following speech: "Magnificent Signori, many of us feared to assemble on private instructions, even though it was for a public cause. We judged that we could be blamed as presumptuous or criticized as ambitious. But then we thought that every day many citizens gather together, regardless, in the loggias and in the houses, not for any public good but to further their own interest, and we felt that since those who meet to bring down the republic have no fear, then neither should those who assemble for the public good and welfare. Nor do we care what others think of us, because they do not respect our opinions about them. Magnificent Signori, the love we bear our country first brought us together and has now made us come to you to speak of the evil in our republic, which is already great and which is still growing, and to offer ourselves in readiness to help you put it down. Although it seems a difficult task, you could manage it if you put aside private considerations and used your authority and the civic forces. The corruption common to all the cities of Italy has corrupted and is still corrupting your city. Since this province threw off the yoke of the Empire, its cities have had no powerful curb to restrain them, and they have set up their regimes and governments not as democracies but as cities with factions. This has been at the root of all the other evils and irregularities that occur in them. First of all, there is no unity or friendship among their citizens, except among those who are a party to some wickedness committed against the country or against private citizens. And because religion and the fear of God are lacking in everyone, an oath or a promise

122

last as long as they are expedient. Men make them not to observe them but as a means to deceive others more easily. The easier and more successful the deception, the more glory and praise it wins. So dangerous men are praised for their industry, and the good are condemned as fools. It is quite true that in the cities of Italy everything that can be corrupted and everything that can corrupt others are joining forces: The young are lazy, the old are dissolute, and people of both sexes and all ages are completely without morals. Good laws can do nothing about this because they are ruined by bad customs. This is the cause of the greed apparent in the citizens, and the desire not for true glory but for shameful honors, which is the reason for the hatred and the quarrels, the feuds and the factions. These in turn bring about death, exile, the oppression of the good, and the exaltation of the wicked. The good, trusting in their innocence, do not try to find someone to defend and honor them in any special way, as the wicked do, and they come to a bad end, undefended and unhonored. Their example gives rise to the desire for factions and it makes the factions powerful. Bad men join them out of greed and ambition, good men out of necessity. Even more pernicious is the way in which the party leaders and backers dress up their aims and intentions with pious words; because although they are all enemies of liberty, they suppress it while making a pretense of defending an oligarchy or a democracy. The prize they look for from victory is not the glory of having liberated the city, but the satisfaction of having worsted the others and taken command of the city. Once they have done this, nothing is too unjust, cruel, or mean for them. This means that regulations and laws are made not for public but private good; and wars, peace treaties, and alliances are decided upon not for the common glory but for the satisfaction of the few. If other cities are full of these disorders, ours is more tainted than any other, because laws, statutes, and civil ordinances are made, and always have been, not according to a democratic system but according to the ambition of the party that has come out on top. The result is that as soon as one party is expelled and one conflict has ended another always appears in its place. A city that seeks to maintain itself by factions rather than by laws is bound of necessity to be divided against itself, when one faction is left without opposition. It cannot defend itself by means of those private methods which it had set up in the first place for its own good. The truth of this is proved by past and present dissension within our city. Everyone thought that once the Ghibellines had been destroyed the Guelphs would live happily and well respected for a long time; and yet, in a short while they divided into Blacks and Whites. Later when the Whites were beaten, the city was never without factions. We went on fighting, sometimes on behalf of the exiles, sometimes because of the enmity between the people and the nobles. We placed our liberty now in King Robert's hands, now in his brother's, now in his son's, and finally in those of the Duke of Athens, giving to others what we would not or could not agree to keep for ourselves. Yet still we never achieved a stable form of government, for we have never been able to agree to live in freedom, yet we are not satisfied to be slaves. Our political traditions are so bound up with party politics that we did not hesitate to confer the power of the King, while we still owed allegiance to him, on a man of very humble birth from Gubbio. One should not mention the Duke of Athens for the sake of the city's honor. His harsh, despotic character should have made us wise and taught us how to live; and yet no sooner was he expelled than we grasped our weapons and fought each other with more hatred and greater fury than ever before. Our ancient nobility was conquered and placed itself under the control of the people. Many people thought that nothing would give rise to trouble or party feeling in Florence ever again, once the people who had caused them with their pride and intolerable ambition had been curbed. But now we can see by experience how untrustworthy men's opinion is, and how wrong their judgment. The nobles' pride and ambition were not destroyed but taken from them by the *popolani*, and now, as ambitious men will, they are trying to lay hands on the top ranks of the republic. Having no other way to achieve them but

124

by creating strife, they have split the city again and have brought back the names of Guelph and Ghibelline, which had been forgotten, and which had better never been introduced into the republic. It is decreed above that all republics should have their marked families, who are destined to bring about the republic's ruin, so that nothing is everlasting or settled in human affairs. Our republic has been more prolific in these families than any other. It has been disturbed and afflicted not by one but by many: The Buondelmonti and the Uberti first, then the Donati and the Cerchi, and now, which is shameful and ridiculous, the Ricci and the Albizzi are upsetting and dividing the city. We have not pointed out the corrupt practices and earlier continual conflicts within the city in order to frighten you, but to remind you of their cause, to show you that just as you may remember them we also remember, and to tell you that the example of those disputes should not make you despair of being able to control the present ones. The power of those old families was so great, and so great were the favors they enjoyed from princes, that civic institutions and customs were not enough to check them; but now that the Empire has no troops here, and the Pope is no threat, and the whole of Italy and this city has reached such a state of equality that it can stand on its own, there will not be much difficulty. Despite earlier examples to the contrary, this republic of ours especially can not only be kept united but its morals and civic structure can be reformed, provided that your Lordships are disposed to accept the task. We recommend this course to you not out of any private feeling but for love of our country. Although her corruption is very great, destroy the disease that is weakening us, the rage that consumes us, and the poison that is killing us. Do not impute the feuds of old to the nature of men, but to the times. These have now changed, and you may hope for better fortune for our city, with the help of better institutions. The malice of Fortune can be overcome by prudence which would check those men's ambitions, abolish institutions which create factions, and keep those which are consonant with true democracy. And be content to do it now, gently, by using the laws, rather than put it off until later when men will be forced into it by violent methods."

VI

Prompted first by their own knowledge and then by the authority and recommendations of these men, the Signori appointed fifty-six citizens to look into the safety of the republic. It is very true that a large number of men is better suited to maintaining a good institution than to creating one by themselves. These citizens were more concerned about destroying present factions than rooting out the causes of future ones; and they achieved neither of the two aims, because they did not do away with the causes of recent feuds, and aggravated the underlying causes, which was more dangerous to the republic. Three of the Albizzi family and three of the Ricci, among whom were Piero degli Albizzi and Uguccione de' Ricci, were deprived of all offices, except those of the Guelph party, for three years. They forbade all the citizens to enter the palace, except when the magistracies were in session. They laid down that if anyone was beaten or had his property interfered with he could denounce the culprit to the Councils, have him declared a noble, and then have him placed under their jurisdiction. This regulation put an end to the effrontery of the Ricci family, but added to that of the Albizzi. Although they were both equally indicted, the Ricci still came off worse, because even though the palace of the Signori was closed to Piero, the Guelph palace, where he had immense authority, remained open to him. And where before he and his followers had been keen on warning others, they became even keener after this insult. Then new causes arose to add to their malevolence.

VII

Gregory XI was Pope at this time, and being at Avignon, like his predecessors he ruled Italy by means of legates, men full of greed and pride who had ill-treated a number of towns. One of them, who was at Bologna at that time, hoped to gain control of Tuscany by taking advantage of the famine that year in Florence. Not only did he fail to help the Florentines with food, but to take away any hope of future harvests he attacked them with a large army when spring first appeared, hoping to overcome them easily while they were hungry and unarmed. Perhaps he would have succeeded if the troops he used for the attack had not been unreliable and bribable, because the Florentines had no better remedy than to give one hundred and thirty thousand florins to his soldiers in order to make them give up their task. Wars begin when someone wants them to, but they do not end when he wants. This war, begun because of the legate's ambition, was carried on because of the Florentines' anger. They made an alliance with Bernabò and all the cities who were enemies of the Church. And they appointed eight citizens to supervise the conduct of the war, with power to operate without appeal, and to spend money without giving an account of it.

This war against the Pope caused the rise of those who had belonged to the Ricci faction, even though Uguccione was dead. They had always favored Bernabò and had opposed the Church, against the Albizzi; and they did so all the more because the Eight were all enemies of the Guelph faction. This meant that Piero degli Albizzi, Lapo da Castiglionchio, Carlo Strozzi, and the others cooperated more closely to bring down their enemies. And while the Eight were waging war, they went on warning people. The war lasted three years and did not end until the Pope's death. And it was managed with such *virtù*, and so much to the general satisfaction that the Eight were maintained in office each year. They were called Saints, even though they had paid little heed to censure, robbed the churches of their property, and forced the clergy to conduct services. But the citizens at that time thought more of their country than of their souls. They proved to the Church that whereas before they had defended her as her friends, as her enemies they could

127

attack her, because they made the whole of Romagna, the Marches, and Perugia rebel against her.

VIII

However, even while they were waging this war on the Pope, they could not defend themselves from the Captains of the party and their faction. The envy that the Guelphs bore the Eight increased their effrontery, and they did not refrain from insulting other noble citizens and even some of the Eight. The Captains of the party reached such heights of arrogance that they were more feared than the Signori; the people went to them with greater reverence than to the Signori; and the party's headquarters was more respected than that of the Signori. No ambassador came to Florence who had not some business with the Captains. After the Pope's death, when the city was no longer involved in a foreign war, there was great confusion at home. On the one hand, the insolence of the Guelphs was intolerable; on the other hand, nobody could think of a way of controlling them. Yet it was felt that there was bound to be a fight to see which of the two authorities would win. On the Guelph side were all the old nobles and most of the more powerful *popolani*, with, as we said, Lapo, Piero, and Carlo as leaders. On the other side were all the lesser *popolani*, whose leaders were the Eight for war, Giorgio Scali, and Tommaso Strozzi; and with them were the Ricci, the Alberti, and the Medici. The rest of the masses gathered to the protesting side, as almost always happens. The leaders of the Guelph faction felt that the enemy forces were strong and that they would be in great danger if ever an ill-disposed Signoria should want to humble them. Thinking that it was best to be prepared, they met together and examined their own position and conditions within the city. They felt that the *ammuniti* had greatly increased in numbers, and had heaped up so much resentment against them that the whole city was against them. They could see no remedy for this, other than depriving the *ammuniti*, whose privileges they had already taken away, of their rights of citizenship, occupying the palace of the Signoria by force, and bringing the whole state under the party's control, thus imitating the old Guelphs who only lived in safety in the city because they had expelled their enemies. Everyone agreed on this, but they could not decide on a time.

IX

It was now April 1378, and Lapo felt that things should not be postponed any longer. He said that nothing harmed time so much as time and that this applied particularly to them because Salvestro de' Medici could easily be made Gonfalonier in the next Signoria, and they knew he was opposed to their faction. Piero degli Albizzi, on the other hand, felt that they should wait, because he thought that troops were needed and they could not be recruited without some show being made, and if their plan was discovered they would run into certain danger. So he thought they should wait until the next St. John's Day. On that day, because it is the city's most important feast day, a great number of people would gather in the city, and they could then hide as many soldiers as they liked in the crowd. To take care of the danger from Salvestro, he should be warned. And if they did not feel like doing this, then some member of the college from his quarter should be warned, and when the lots were drawn for a replacement, because the purses were empty, Fate could easily arrange for him or one of his relatives to be drawn, and this would make him ineligible for the office of Gonfalonier. So they settled on this plan, although Lapo consented unwillingly, reckoning that it would be harmful to wait and that time is never quite right for anything, so that anyone who waits for all the advantages either never attempts anything or, if he does, most often it is to his own disadvantage. They warned the member of the college; but they did not manage to stop Salvestro, because the Eight discovered the reasons and stopped the replacement from being drawn. And so Salvestro, son of Alamanno de' Medici, was drawn as Gonfalonier.

He belonged to a noble *popolano* family, and he could not bear the people to be oppressed by a few powerful men. He thought of a way to put a stop to their insolence, and seeing that the people were on his side, as were many of his noble *popolano* friends, he communicated his plans to Benedetto Alberti, Tommaso Strozzi, and Giorgio Scali, who promised to give him all the help they could. They agreed in secret on a law which brought back the Ordinances of Justice against the nobles, lessened the authority of the Captains of the party, and gave the *ammuniti* the chance of being eligible for office. Since it had first to be discussed in the colleges and then in the councils, Salvestro, who was *proposto* (a rank which makes one almost ruler of the city while it lasts), arranged for the colleges and the councils to meet on the same morning, in order to test the proposal and have it passed all at the same time. He proposed the draft of the law to the colleges first, which were sitting separately from the council. As it was something new, this small number of men disapproved of it so strongly that it was not passed. Seeing that the first means of getting it through had been denied him, Salvestro pretended to leave the room for personal reasons, and without anyone realizing he went into the council chamber. Climbing up where everybody could see and hear him, he said he believed that he had been made Gonfalonier not to judge private cases, for which there were ordinary judges, but to look after the state, punish the powerful for their arrogance, and alter those laws which seemed to be leading to the downfall of the republic. He said that he had thought carefully about these duties and had done his best to carry them out, but men's wickedness was opposed to his just endeavors and he had been deprived of any way of doing good, while they had lost the chance not only of discussing it but even of hearing about it. Seeing that he could be of no further use either to the republic or to the general welfare, he saw no reason for staying in an office that either he did not deserve or others thought he did not deserve. So he was going home to let the people put someone in his place who had either greater *virtù* or better Fortune. After this speech, he left the council to go home.

X

The people in the council who were in on the secret and some others who were anxious for change started to create a disturbance. At this the Signori and the colleges collected, and seeing their Gonfalonier going away, they held him back with entreaties and threats, and made him go back into the council, which was in uproar. Many noble citizens were threatened with very insulting language, among them Carlo Strozzi, who was manhandled by an artisan who wanted to kill him; and the people standing by were hard put to it to defend him. But Benedetto degli Alberti was the one who caused the most rioting, and he got the whole city up in arms. He called the people to arms in a loud voice from the palace window, and immediately the square filled with armed men. After they had been threatened and scared, the colleges did what they had not wanted to do before when they had been asked. At the same time the Captains of the party had assembled a large number of citizens in their palace to decide how they were to defend themselves against the Signoria's new regulation. But when they heard that rioting had broken out and they were informed of the councils' decision, they all took refuge in their own houses. Let no one think that if he starts a revolution in a city he will be able to control it as he likes or regulate it in his own way. It was Salvestro's intention to bring in that law and calm the city, and things turned out quite differently. The emotions roused had affected everybody, so that the shops did not open, citizens were barricading themselves in their houses, many of them hid their furniture in monasteries and churches, and everyone seemed to be afraid of some approaching trouble. The corporations of the Guilds met and each appointed a syndic. The Priors summoned their colleges together with these syndics, and they conferred for a whole day to see how the city could be pacified to every-body's satisfaction. But opinions differed and they came to no agreement.

The next day the Guilds brought out their banners. When they heard this, the Signori were afraid of what did in fact happen, and they called the council to take preventive measures. Hardly had it assembled when riot-ing broke out, and immediately the Guilds' standards came into the square followed by a great number of armed men. To give the Guilds and the people hope of satisfaction and to keep them out of trouble, the council gave special authority, which is called *balìa* in Florence, to the Signori, the colleges, the Eight, the Captains of the party, and the syndics of the Guilds to reform the consti-tution of the city for its own general good. While this was being arranged, some of the Guilds' standards and those belonging to lower classes of people detached them-selves from the main group, and led by people who wanted revenge for recent insults from the Guelphs, they sacked and burned Lapo da Castiglionchio's house. When he heard that the Signoria had taken a stand against the Guelph establishment, and when he saw the people up in arms, Lapo could do nothing but hide or escape. First he hid in Santa Croce, then fled into the Casentino dressed as a monk. There he was often heard to lament the fact that he had given in to Piero degli Albizzi and that Piero had wanted to wait until St. John's Day to attempt the *coup*. Piero and Carlo Strozzi, how-ever, hid during the first rioting, thinking that once it was over they would be safe in Florence because they had plenty of friends and relatives. After Lapo's house was burned down, many other men's houses were sacked and burned, either because they were universally hated or because of some private vendetta. It is difficult to start trouble, but it easily grows. The rioters broke into the public prisons so that they would have company with an even greater thirst for robbing other people's property, and then they sacked the Monastery degli Agnoli and the Monastery of Santo Spirito where many citizens had hidden their furniture. Not even the public Chamber would have been safe from these robbers if it had not been defended by the respect in which one of the Signori was held. On horseback, with a large armed following, he resisted the anger of the mob as best he could. The people's fury was tempered a little, both by the authority of the Signori and by the coming of darkness. The next day the *Balìa* raised the ban on *ammuniti*, with the proviso that they could not hold any office for three years. They cancelled the laws made against the citizens by the Guelphs, and they declared Lapo da Castiglion-chio and his relatives to be rebels, and with them several others who were hated by the mob. After these decisions, the new Signori were made known, with Luigi Guicciar-dini as Gonfalonier. When their names were known, hope grew that rioting would cease, because everyone felt that they were peaceloving men.

XI

Nevertheless, the shops did not open, the citizens did not lay down their arms, and everyone set up strong guards all over the city. So the Signori did not assume office outside the palace with the usual pomp, but inside without any ceremony. These Signori thought that they could do nothing more useful at the beginning of their period of office than restore peace to the city. They had the citizens disarm, got the shops to open, and sent back to the *contado* many people who had been called in by the citizens to help them. They ordered a watch to be kept in many parts of the city. If they had been able to appease the *ammuniti*, then peace would have been re-stored to the city. But the *ammuniti* were not content to wait three years before having their privileges restored. To satisfy them, the Guilds met again and asked the Signori, for the sake of peace and quiet in the city, to decree that no citizen who at any time had been one of the Signori, a member of a college, a captain of the party, or consul of any Guild, could be warned as a Ghibelline; and also to have new voting bags made up for the electoral scrutinies within the Guelph party, and to have the old ones burned. These requests were imme-

133

diately granted, not only by the Signori but also by all the councils, and it looked as if the riots which had already broken out would be stopped. However, it is not enough for men to get their property back, they also want to take what belongs to others and have their revenge. Those who stood to gain out of the disorders persuaded the artisans that they would never be safe unless a lot of their enemies were expelled and destroyed. The Signori foresaw this and had the officers of the Guilds appear before them with their syndics. The Gonfalonier, Luigi Guicciardini, spoke to them and said: "If these Signori and I had not already been well acquainted with the city's fortune, which makes wars start at home as soon as foreign ones are over, we would have been much more surprised and disturbed by the rioting that has taken place. However, since familiar things worry one less, we have borne the recent disturbances patiently, because they began through no fault of ours, and we hoped they would eventually come to an end like the previous ones, after we had agreed to your numerous, weighty requests. But we anticipate that you are not going to calm down and that you even want your fellow citizens to suffer fresh abuses and be condemned to further exile; and our annoyance increases with your bad faith. Certainly if we had known that during our period of office our city was going to fall, either because we opposed or complied with your wishes, we would have avoided these honors by flight or exile. We hoped that we would be dealing with men who had some decency and some patriotic feeling, and we accepted office willingly, thinking that we would be sure to overcome your ambition by our goodwill. We have now learned by experience that the more humbly we behave and the more we give in to you, the more arrogant you become and the more extreme your demands. If we speak to you like this, it is not to offend you but to give you pause; we leave others to tell you what you would like to hear, we want to speak for your own good. Tell us, on your honor, what more you can rightly ask of us? You wanted to deprive the Captains of the party of their authority: It has been taken from them. You wanted their voting bags to be burned and new reforms to be made: We agreed. You wanted the *ammuniti* to be granted their privileges again: We allowed it. On your request we have pardoned those people who have burned down houses and robbed churches, and to satisfy you a great many revered and powerful citizens have been sent into exile; for your sake the nobles have been curbed by new regulations. How will these demands of yours end, and how much longer will you trade on our generosity? Do you not see that we can bear defeat more patiently than you can victory? Where will these quarrels of yours lead your city? Do you not remember that when she was divided, Castruccio, a base citizen of Lucca, defeated her? A Duke of Athens, one of your private soldiers of fortune, subjugated her? But when she was united, an Archbishop of Milan and a Pope could not get the better of her, and after years of war they were left discomfited. Why do you want your feuds to enslave in peacetime a city which so many powerful enemies have left free in times of war? What will you gain from your dissensions but slavery? What will you get from the property you have robbed or may rob from us but poverty? They are things that nourish the whole city with our industry: If we are deprived of them we cannot nourish her; those who occupy them will not be able to preserve them because they will have been wrongly acquired, and the result will be hunger and poverty in the city. I and these Signori order you, and entreat you, if honor will allow, to make up your minds once and for all to abide by what we have decreed, and if something else is needed to ask for it constitutionally and not with rioting and violence. If they are fair requests they will be complied with, and you will not give evil men the chance to ruin your country to your own cost and shame."

The citizens were moved by these words because they were true. They thanked the Gonfalonier warmly for having acted toward them as a good Signore and for being a good citizen to the city, and they said they were ready to obey his recommendations. To give them the opportunity, the Signori deputed two citizens to each of the more important magistracies, who with the syndics of the Guilds were to find out if there was anything that should be reformed in order to achieve peace at home, and to report back to the Signoria.

XII

While these things were going on another riot broke out, which did much more harm to the republic than the first. Most of the burning and looting carried out during the following days was the work of the very lowest classes of the city, and those who had been the boldest among them feared that once the major differences were settled peacefully they would be punished for the crimes they had committed, and that, as always happens, they would be deserted by those who had incited them to do wrong. To this fear was added the *popolo minuto*'s hatred of the rich citizens and the leaders of the Guilds, due to their feeling that they were not rewarded for their labors as well as they deserved. Because when, in Carlo I's time, the city was divided into Guilds, each one was given a free hand, and it was laid down that the subjects of each Guild should be judged by the heads of the Guild in civil matters. As we have already said, these Guilds numbered twelve to begin with. In time the number grew to twenty-one; and they were so powerful that in a few years they took over the government of the city. Because some were more important, and some less, they were divided into Greater and Lesser Guilds, seven being called Greater, and fourteen Lesser. The arrogance of the Captains of the party was caused by this division and the other reasons related above: The citizens who belonged to the old Guelph families, and among whom this office circulated, favored the *popolani* of the Greater Guilds and perse-cuted those of the Lesser Guilds and their defenders. And the riots we have been describing above were directed against these citizens. When the corporations of the Guilds were created, many of those trades carried on by the *popolo minuto* and the working classes were left without their own Guilds. These men joined different

Guilds according to their own type of craft, and as a result when they were either not rewarded for their work or oppressed in any way by their masters, they had no one else to complain to but the official of the Guild who controlled them. And they did not feel that he dispensed justice fairly. Of all the Guilds the one that had, and still has, the most of these members was, and still is, the Wool Guild. Because it was very powerful, and considered by all the others as the most important, it looked after, and still looks after, the interests of most of the working classes and the *popolo minuto*.

XIII

For the reasons explained above then, the men of the proletariat, both those in the Wool Guild and in other Guilds, were very angry. Added to this was the fear caused by the burning and looting they had committed. They met several times at night to discuss recent events and to persuade each other of the danger they were in. Some of the boldest and most experienced spoke these words to encourage the others: "If we had to decide now whether to arm, burn and rob citizens' houses, and pillage churches, I would be one of the ones who would consider it needed thinking about, and perhaps I would decide that peaceful poverty was preferable to a dangerous prize. But since violence has already broken out and much damage has been done, I feel we should be discussing ways of keeping people armed and profiting by the harm done. I certainly believe that if there is no one else to guide us then we ought to be guided by necessity. You can see that the whole of the city is full of complaints against us and hatred of us. The citizens are closing their ranks and the Signori are always with the officials. You can well believe that they are laying traps for us and are preparing to attack our strongholds with new forces. So we must aim at two things and have two goals in our deliberations: one, to avoid being punished for what we have done in the days to come; and the other, to live with more freedom and better rewards than

137

we have in the past. In my opinion, to make sure that we are forgiven for past crimes, we must commit new ones, increasing the damage, stepping up the burning and pillaging, and try to have a lot of companions in this, because when a number of people do wrong no one is punished, and small crimes are punished while great and serious ones are rewarded. When many suffer, few try to be revenged, because general oppression is more tolerable than the oppression of a few individuals. So an increase in violence will mean that we are forgiven more readily, and it will give us a way of getting what we want in order to gain our liberty. I feel that we are certain to achieve it, because those who might stop us are disunited and rich. Their disunity will give us victory, and when their wealth has become ours it will maintain us in power. Do not worry about the ancient lineage which they say we lack. All men had the same beginning and are equally ancient, and they were all made alike by nature. Naked, you will see that we are all the same. If they were dressed in our clothes and we in theirs, we would certainly look noble and they would look common. The only difference between us is that they are rich and we are poor. I am sorry to hear that many of you are conscience-stricken and regret what has been done, and that you do not want to do anything more. If this is so you are certainly not the men I took you for. You should not be afraid of conscience or infamy. The winners never bear any shame, whatever means they have used. We must pay no attention to conscience, because while we fear hunger and prison, we cannot and should not find room for the fear of hell. If you will notice the way men behave, you will see that everyone who achieves great wealth or power does so either by deceit or violence. Later, to hide the ugliness of the method of acquiring what they had taken by fraud or force, they whitewash it with a false claim of ownership. People who will not use these methods because they are too imprudent or too stupid always end in slavery and poverty. Faithful slaves are always slaves, and good men are always poor. The only people to escape from servitude are the bold and dishonest, and from poverty the grasping and deceitful. God and Nature put all the fortunes of men among them, and they are affected more by plunder than by industry, more by wicked than by good arts. This is why men eat one another, and the weakest always comes off worst. So force should be used when there is a chance. Fortune could not offer us a better chance now, with the citizens still divided, the Signoria in doubt, and the officials frightened. They can easily be crushed before they unite and make up their minds. We will either be in absolute control of the city or we will have so much power that not only will our earlier crimes be pardoned but we will be able to threaten them with new attacks. I admit that this course is bold and dangerous, but when the need is urgent, boldness is reckoned as prudence; and in great events men never paid any attention to danger. Exploits that begin with danger end with a prize, and no one ever escaped danger without danger. I believe that when you see prison, torture, and death being prepared, it is more dangerous to wait than to try to protect yourself. In the first case trouble is certain, in the second it is doubtful. How many times have I heard you complaining about your employers' meanness and your officers' unfairness? Now is the time not only to free yourselves of them but to become so superior to them that they will have to complain about and fear you instead. The opportunity that chance has brought us is passing; when it has gone there is no way of taking it again. You can see your enemies' preparations. We have got them worried. The one who first takes up arms again among us will certainly be a conqueror bringing ruin to the enemy and glory to himself. Many of us will gain honor, and all of us security."

These persuasive words inflamed hearts that had already warmed to evil, and they decided to arm since they had drawn a number of comrades to their side. They bound themselves by oath to help each other if one of their number was ill-treated by the officials.

XIV

While these men were preparing to take over the republic, their plan came to the notice of the Signori. The Signori got their hands on one Simone dalla Piazza and heard all about the conspiracy from him and about how they meant to start rioting the following day. They saw the danger and assembled the colleges and those citizens who, with the syndics of the Guilds, were trying to bring about the unity of the city (and before everybody was gathered, it was already evening). These people advised the Signori to call the consuls of the Guilds; and the consuls all advised that all the men at arms should be ordered into Florence and that the Gonfaloniers of the People should parade in the square the next morning with their armed companies. While Simone was being tortured, one Niccolò da San Friano was regulating the palace clock; and having realized what was going on, he went home and filled his whole neighborhood with uproar. In a moment, more than a thousand armed men thronged the Square of Santo Spirito. News of this rioting spread to the other conspirators, and San Piero Maggiore and San Lorenzo, both places they had agreed upon, were filled with armed men.

It was already light on the twenty-first of July, and more than eighty men at arms had appeared in the square in favor of the Signori. None of the Gonfaloniers had come, because they were afraid to leave their houses, having heard that the whole city was up in arms. The first of the masses to come into the square were the ones who had assembled at San Piero Maggiore; and when they arrived, the men at arms did not move. The other mob appeared beside them and meeting no resistance, they demanded their prisoners from the Signoria with loud threats. To get them by force, since they had not been freed after threats, they burned Luigi Guicciardini's house. The Signori handed the prisoners over to them for fear of worse. When they had got the prisoners back, they took the standard of justice from the executor; and bearing it before them, they burned many more citizens' houses, hunting down men who were hated for public or private reasons. Many citizens led the mob to their enemies' houses to be revenged for some private insult: for it was enough for a voice to shout from among the mob "so and so's house," or for the men who held the standard to turn in a certain direction. They also burned all the Wool Guild's documents. In order to accompany the great damage done with some praiseworthy deeds, they knighted Salvestro de' Medici and many other citizens. Altogether there were sixty-four, among whom were Benedetto and Antonio degli Alberti, Tommaso Strozzi, and other friends of theirs, though some of them had to be forced. The most remarkable thing about this occurrence was that many people had seen their houses burned down and then shortly afterwards were knighted on the same day by the same people (so near was the benefit to the injury). This happened to Luigi Guicciardini, Gonfalonier of Justice. The Signori did not know which way to turn among so much rioting, and they found themselves deserted by the men at arms, the leaders of the Guilds, and their own Gonfaloniers. No one had obeyed orders and helped them; and of the sixteen standards, the Golden Lion and the Squirrel were the only ones to appear, under Giovenco della Stufa and Giovanni Cambi. They stayed in the square for a short time, then they also left when they saw that no one was following them. On the other hand, seeing the fury of this undisciplined mob and seeing the Palace deserted, some of the citizens stayed in their homes, and others followed the hordes of armed men in order to defend their own and their friends' houses better by being among them. So it happened that their influence increased and that of the Signori grew less. The rioters went on all day, and when night fell they stayed at Stefano's palace behind the church of San Barnaba. They numbered more than six thousand; and before daybreak they threatened the Guilds and made them send them their standards. When morning came they went to the palace of the Podestà, bearing the standard of justice and the banners of the Guilds before them. The Podestà refused to hand the palace over to them, but they fought him and won.

XV

The Signori wanted to try to come to terms with the mob because they could see no way of restraining them by force. They called together four of their collegiate members and sent them to the palace of the Podestà to find out their intentions. They found that the leaders of the proletariat had already decided with the syndics of the Guilds and some other citizens what they wanted to demand of the Signoria. So they returned to the Signoria with four representatives from the masses, bearing these requests: that the Wool Guild should no longer have a judge from outside; that three new craft Guilds should be created, one for the carders and dyers, one for the barbers, doublet makers, tailors, and for similar mechanical crafts, and the third for the *popolo minuto;* and that these three new Guilds should always have two of their members among the Signori, and the fourteen Lesser Guilds should have three; that the Signoria should provide meeting places for these new Guilds; that no one belonging to these Guilds could be forced to pay a debt of less than fifty ducats for two years; that the *Monte* should stop paying interest and only pay back capital; that the exiles and those condemned should be pardoned; and that all the *ammuniti* should have their privileges restored. They demanded many other things as well for their own particular supporters, and then wanted a number of their enemies to be exiled and warned. Although these demands were a disgrace and a blow to the republic, they were immediately granted by the Signori, the colleges, and the Council of the People, for fear of worse. Before they could become law they had to be passed by the Council of the Commune, and this had to be postponed to the next day, as two councils could not meet in one day. But it seemed that the Guilds were happy and the working classes were satisfied with the arrangements. They promised that once the law was passed all rioting would cease.

The next morning, while the Council of the Commune was debating, the impatient, fickle mob came into the square with the same banners, and frightened all the council and the Signori with their loud, fearsome shouting. One of the Signori, Guerriante Marignolli, prompted more by fear than by any private interest, went downstairs, pretending to look at the ground floor door, and fled home. Coming out, he did not manage to escape the notice of the crowd and he was recognized. No harm was done to him, but the mob shouted, when they saw him, that all the Signori must leave the Palace, otherwise they would kill their children and burn their homes. Meanwhile, the law had been debated and the Signori had returned to their rooms. The council had come downstairs and without going outside, they stood in the loggia and the courtyard despairing of the city's safety, because they saw so much bad faith in the mob and so much wickedness or fear in the only people who could have restrained or mastered it. The Signori were also perplexed and worried about the country's safety, seeing that one of their number had deserted them, and no citizen had brought them any material aid or even advice. While they were still uncertain what they could or should do, Tommaso Strozzi and Benedetto Alberti, prompted either by their personal ambition to be lords of the palace or because they thought it was right, persuaded the Signori to yield to this popular outburst and go home as private citizens. This advice, given by men who had been leaders of the rioting, annoyed Alamanno Acciaiuoli and Niccolò del Bene, two of the Signori, although the others agreed. With a slight return of spirit, they said that if the others wanted to leave they could do nothing about it, but that they were determined not to put aside their authority before their time was up, unless they lost their lives at the same time. These disagreements doubled the fear of the Signori and the people's anger; and the Gonfalonier, preferring to end his period of office shamefully rather than dangerously, turned to Tommaso Strozzi for help. The latter got him out of the

143

palace and took him home. The other Signori left in the same way, one after the other; and Alamanno and Niccolò, finding themselves on their own, also went home in order not to be thought more brave than wise. The palace remained in the hands of the working classes and the Eight for war, who had still not resigned their office.

XVI

One Michele di Lando, a wool comber, had the standard of the Gonfalonier of Justice in his hand when the mob entered the Palace. Barefoot, with very few clothes on and with the whole throng behind him, he climbed upstairs; and when he came to the audience chamber of the Signori, he stopped and, turning to the mob, said: "You see, this place is yours, and this city is in your hands. What do you think we should do now?" To this they all replied that they wanted him to be Gonfalonier and ruler, to govern them and the city as he liked. Michele accepted power and because he was a wise and prudent man, better endowed by Nature than by Fortune, he decided to calm the city and stop the rioting. To keep the people busy and to give himself time to get organized, he ordered one Ser Nuto to be found, a man whom Lapo da Castiglionchio had appointed *bargello*. Most of the people who had gathered about him went off to carry out this task. To begin with justice the rule that he had won by grace, he publicly decreed that no one should burn or steal anything; and to frighten everyone, he raised the gallows in the square. To make a start on the reform of the city, he dismissed the syndics of the Guilds and appointed new ones; he deprived the Signori and collegiate members of office; and he burned the voting bags. Meanwhile, Ser Nuto was brought into the square by the mob, and he was hanged by one foot from the gallows. Everyone who was standing near cut off a piece, and in no time, all that was left of him was his foot. Meanwhile, the Eight for war, thinking that they had been left as rulers of the city now that the Signori had

144

gone, had already nominated the new Signori. When Michele heard this he sent to them to say that they must leave the palace at once, because he wanted to show everyone that he could rule Florence without their advice. Then he called a meeting of the syndics of the Guilds. Besides this, he made a new scrutiny[2] and divided the government into three parts: one for the new Guilds, one for the Lesser and one for the Greater Guilds. He gave Salvestro de' Medici the revenue from the shops on the Ponte Vecchio and made himself Podestà of Empoli. He made a number of other gifts to other citizens who were friends of the working class, not so much to repay them for their help as to make sure they would be prevented from envying him at any time.

XVII

The working class felt that Michele had been too favorable to the more powerful *popolani* in reforming the city. And they did not feel that they had as much say in the government as they needed to maintain power and defend themselves. Spurred on by their usual boldness, they armed again and, carrying their banners, burst into the square. They demanded that the Signori come down onto the rostrum to discuss new plans for the security and welfare of the working class. Seeing their arrogance and not wanting to make them more angry, Michele did not wait to hear what else they wanted but upbraided them for the way they were making their demands, and he urged them to lay down their arms, after which they would be granted requests that the Signoria could not grant honorably if forced. At this the mob became angry with the palace and went to Santa Maria Novella. There they set up eight leaders from among

---

[2] *scrutiny*—the process by which citizens were voted eligible for office. The names of the citizens thus elected were put into voting bags prepared by the *accoppiatori* and drawn out by the Podestà at appointed times.

145

themselves, with officers and other bodies, which gave them both prestige and respect. So the city had two seats of government and was ruled by two different masters.

These latter leaders decided among themselves that eight of them, elected from the corporations of their Guilds, should always remain with the Signori in the palace and that everything decided by the Signoria should be confirmed by them. They deprived Salvestro de' Medici and Michele di Lando of everything that had been granted to them in their other decisions. And they assigned offices and subsidies to many of their own number so that they could keep up their position with dignity. In order to enforce these decisions once they had been made, they sent two of their members to the Signoria to ask for them to be confirmed in the councils, with the intention of using force if they could not get them passed by agreement. These two explained their mission to the Signori with great boldness and greater presumption, and they reproached the Gonfalonier for the ingratitude and lack of respect he had shown them, considering that they had honored him and had given him his office. Finally, when they started to threaten him, Michele could bear such effrontery no longer and, remembering his rank rather than his lowly origins, he decided to put a stop to such extraordinary insolence in an extraordinary way. He drew the sword he wore, wounded them seriously, and then had them bound and imprisoned. When this affair was known, the whole mob was infuriated; and thinking that if they were armed they could achieve what they had been powerless to do unarmed, they armed amid rioting and uproar and set off to force the Signori to give in. Michele, however, foresaw everything and decided to take precautions, feeling that it would be more creditable to attack than to wait for the enemy inside the walls, and then have to flee like his predecessors, bringing dishonor to the Palace and shame on himself. So he collected a large number of citizens who had already begun to think again, mounted his horse, and followed by many armed men went to Santa Maria Novella to fight. The mob, who had come to the same decision, as we have said, left to go to the square almost at the same time as Michele left, which meant that each lot took a different route, and they did not meet on the way. When Michele got back, he found the square taken and fighting going on in the Palace. He joined battle with them and won, expelled some of them from the city, and forced some to lay down their arms and go into hiding. Once the battle was won, the rioting was quelled only through the *virtù* of the Gonfalonier. He surpassed every other citizen of that time for courage, prudence, and goodness, and he deserves to be counted among the few who have benefited their country. If he had had a wicked or ambitious nature, the republic would have lost its liberty completely and would have reached a worse state of despotism than that of the Duke of Athens. But his goodness never allowed a thought to enter his head that was contrary to the common good, and his prudence made him order affairs so that many of his own party gave in to him; and the rest he could control by force of arms. This made the working class scared; and it caused the better artisans to think again and to see how shameful it was for those who had tamed the pride of the nobility to have to tolerate the stink of the proletariat.

XVIII

When Michele won his victory over the working class, the new Signoria had already been drawn. Among them were two men of such base and vulgar origins that people's desire to free themselves from such infamy increased. On the first of September, when the new Signori took office, the square was full of armed men. As soon as the old Signori came out of the Palace, a cry went up from the armed men that they did not want anyone from the *popolo minuto* among the Signori. To satisfy them, the Signori deprived those two of office, one who was called Tria, and the other Baroccio. They elected Giorgio Scali and Francesco di Michele instead of them. They also did away with the Guild of the *popolo minuto* and deprived its members of office, except

Michele di Lando and Lorenzo di Puccio, and some others of better standing. They divided privileges into two parts, and gave one part to the Greater and one part to the Lesser Guilds. As Signori they wanted only five from the Lesser Guilds and four from the Greater, and they wanted the office of Gonfalonier to go now to one member, now to another. This constitution brought peace to the city for the time being. But although the republic had been taken out of the hands of the working class, the lesser guildsmen were still more powerful than the noble *popolani*. The latter were obliged to agree to this in order to woo the Guilds away from the *popolo minuto* by granting the Guilds' wishes. This state of affairs was also approved of by the men who wanted to get the better of those who had done so much harm to so many citizens in the name of the Guelph party. Because Giorgio Scali, Benedetto Alberti, Salvestro de' Medici, and Tommaso Strozzi were among those who were in favor of this type of government, they almost ruled the city. These events and decisions confirmed the division between the noble *popolani* and the lesser guildsmen which began with the ambition of the Ricci and the Albizzi. Very serious consequences followed at different times, and we will have to mention them very often, so we will call one of these parties "popular," and the other "working class." This regime lasted for three years, and it was marked by exiles and executions because the rulers lived in great fear, as there were many discontented people both at home and abroad. The malcontents at home either tried or were believed to be trying something new every day: Those abroad with nothing to hold them back sowed scandal on all sides with the help now of this prince, now of that republic.

XIX

In Bologna at this time was Giannozzo da Salerno, a captain of Carlo di Durazzo's who was a descendant of the Kings of Naples. He was planning an attack on the Kingdom against Queen Joan, and he kept his captain in that city depending on the favors of Pope Urban, an enemy of the Queen. There were also many Florentine exiles in Bologna who were negotiating with Carlo and him. This was why those who were governing Florence were living in great fear and why they easily believed slanders of the citizens who were suspect. While people were in this state of suspense, it was revealed to the government that Giannozzo da Salerno was coming to Florence with the exiles and that many people inside were going to take arms and deliver the city up to him. Because of this report, many people were charged, among whom the first to be named were Piero degli Albizzi and Carlo Strozzi, then Cipriano Mangioni, Iacopo Sacchetti, Donato Barbadori, Filippo Strozzi, and Giovanni Anselmi. All of them were arrested, except Carlo Strozzi, who escaped. The Signori appointed Tommaso Strozzi and Benedetto Alberti with a number of armed men to guard the city and stop anyone from arming in support of these men. The prisoners were examined and they could not be found guilty of any of the charges on the basis of the evidence. The Captain did not want to condemn them, but their enemies roused the people and played on their anger so much that the prisoners had to be condemned to death. The greatness of his house and his earlier standing, when he had been honored and feared above every other citizen, were of no use to Piero degli Albizzi. One day when he had been giving a banquet for some citizens, someone, either a friend who wanted to make him kinder in his prosperity or else an enemy who wanted to threaten him with the fickleness of Fortune, sent him a silver bowl full of sweets, among which a nail was hidden. When this was discovered and all the banqueters saw it, it was interpreted as a reminder to nail down the wheel. Fortune had brought him to the top of the wheel, and if it completed its circle it could not help dragging him down to the bottom again. This interpretation was confirmed first by his downfall, then by his death.

After this execution the city remained in a state of confusion because both winners and losers were afraid. But more evil resulted from the rulers' fear, because the slightest thing made them heap fresh abuses on the party, condemning, warning, or sending citizens into exile. Added to this were new laws and new regulations, which they made frequently to strengthen the regime. All this was carried out to the detriment of those whom their faction suspected. They appointed forty-six men who with the Signoria were to rid the republic of suspects. They warned thirty-nine citizens, and made many *popolani* nobles and many nobles *popolani*. In order to withstand a foreign attack, they hired John Hawkwood, English by birth, and very famous for his military prowess, who had already fought for the Pope and other people in Italy for some time. The fear of a foreign attack arose from the news that several companies of men at arms were being drawn up by Carlo di Durazzo to invade the Kingdom, and with him there were said to be many Florentine exiles. Provision was made against these dangers not only in troops but also in money. When Carlo reached Arezzo, he got forty thousand ducats from the Florentines, and he promised not to molest them. He carried on with his expedition, succeeded in occupying the Kingdom of Naples, and sent Queen Joan a prisoner to Hungary. This victory increased the fears of the government in Florence, because they could not believe that their money would have more power over the King than the old friendship which his house bore the Guelphs, whom they were oppressing so heavily.

XX

As this fear grew it made the oppression heavier, and this in turn did not end the fear but rather increased it. So most people were very discontented. The disorderly behavior of Giorgio Scali and Tommaso Strozzi added to the discontent. They overruled the officials with their authority, and everyone was afraid of being bullied by them, with the backing of the working classes. That government seemed tyrannical and violent, not only to the good but also to the rebellious. However, since Giorgio's insolence had to come to an end sometime, it happened that Giovanni di Cambio was accused by one of Giorgio's friends of having plotted against the state. The Captain found him innocent, and the judge wanted to punish the plaintiff in the same way as the prisoner would have been punished if he had been found guilty. Giorgio could not save his friend by his entreaties or by his authority, and he and Tommaso Strozzi went with a crowd of soldiers and set him free by force. They sacked the Captain's palace and forced him to hide in order to save himself. This deed roused the city's hatred against Giorgio so much that his enemies thought they would be able to get rid of him and get the city not only out of his hands but also out of the hands of the working classes who had tyrannized it with their arrogance for three years.

The Captain gave them a good opportunity for this. When the disturbance was over, he went to the Signori and told them that he had willingly accepted the office to which the Signori had appointed him, because he thought he would be serving just men who would take up arms to help and not to hinder justice. But now that he had experience of the way the city was governed and its way of life, he would willingly forfeit the dignity that he had accepted for his own honor and profit, in order to escape danger and injury. The Captain was supported by the Signori and was encouraged by promises that he would be compensated for earlier damages, and he was given assurances of his future security. A number of them met with some of the citizens who they felt respected the common good and who were least suspect to the regime, and they concluded that they had a good opportunity of wresting the city from the grip of Giorgio and the working classes, since he had alienated the whole populace by his latest piece of insolence. They decided to grasp the opportunity before the two sides were reconciled, because they knew that the people's favor is lost and won over the slightest thing. They thought that in order to achieve their aim they must win Benedetto Alberti over to their side, as it would be a dangerous task without his support.

Benedetto was a very rich man, kind, strict, a lover of

151

his country's liberty, who much disliked despotic methods. So it was easy to pacify him and get his consent to Giorgio's downfall. The reason why he had become the enemy of the noble *popolani* and the Guelph faction, and the friend of the working classes, had been the former's insolence and tyrannical behavior. Then when he saw that the proletarian leaders had become just like them, he had left their party sometime before, and the wrongs that many citizens had suffered had been committed entirely without his consent. So the same reasons that had made him take up the cause of the working classes now made him reject it. Once they had won Benedetto and the leaders of the Guilds over to their side and had provided themselves with arms, Giorgio was arrested and Tommaso fled. The next day Giorgio was beheaded, and his own party was so terrified that nobody did anything, rather they did their best to bring about his downfall. Seeing himself brought out to die in front of the people who a short time before had worshipped him, Giorgio complained of his evil fate and the wickedness of the citizens, who because they had wrongly abused him had forced him to favor and honor a mob that knew neither faith nor gratitude. Recognizing Benedetto Alberti among the armed men, he said to him: "Are you, Benedetto, going to allow an injustice to be done to me, which I would never allow to be done to you if I was out there? I prophesy to you that this day marks the end of my troubles and the beginning of yours." Then he reproached himself for having trusted too much in a people who are affected and corrupted by every rumor, every deed, and every suspicion. After these complaints he died amid his armed enemies who rejoiced at his death. After him some of his closest friends were executed and then dragged along by the people.

XXI

The whole city was affected by the death of this citizen, because when the sentence was carried out many people armed in support of the Signoria and the Captain of the People, and many others did so out of ambition or because of their private fears. The city was full of different factions, each one with a different aim, and they all wanted to achieve these aims before they disarmed. The old nobility, called *Grandi,* could not bear to be deprived of their state dignities, and they were trying all ways to get them back. They wanted the Captains of the party to be given back their authority for this reason. The noble *popolani* and the Greater Guilds disliked sharing the government with the Lesser Guilds and the *popolo minuto.* The Lesser Guilds, on the other hand, wanted to increase their privileges rather than diminish them, and the *popolo minuto* were afraid of losing the Colleges of their Guilds. These differences caused frequent rioting in Florence for a year; now the nobles armed, now the Greater or Lesser Guilds, and with them the *popolo minuto.* Several times everyone was armed at the same time in different parts of the city. A number of clashes resulted both between factions and with the Palace soldiers, because the Signoria did its best to put things right, sometimes by giving in, sometimes by fighting. Finally, after two popular assemblies and several *Balìe* were set up to reform the city, and after a great deal of destruction and distress and serious danger, a government was established. This government recalled from exile all those who had been banished since Salvestro de' Medici had been Gonfalonier; it took away rights of precedence and pensions from people who had been given them by the *Balìa* of 1378; privileges were restored to the Guelph party; the two new Guilds were deprived of their functions, and all their members were reassigned to their former Guilds; members of the Lesser Guilds were excluded from the rank of Gonfalonier of Justice and their share of the dignities went down from a half to a third, and those they lost were of the most important kind. So the party of the noble *popolani* and Guelphs resumed power, and the party of the working classes lost it. But the latter had ruled the state from 1378 to 1381, during which time these strange events took place.

153

XXII

This new regime was no less harsh to its subjects nor less oppressive in its early stages than the regime of the working classes. Many of the noble *popolani* who were well-known defenders of the proletariat were exiled together with a large number of working-class leaders, among whom was Michele di Lando. The good that he had done by using his authority when the rabble had plundered the city unchecked could not save him from the fury of the parties. His country showed him no gratitude for his good deeds. Because princes and republics often make this mistake, men are frightened by similar examples, and they strike at their rulers before they can experience their ingratitude. Benedetto Alberti disliked these exiles and deaths, as he had disliked the earlier ones, and he criticized them publicly and privately. The leaders of the government feared him because they thought he was one of the chief friends of the working classes, and they thought he had consented to Giorgio Scali's death not because he disliked his behavior but because he wanted to remain in power alone. Then his words and his actions increased their fear, and the whole of the ruling party kept their eyes on him to find some opportunity of getting the better of him.

While this state of affairs continued, foreign affairs were fairly quiet. What did happen caused more alarm than damage. At this time Louis of Anjou came to Italy to restore the Kingdom of Naples to Queen Joan and to expel Carlo di Durazzo. His arrival frightened the Florentines a great deal because Carlo, an old friend, asked them for help, and Louis, looking for allies, asked them to remain neutral. So the Florentines, to make a show of satisfying Louis and of helping Carlo, dismissed John Hawkwood from their service and made him captain an army for Pope Urban, who was a friend of Carlo's. Louis easily saw through the trick and considered that the Florentines had treated him badly. While war was being waged in Apulia between Louis and Carlo, new reinforcements arrived from France for Louis. When they reached Tuscany, they were taken to Arezzo by the Aretine exiles, and the party that ruled on Carlo's behalf was expelled. When they were planning a revolution in Florence like the one in Arezzo, Louis died; and with this change of fortune, affairs in Apulia and Tuscany changed correspondingly. Carlo tightened his hold on the kingdom that he had almost lost and the Florentines, who had wondered whether they could defend Florence, won Arezzo, because they bought it from the soldiers who were holding it for Louis. So Carlo, once he was sure of Apulia, went off to the Kingdom of Hungary, which was his by heredity, and left his wife in Apulia with his two children Ladislaus and Joan, who were still young, as we have already explained. Carlo won Hungary, but soon afterwards he was killed there.

XXIII

Florence arranged solemn celebrations for the acquisition of Arezzo, as any city might have done for a real victory. Both public and private splendor could be seen because many families competed with the public in their merrymaking. But the family that outdid all the others in pomp and magnificence was the Alberti family, because the displays and the jousting that they put on were worthy not of a private family but of some prince. These things increased the envy felt toward the family, and this, added to the regime's fear of Benedetto, was the cause of his downfall. Those who were ruling felt they could not rely on him, because at any time he might trade on his reputation and expel them from the city. During this period of mistrust, while he was a Gonfalonier of the Companies, his son-in-law, Filippo Magalotti, happened to be drawn as Gonfalonier of Justice. The fear of the rulers of the state doubled at this, as they thought that too much power was in Benedetto's hands and that this implied too much danger for the state. Hoping to settle matters without any disturbances, they prompted Bese Magalotti, a relative and enemy of his,

155

to report to the Signori that Filippo could not and should not hold the office because he did not have the time necessary to carry out his duties. The Signori examined the case and ruled, some of them out of spite, some to avoid trouble, that Filippo was ineligible for the honor. In his place Bardo Mancini was drawn, a man who was entirely opposed to the working-class party and a bitter enemy of Benedetto's. After he had taken office he appointed a *Balìa* which, when it took control of the state and reformed it, banished Benedetto Alberti and warned the rest of the family, except Antonio.

Before he left, Benedetto called all his relations together, and seeing them sad and tearful he said to them: "My fathers and elders, you see how Fortune has ruined me and threatened you. This does not surprise me, nor should it surprise you, because this always has happened to people who want to be good among the wicked and who want to uphold what most people want to destroy. Love of my country made me side with Salvestro de' Medici and later quarrel with Giorgio Scali. It also made me hate the methods of our present rulers, who, because they had no one to punish them, did not want anyone to criticize them either. I am happy with my exile to free them of the fear they had, not only of me but of anyone who they know can recognize their despotic and evil ways; with the blows they have dealt me they have threatened the others. I am not worried about myself, because the honors my country gave me when she was free she cannot take from me now that she is in chains, and the memory of my past life will always give me more pleasure than the unhappiness of my exile can bring me pain. I am sorry that my country remains in the grip of a few men, and subject to their pride and greed. And I am sorry for your plight, because I am afraid that the troubles that for me are ending today are beginning for you and that they will persecute you and do you more harm than they have done me. So I advise you to keep a steadfast heart against all misfortunes and to behave in such a way that if you are attacked, as you will be, everyone will know that you were innocent and blameless." Then to win no less a reputation for goodness

outside Florence than he had inside, he went to the
Sepulchre of Christ and died at Rhodes on his way back.
His bones were brought to Florence and buried with great
pomp by those who had persecuted him with all kinds of
slander and insults when he was alive.

XXIV

During these upheavals in the city, the Alberti family
was not the only one to suffer. Many citizens were
warned and banished with them, among whom were
Piero Benini, Matteo Alderotti, Giovanni and Francesco
del Bene, Giovanni Benci, Andrea Adimari, together with
a great many lesser artisans. Among those warned
were the Covoni, Benini, Rinucci, Formiconi, Corbizzi,
Mannelli, and the Alderotti. It was customary to appoint
a *Balìa* for a certain period of time, but once those citizens had done what they had been deputed to do, they
would resign out of public spirit even though their time
was still not up. So when those men felt that they had
done their duty by the state, they wanted to resign in the
usual way. When they heard this, many people ran to
the Palace armed and asked them to outlaw and warn
many more people before they resigned. The Signori
were greatly annoyed by this and kept them quiet with
promises until they had strengthened their position; then
they acted so that the people who had taken up arms in
anger were forced to lay them down in fear. However, to
placate this angry feeling partially, and to deprive the
working-class guildsmen of still more power, they decreed
that where before they had had a third of the honors they
should now have a quarter. And so that there would
always be two people that the regime could trust among
the Signori, they gave the Gonfalonier of Justice and four
other citizens authority to make up a bag of specially
selected names from which two would be drawn in every
Signoria.

XXV

After the regime that had been set up in 1381 was established in this way six years later, the city remained fairly quiet at home until 1393. During this time Giovan Galeazzo Visconti, called the Count of Virtù, imprisoned Bernabò, his uncle, and so became prince of all Lombardy. He thought he could become King of Italy by using force, just as he had become Duke of Milan by trickery. In 1390 he started a very serious war against Florence, and he changed his conduct of the war so much that very often he was in greater danger of losing than the Florentines, who would have lost in fact, however, if he had not died. Nevertheless, they put up a wonderfully courageous defense for a republic, and the outcome was much less bad than the war was frightening. Because when the Duke had occupied Bologna, Pisa, Perugia, and Siena, and had prepared the crown for his coronation as King of Italy in Florence, he died. His death stopped him from enjoying his past victories and prevented the Florentines from feeling their present losses.

While this war with the Duke was being waged, Maso degli Albizzi was made Gonfalonier of Justice. Piero degli Albizzi's death had made him an enemy of the Alberti. As party feeling was still rife, Maso thought he would have his revenge on the rest of the family, even though Benedetto had died in exile, before he laid down his office. He took his opportunity when someone was questioned for carrying on negotiations with the rebels, who named Alberto and Andrea degli Alberti. The latter were arrested immediately, which angered the whole city. The Signori armed themselves, called the people to an assembly, and appointed a *Balìa*, through which they outlawed a number of citizens and made up new voting bags. Among those banished were almost all the Alberti; and a great many artisans were warned or executed. This caused the Guilds and the *popolo minuto* to rise up in arms, seeing that they had lost their honor and their lives. Part of them came into the square, and another group ran to Veri de' Medici's house. He had become head of that family after the death of Salvestro. To quieten those who came into the square, the Signori gave them as leaders Rinaldo Gianfigliazzi and Donato Acciaiuoli, who carried the standards of the Guelph party and of the People, as being the *popolani* most acceptable to the working classes. Those who went to Veri's house begged him to take over the government and free them from the tyranny of those citizens who were ruining good people and destroying the welfare of all. All those who have left a record of this time agree that if Veri had been more ambitious than good he would have had no difficulty in making himself ruler of the city. The grave injustices that rightly or wrongly had been done to the Guilds and their supporters had so kindled their desire for revenge that all that was needed to satisfy their desires was a leader. Nor was Veri without people who could remind him what he could do, because Antonio de' Medici, who had nourished a particular enmity for him for some time, was trying to persuade him to take control of the republic. To him Veri said: "Your threats never frightened me when you were my enemy, now that you are my friend your advice will do me no harm." He turned to the mob and told them to take heart, and he would defend them if they would take his advice. He went into the midst of them in the square, and then up to the palace; and before the Signori he said he did not at all regret having lived so that the people of Florence loved him, but he did regret their having judged him in a way unwarranted by his past life. He had never done anything to make people think that he was rebellious or ambitious, and he did not know how anyone could think he would make trouble like a rebel, or take over the state like an ambitious man. He begged their Lordships not to make him responsible for the mob's ignorance, because as far as he was concerned he had put himself at their disposal as soon as he could. He reminded them to be content to use their good fortune modestly and to be satisfied to enjoy a moderate victory rather than destroy the city for the sake of a complete one. Veri was praised by the Signori and was urged to get the people to disarm. Afterwards they would not fail to do what he and the other citizens advised. After these words Veri went back into the square and added his bands of men to those that were led by Rinaldo and Donato. Then he told everyone that he had found the Signori very well disposed toward them and that they had discussed a number of things together without reaching any conclusions because of lack of time and the absence of the officials. He begged them to put down their arms and obey the Signori, and he promised them that the Signori would be more likely to be touched by gentleness than by arrogance and by requests rather than threats. He said that their status and security would not be endangered if they followed his advice. So he got everyone to go home on the strength of his promises.

XXVI

After these people had disarmed, the Signori first fortified the square, then listed two thousand citizens regarded as trustworthy by the regime, divided them equally into companies with standards, and commanded them to be ready to help them whenever they were called upon. Those not on the list were forbidden to bear arms. Having made these preparations, they outlawed and executed many of the artisans who had been more violent than the others during the rioting. So that the Gonfalonier of Justice should have more dignity and respect, they decreed that a man must be forty-five years old to hold the position. To strengthen the government further, they made many other provisions that were intolerable to those against whom they were directed. The good citizens of their own party disliked them because they judged that a state that needed to be defended with such violence could be considered to be neither good nor secure. And it was not only those Alberti who were left in the city, or the Medici, who felt they had deceived the people, that disliked so much violence, but many others as well. The first person who tried to oppose it was Donato, son of Iacopo Acciaiuoli. Although he was important in the city and superior rather than equal to Maso degli Albizzi, who was as good as head of the republic because of what had been done while he was Gonfalonier, he could not live happily amid so much dissatisfaction, nor turn public misfortune into private gain, as most people do. So he thought he would try to have the exiles brought home, or at least give the *ammuniti* their offices back. He went about putting his views to one citizen after another, telling them that the people could not be placated and party feeling stifled in any other way. He was only waiting to be made one of the Signori to put his wishes into practice. But because where our actions are concerned, delay means boredom and speed danger, to avoid boredom he decided to risk danger. Among the Signori were Michele Acciaiuoli, a relative of his, and Niccolò Ricoveri, a friend. Donato felt that this was an opportunity not to be missed, and he asked them to propose a law in the Councils that would permit the citizens' reinstatement. He convinced them and they mentioned it to their colleagues, who replied that they were not going to try out anything new where the gain was doubtful and the danger certain. Donato was angry, and having first tried all ways in vain, he gave them to understand that if they did not want the city to be put right by peaceful methods, then it would be put right by force of arms. These words caused a great deal of concern, and when the affair was reported to the leaders of the government, Donato was cited. When he appeared, he was convicted by the man to whom he had entrusted his recommendations. He was outlawed to Barletta. Alamanno and Antonio de' Medici were also outlawed, with everyone of that family who descended from Alamanno, as well as many common artisans who had prestige with the working classes. These events happened two years after Maso had taken over the government.

XXVII

So the city remained with many discontented people inside and many exiles outside. Among the outlaws at Bologna were Picchio Cavicciuli, Tommaso de Ricci, Antonio de' Medici, Benedetto degli Spini, Antonio Girolami, Cristofano di Carlone, and two other men of low birth, but all spirited young men, willing to try anything to get back home. Piggiello and Baroccio Cavicciuli, who were *ammuniti* living in Florence, communicated in secret with these men and said that if they came to the city secretly they would receive them in their own house, and from there they could go out and kill Maso degli Albizzi and call the people to arms. The people were dissatisfied and could easily be roused, especially as they would be followed by the Ricci, Adimari, Medici, and Mannelli, and many other families. The men were attracted by this hope and on the fourth of August 1397, they came to Florence, going secretly where they had been told, and they had Maso watched because they wanted to kill him and start a revolution. Maso came out of his house and stopped at a grocer's near San Piero Maggiore. The man sent to watch him ran to tell the conspirators, who came to the place armed, but found that he had already gone. They were not dismayed to find that their first plan had failed, and they turned toward the Old Market, where they killed a man of the opposing party. They created an uproar shouting "People, arms, liberty" and "Death to the tyrants," and turning toward the New Market, they killed another man at the end of Calimala. They went on their way shouting the same slogans, but no one took up arms, and they ended up in the loggia della Nighittosa. There they climbed up high, and were surrounded by a huge crowd that had come out to look at them rather than to side with them. In a loud voice they urged the men to arm and throw off the slavery they had hated so much, and they told them that they had been moved to free them more by the grievances of those in the city who were dissatisfied than by the injustice they themselves had suffered. They said they had heard that many people begged God to give them a chance for revenge, which they would take if ever they had a leader. Now that the chance had come and they had the leaders, they stood looking at each other stupidly, waiting for the promoters of their freedom to die and the oppression they suffered to become heavier. They said they were surprised that people who used to arm over the slightest abuse, now after so many abuses made no move, and that they could tolerate so many of their citizens being outlawed and warned. But it was in their power to bring the exiles back to their country and to give the *ammuniti* their places in the government again. Although these words were true, they did not move the mob at all, either because they were afraid or because the deaths of those two men had made them hate the murderers. When the instigators of the rioting saw that neither words nor deeds had any power to move anyone, they realized too late how dangerous it is to try to free a people that wants to be enslaved at all costs. They gave up all hope of success and withdrew to the church of Santa Reparata and shut themselves in, not in order to save their lives but to postpone death. The Signori had been worried at the first disturbances and had armed and shut the palace. Then when the affair had been reported and they knew who the troublemakers were, and where they had gone, they were reassured. They ordered the Captain to go and arrest them with many other armed men. The doors of the church were forced open without much trouble; some of the men were killed defending themselves, and some were arrested. When they were questioned the only others who were found guilty besides them were Baroccio and Piggiello Cavicciuli, and they were executed with them.

XXVIII

After this event there came another of greater importance. At this time the city was at war with the Duke of Milan, as we said earlier. When he saw that main force was not enough to subdue Florence, he turned to secret means, and through the Florentine exiles, of which Lombardy was full, he drew up a treaty which many people inside knew about. It was agreed that on a particular day a large number of exiles able to bear arms should leave from the places nearest to Florence and enter the city by the river Arno. With the friends inside, they would run to the homes of the leaders of the government, and when they had killed them, they could reform the republic as they liked.

Among the conspirators inside the city was one of the Ricci family who was called Saminiato. And as often happens in conspiracies, a small number is not enough and a large number gives it away. While Saminiato tried to win friends, he found someone to inform against him. He confided in Salvestro Cavicciuli, who should have been trustworthy because of what he and his family had suffered. However, he thought more of the immediate danger than of any future hope, and he laid the whole affair of the treaty before the Signori immediately. They had Saminiato arrested and forced him to reveal the whole organization of the plot. None of those who were in the know were taken except Tommaso Davizi, who was arrested on his way from Bologna, before he knew what had happened in Florence. All the others fled terrified after the capture of Saminiato. After Saminiato and Tommaso had been punished according to their crimes, a *Balìa* of several citizens was set up with authority to seek out criminals and to ensure the safety of the state. They declared as rebels six of the Ricci family and six of the Alberti, two of the Medici, three of the Scali, two of the Strozzi, Bindo Altoviti, Bernardo Adimari, with many commoners. And they warned the whole of the Alberti, Ricci, and Medici families for ten years, except for a few of them. Among the Alberti who were not warned was Antonio, as he was thought to be a quiet, peaceful man. Then before the fear of conspiracy had died down, a monk happened to be captured who had been seen going several times from Bologna to Florence at the time when the conspirators were active. He confessed that he had carried letters to Antonio several times. So the latter was arrested immediately; and although he denied it at first, the monk's evidence convicted him, and he was fined and exiled to three hundred miles from the city. To stop the Alberti from endangering the state every day, all those of the family who were more than fifteen years old were exiled.

XXIX

These events happened in 1400. Two years later Giovan Galeazzo, Duke of Milan, died, and his death put an end to the war that had lasted ten years, as we said above. During this time, with a more powerful government which had no enemies at home or abroad, there was the campaign for Pisa, which was gloriously won, and there was peace at home from 1400 to 1433.

Only in 1412 a new *Balìa* was set up against the Alberti, because they had broken their bounds. It strengthened the regime with new laws and directed heavy taxes against the Alberti. During this time the Florentines also waged war on Ladislaus, King of Naples, but this finished in 1414 because of the King's death. During the course of the war the King felt himself to be losing, and he surrendered his city of Cortona to the Florentines. But soon after, he regained strength and started the war again, and it was much more dangerous than at first. If it had not finished because of his death, as the war with the Duke of Milan had finished, he, like the Duke, would have brought Florence to the brink of losing her liberty. This war finished with no less luck than the earlier one, because when he had taken Rome, Siena, all the Marches and Romagna, and when he only needed Florence before turning with all his strength on Lombardy, he died. So death was always more of a friend to the Florentines than any other ally, and it did more to save them than any *virtù* of theirs. After this King's death, the city remained at peace at home and abroad for eight years. At the end of that time, party politics began again, at the same time as the wars with Filippo, Duke of Milan. Party strife did not come to an end before the downfall of the old regime which had ruled from 1381 to 1434, and which had waged so many wars so gloriously and had acquired Arezzo, Pisa, Cortona, Leghorn, and Monte Pulciano. It would have done greater things if the city had kept united and the old feelings had not broken out again, as will be shown in detail in the next book.

BOOK IV

Cities which have a republican political structure, and especially those which are not well governed, often alter their governments and constitutions, not, as many people believe, by interchanging liberty and oppression, but oppression and anarchy. Only the name of liberty is worshipped by the upholders of anarchy who are the people, and by the upholders of oppression who are the nobles, as neither of them wants to be subject either to laws or to men. It is true that when it does happen (as it does very rarely) that a city is lucky enough to number among its citizens a wise, good, and powerful man who can make laws which will calm the aspirations of the nobles and the people, or so restrain them that they can do no harm, then that city can be called free, and its regime can be considered to be stable and firm. Being based on good laws and good institutions, it has no need of one man's *virtù* to maintain it, as the others have. Many ancient republics which lasted for a long time were blessed with laws and institutions of this kind. These laws and institutions were lacking and are still lacking in those republics which have changed and still change their form of government from the despotic to the anarchic and from the anarchic to the despotic. These governments have no stability and cannot achieve it at all because they all make powerful enemies: Good men dislike one form of government, wise men the other; one can do evil easily, the other can only do good with difficulty; in one too much power goes to insolent men, in the other to fools; and both of them must be upheld by the *virtù* and fortune of one man, who can fail through death or become useless because of political trouble.

167

II

In Florence the regime which originated after the death of Giorgio Scali in 1381 was upheld first by the *virtù* of Maso degli Albizzi, then by that of Niccolò da Uzano. The city remained peaceful from 1414 until 1422. King Ladislaus was dead, the state of Lombardy was divided up, and there was nothing for Florence to fear at home or abroad. After Niccolò da Uzano, the citizens with influence were Bartolommeo Valeri, Nerone di Nigi, Rinaldo degli Albizzi, Neri di Gino, and Lapo Niccolini. The factions which sprang up because of the enmity between the Albizzi and the Ricci, and which Salvestro de' Medici later resuscitated, causing so much trouble, never died out. Although the party that was most favored by the common people only ruled for three years and was beaten in 1381, the greater part of the city sympathized with its aims, and it was never entirely suppressed. It is true that frequent popular assemblies and continual persecutions directed against its leaders from 1381 to 1400 reduced it to almost nothing.

The chief families who were persecuted as leaders of the party were the Alberti, the Ricci, and the Medici. Their members were exiled or fined several times. If some of them did remain in the city, they lost their privileges; and these blows humbled the faction and almost finished it off. But many men still had memories of wrongs suffered, and the desire to be revenged for them remained hidden in their breasts, since it found no one to support it. The noble *popolani* who were ruling the city peacefully made two mistakes which caused the collapse of their regime: One was to become overbearing because of their prolonged rule, the other to underestimate those who could harm them, because of the envy they bore each other and because of their long period in power.

III

These men stirred up the people's hatred every day with their crooked ways. They did not watch out for trouble because they did not fear it, or sometimes they fostered it out of envy for each other. So they were responsible for the Medici family's regaining power. The first of the family to begin to reassert himself was Giovanni, son of Ricci. He had become very rich, and being by nature kind and benevolent, he was appointed to the supreme office after the government had made a concession. The common people of the city rejoiced so much, since the mob felt it had won a defender, that the wise were quite rightly suspicious because they saw all the old feelings being roused again. Niccolò da Uzano did not fail to warn the other citizens, telling them how dangerous it was to support someone who had such prestige with the people; how easy it was to withstand irregularities at the beginning, but if they were left to grow it was difficult to control them; and that he knew that Giovanni had many supporters, more than Salvestro. Niccolò was not heeded by his peers because they envied his reputation and were looking for allies with whom to beat him. While Florence was beset by these differences which were beginning to come to a head, Filippo Visconti, Giovanni Galeazzo's second son, had become Lord of all Lombardy through the death of his brother, and feeling that he could undertake a campaign, he particularly wanted to regain control of Genoa, which was then independent under the Doge Tommaso da Campo Fregoso. But Filippo had no hope of succeeding in this or anything else unless he first made a new agreement with the Florentines. He believed that once this was known of, it would be enough to get him everything he desired. So he sent ambassadors to Florence to ask for an agreement. Many citizens advised against it, but said that the peace that had been kept between them for many years should be maintained without an agreement. They knew how useful an agreement would be to Filippo and how comparatively useless it would be to the city. Many others felt they should make an agreement in which terms would be imposed, and then if he violated these everyone would know of his bad faith, and when he broke the peace there would be more justification for waging war against him. After the question had been much debated, an agreement was signed. Filippo promised not to touch territory between here and the Magra and the Panaro.

IV

Once this agreement was made, Filippo occupied Brescia, and Genoa soon after, much to the surprise of those people in Florence who had advised peace, because they thought Brescia would have been defended by the Venetians and Genoa would have defended herself. In the agreement Filippo had made with the Doge of Genoa, he had been given Serezana and other towns on this side of the Magra, on condition that if he wanted to get rid of them he had to give them to the Genoese. This meant that he had violated the treaty with Florence. Besides this he had made an agreement with the Legate of Bologna. These things made our citizens change their minds and think of new remedies for fear of new evils. Their fears came to Filippo's notice, and either to justify his actions or to find out the Florentines' intentions, or else to fob them off, he sent ambassadors to Florence, pretending to be very surprised at their suspicions and offering to cancel anything that he had done that could have given occasion for fear. These ambassadors had no other effect than to divide the city. One party, those who had most reputation in the government, thought that they should arm and prepare to foil the enemy's plans, and then if preparations had been made and Filippo remained quiet, a war would not have been started and there would be all the more reason for peace. Many others, either out of envy of those in power or for fear of war, thought that they should not suspect a friend so easily and that he had not done anything to arouse so much suspicion, whereas everyone knew that to appoint the Ten and hire soldiers meant war. If the city went to war with such a great prince, it was certain to be defeated without any hope of gain. We could not become masters of the acquisitions that might be made, because Romagna lay in between, and Romagna territory was out of the question because of the proximity of the Church. Those who wanted to prepare for war were more influential than those who wanted peace, and they appointed the Ten, hired soldiers, and levied new taxes. These last weighed more heavily on the lower classes than on the upper, and the city was full of complaints. Everyone criticized the greed and ambition of those in power, and they were accused of wanting to embark on an unnecessary war in order to satisfy their own appetites and to oppress and dominate the people.

V

There had still not been an open break with the Duke, but the air was full of suspicion, because Filippo had sent troops to Bologna at the request of the Legate, who was afraid of Antonio Bentivogli who had left the town and was at Castel Bolognese. These troops were near Florentine territory and were causing the Florentine government some concern. But what frightened everyone more and was an important cause of war breaking out, was the Duke's campaign against Forlì. Giorgio Ordelaffi was Lord of Forlì, and when he died he left his son, Tibaldo, under the guardianship of Filippo. His mother was suspicious of the guardian and sent her son to her father, Lodovico Alidose, who was Lord of Imola. But the people of Forlì forced her to observe the father's will and put the boy back into the Duke's hands. To cause less suspicion or hide his intentions better, Filippo arranged for the Marquis of Ferrara to send Guido Torelli as his proxy with soldiers to take control of Forlì: So the town passed into Filippo's hands. When this was known in Florence, together with the news of the troops in Bologna, it made it more easy to decide in favor of war. Nevertheless, the decision was bitterly opposed, and Giovanni de' Medici advised against it publicly, saying that even if they were certain of the Duke's evil intentions, it would be better to wait for him to attack than to go out to meet him with an army. If they did that, the war would be justified in the eyes of the Italian princes both on the Duke's side and our own. Nor could they ask for help with such conviction as they could if his ambition was plainly revealed. And they would defend their own property with more courage and more strength than they would other people's. The others said that they should not wait for the enemy at home but go out and find him, that Fortune favors the attacker rather than the defender, and that there is less damage, though more expense, if you make war in someone else's house rather than in your own. The latter opinion prevailed and it was decided that the Ten should do everything in their power to get the city of Forlì out of the Duke's hands.

VI

Seeing that the Florentines wanted to occupy the territory that he had begun to defend, Filippo laid his scruples aside and sent Agnolo della Pergola with a large army to Imola, so that its Lord would have to think of defending his own and would have no time to spare for taking care of his grandchild. While the Florentine forces were still at Modigliana, Agnolo arrived near Imola; and because it was very cold and the moat around the city was frozen, he took the city by stealth one night and sent Lodovico a prisoner to Milan. Seeing that Imola was lost and open war was being waged, the Florentines sent their army to Forlì, and besieged the city, pressing it on all sides. To prevent the Duke's army from uniting to help the city, they had hired Count Alberigo, who scoured the country from Zagonara, his town, up to the gates of Imola every day. Agnolo della Pergola saw that he could not safely come to the aid of Forlì because of the strong hold our army had taken on the place. He decided to go and capture Zagonara, judging that the Florentines

172

would not allow that town to be lost. If they wanted to help it, they would have to give up the Forlì campaign and do battle at a disadvantage. So the Duke's army forced Alberigo to ask for terms. These were granted to him, and he promised to give up the city within fifteen days unless the Florentines came to his aid before then. News of this setback reached the Florentine camp and the city, and everyone wanted to stop the enemy from gaining the victory, but they managed things so badly that the enemy's victory was even greater. The army left Forlì to go to the aid of Zagonara, and when they clashed with the enemy they were beaten, not so much by the *virtù* of their foes as by the bad weather. Our men had walked through deep mud for several hours; soaking wet, they found the enemy fresh and easily able to beat them. Nevertheless, in this defeat, famous throughout Italy, no one died but Lodovico degli Obizzi and two of his men, and they fell from their horses and were drowned in the mud.

VII

The whole city of Florence was saddened by the news of this defeat, particularly the *Grandi* who had counseled war, because they saw that the enemy was strong while they were unarmed, friendless, and without popular support. The people criticized them harshly in all the public squares, complaining about the taxes they bore and the war that had been begun without reason, saying: "Did they appoint the Ten to frighten the enemy? Did they bring help to Forlì and take it out of the Duke's hands? Now we know about their advice and their aims. It was not to defend liberty, which is their enemy, but to increase their own power, which God has justly restricted. And this is not the only campaign they have burdened the city with. There have been many more. The one against King Ladislaus was like this one. Now who will they go to for help? To Pope Martin whom they wronged in the sight of Braccio? To Queen Joan whom they abandoned and forced into the arms of the King of

Aragon?" And besides all this, they said everything that an angry populace usually says. So the Signori felt they should assemble a number of citizens who would calm the passions of the mob with gentle words. Rinaldo degli Albizzi, who was now Maso's eldest son, and with his own virtues and his father's memory aspired to the first rank in the city, spoke for a long time, explaining that it was not prudent to judge things by their effects, because often many things which have been rightly advised do not turn out right, while those that were ill-advised do. And if bad advice is praised for its good results, this does nothing but encourage men to make mistakes. This does a great deal of harm to republics, because bad advice is never successful. In the same way it was wrong to blame a wise decision which had a bad result, because it discouraged citizens from giving advice to the city and from saying what they meant. Then he explained how necessary it had been to embark on the war, because if it had not been begun in Romagna it would have been fought in Tuscany. God had willed that their troops should be defeated, but if more people had been deserted the loss would have been even more serious. But if they showed Fortune a brave face and took what precautions they could, they would not notice their losses and the Duke would not benefit from his victory. They must not be frightened by the expenditure and the taxes to come; expenditure would be much less than before because defense requires much less machinery than attack, and it would be reasonable to alter the taxes. Finally, he urged them to imitate their fathers, who had always stood up to every prince, because they had never lost heart—whatever had gone wrong.

VIII

The citizens were heartened by **his** authority and they hired Count Oddo, Braccio's son, and gave him as an adviser Niccolò Piccino, a pupil of Braccio's, and the most famous of all the men who had fought under his colors. Other captains were also appointed, and some of those who had been plundered were re-horsed. Twenty citizens were appointed to impose a new tax. They were encouraged by seeing the powerful citizens affected by the defeat, and they taxed them without making any allowances. The *Grandi* were badly hit by this tax, but at first they did not complain about their own taxes in order to seem more public-spirited. They criticized it in a general way as being unfair, and they advised a reduction. But many people heard about this and their plan was stopped in the councils. So that its harshness should be felt while it was operating and so that it would come to be widely hated, the nobles arranged for the receivers to use force while collecting the tax, and they gave them power to kill anyone who resisted the public sergeants. This gave rise to many sad accidents involving the death and wounding of citizens. It looked as if fighting would break out between the parties, and wise men feared trouble in the future, since the nobles, used to being respected, could not bear to be manhandled, and the others wanted everyone to be taxed equally. Many high-ranking citizens came together and decided that they must take over the state because their carelessness had encouraged men to criticize public affairs and had given confidence to men who at one time had been leaders of the mob. They discussed things a number of times and decided to meet again shortly. More than seventy citizens assembled in the church of Santo Stefano with the permission of Lorenzo Ridolfi and Francesco Gianfigliazzi, who were among the Signori at that time. Giovanni de' Medici was not among them, either because he was not asked, being suspect to them, or because he did not want to take part, not being of their opinion.

IX

Rinaldo degli Albizzi spoke to them all. He discussed the state of the city, and how through their negligence it had fallen into the hands of the working classes again after their fathers had taken it from them in 1381. He reminded them of the iniquity of the regime that had ruled from 1378 to 1381, and how all those present had lost a father or grandfather because of it. The same dangers were returning, and the city was falling into the same disorders; the mob had already levied a tax as it wanted, and very soon, if it was not checked by a greater force or by a better system of government, it would be setting up magistracies as it liked. If this happened their places would be taken, and the regime that had ruled Florence for forty-two years and had brought so much glory to the city would be destroyed. Florence would either exist in a state of anarchy and be ruled according to the whim of the mob, and life would be licentious on the one hand and dangerous on the other, or it would be governed by one man who would make himself ruler. He said that everyone who loved his country and his honor must pull himself together and remember the *virtù* of Bardo Mancini, who rescued the city from danger by bringing down the Alberti; and that the reason for the mob's boldness was that broad scrutinies had been held owing to their own negligence, and the Palace had been filled with new, base men. In conclusion, he said that he saw only one way of putting things right: to hand the government back to the nobles and take away the influence of the Lesser Guilds, reducing them from fourteen to seven. This would mean that the working classes would have less say in the councils, because their numbers would be less, and also the nobles would have more authority there, and would oppose them because of their old enmity. He said that it was prudence to know how to use men at different times; if their fathers had used the working classes to quell the arrogance of the nobles, now that the nobles had grown humble and the working classes arrogant, their arrogance should be checked with the nobles' help. To achieve these ends, deceit or force could be used, and they could easily rely on the latter since some of them were members of the Ten and could bring troops into the city secretly. Rinaldo was applauded, and everybody approved his advice. Niccolò da Uzano said that everything Rinaldo had said was true, and his remedies were good and safe if they could be put into practice without openly dividing the city. A division would take place, however, if they did not win Giovanni de' Medici over to their side. If he agreed, the mob could do no harm without a leader and without arms, but if he did not agree, it could not be done without using force, and if they used force then there was a danger either of not winning or of not being able to enjoy the fruits of victory. He modestly called to mind his own past experiences: how they had not wanted to put these things right when they could easily have done so. Now they were no longer in time to do it without running a greater risk, so there was no other way but to win Giovanni over. So Rinaldo was given the job of seeing Giovanni and making sure of winning him over to their point of view.

X

The knight carried out his task and used all his best arguments to try to persuade Giovanni to join them in their enterprise, rather than side with the mob and encourage it so that it brought down the government and the city. Giovanni replied that he believed it was the duty of a wise and good citizen not to change his city's traditional institutions, as nothing upset men so much as such a change. Many people were bound to be upset and when many are dissatisfied, trouble is to be feared every day. He felt that this decision of theirs would do two very bad things: one, give honors to men who because they had never possessed them would respect them less, and who would also have less reason to complain because they did not possess them now; and two, take away honors from people who were used to possessing them, and who would never rest until they were returned. So the wrong done to one side would be much greater than the benefit received by the other. Whoever was responsible for it would make few friends and many enemies, and the enemies would be more ready to harm him than the friends would be to defend him, since men are naturally more ready to seek revenge for an injury than to express gratitude for a favor, because they feel that revenge brings pleasure and gain, while in expressing

177

thanks they are the losers. Then he turned back to Rinaldo and said: "And if you remembered the things that have happened and what deceits are being practiced in this city, you would be less keen to carry out this decision. Once the men who advise this action had taken the power away from the people with your help, they would take it from you with the help of the people, who would have turned against you because of this injustice. And the same thing would happen to you as happened to Benedetto Alberti, who was persuaded by his enemies to consent to the downfall of Giorgio Scali and Tommaso Strozzi, and soon after he was sent into exile by those same men who had persuaded him." He advised Rinaldo to think things over more carefully and to try to imitate his father who lowered the price of salt to gain popular goodwill, laid it down that anyone who was taxed less than half a florin could pay or not as he liked, and wanted everyone to be safe from his creditors on the day the councils met. He concluded by saying that as far as he was concerned, he was in favor of letting the city keep its traditional political structure.

XI

News of these discussions was heard outside and Giovanni's reputation increased, as did the hatred felt toward the other citizens. Giovanni did not acknowledge his popularity in order not to encourage those who were planning changes in his favor. Whenever he spoke he let everyone know that he had no intention of building up factions but that he wanted to put an end to them, and that as far as he was concerned he only wanted the city to be united. Many of those who favored him were dissatisfied with this because they would have liked him to play a more active part in politics. Among them was Alamanno de' Medici who had an aggressive character and never stopped urging him to persecute his enemies and favor his friends, and who condemned his coldness and his slow way of going about things. He said this was why Giovanni's enemies were plotting against him

openly, and these plots would one day result in the downfall of his house and his friends. He encouraged Giovanni's son, Cosimo, in the same opinion. Nevertheless,
Giovanni did not move from his point of view whatever
had been disclosed or prophesied to him. However, the
party had come out into the open, and the city was
clearly divided. There were two chancellors in the service
of the Signori at the Palace, ser Martino and ser Pagolo;
the former favored the Medici, and the latter da Uzano's
party. Seeing that Giovanni had not wanted to agree
with them, Rinaldo thought that ser Martino should be
deprived of his office and that the palace would be more
favorable to him after this. Rinaldo's adversaries got wind
of this and not only was ser Martino defended but ser
Pagolo was dismissed, much to the annoyance and cost
of his party. This would have produced a bad effect immediately if it had not been for the war that was threatening the city. The city was afraid because of the defeat
at Zagonara, because while these things had been boiling
up in Florence, Agnolo della Pergola with the Duke's
army had taken all the towns that the Florentines possessed in Romagna, except Castrocaro and Modigliana,
partly because of the weakness of the towns, partly because of failures on the part of their garrisons. In the
occupation of these towns, two things happened which
proved how an enemy admires *virtù* in men, and how he
dislikes cowardice and malice.

XII

The governor of the stronghold of Monte Petroso was
Biagio del Melano. He was surrounded by enemies who
had set the place on fire. Seeing no way of saving the
castle, he threw clothes and straw out on the side that
was still not alight, and onto them threw his two small
children, saying to the enemy: "Take for yourselves the
good things Fortune has given me, which you can take
from me: those that I have in my heart, where my glory
and honor lie, I will not give you, nor will you take them
from me." The enemies ran to save the children, and

179

placed ropes and ladders for him to save himself. But he refused and preferred to die in the flames rather than to escape by the hands of his country's enemies. This example is really worthy of ancient times that are so much praised, and even more remarkable because such things are so much rarer. The enemy gave back to his sons everything that could be saved, and they were sent back to their relatives with the greatest care. Nor was the republic any less considerate to them, and while they lived they received a pension from the state. The exact opposite happened in Galeata where Zanobi del Pino was Podestà. He gave the castle up to the enemy without putting up any resistance, and what is more, he urged Agnolo to leave the mountains of Romagna for the Tuscan hills, where he could wage war less dangerously and more profitably. Agnolo hated his cowardice and wickedness and handed him over to his servants, who taunted him and gave him nothing but painted paper snakes to eat, saying that they wanted to turn him from a Guelph into a Ghibelline by that method. So in a short time he died of hunger.

XIII

Meantime Count Oddo had entered the Lamona Valley with Niccolò Piccino to see if he could persuade the Lord of Faenza into an alliance with the Florentines, or at least to try and stop Agnolo della Pergola from raiding Romagna as he pleased. But because the valley is very well fortified and the people are good soldiers, Count Oddo was killed and Niccolò Piccino was taken prisoner to Faenza. But Fortune willed that the Florentines should achieve by losing what perhaps they would not have achieved if they had won. Niccolò was so successful with the Lord of Faenza and his mother that they became allies of the Florentines. By this agreement Niccolò Piccino was freed, but he did not observe the advice that he had given others, because in negotiating with the city over his army, either the conditions seemed unfavorable to him or he found better ones elsewhere, and he very abruptly left Arezzo, where he was encamped, and went to Lombardy, where he took up service with the Duke. The Florentines were dismayed by this event and by their frequent losses, and decided they could no longer carry on the war single-handed, so they sent ambassadors to the Venetians to ask them to stand up to the power of one man while it was still possible, for if it was allowed to grow, it would be as dangerous to them as to the Florentines. Francesco Carmignuola was urging the Venetians to undertake the same task. He was a man who was considered to be a very great soldier in those days, and he had been in the Duke's service, but had since turned against him. The Venetians were in doubt as to how much they could trust Carmignuola, suspecting that the enmity between him and the Duke was a pretense. While they hesitated the Duke had Carmignuola poisoned by one of his servants. The poison was not strong enough to kill him, but it brought him to death's door. The Venetians forgot their suspicions when they discovered the reason for his illness, and they went into league with the Florentines, who had continued to press for this. Both sides pledged themselves to share the expenses of the war. The gains in Lombardy were to go to Venice, and those in Romagna and Tuscany to Florence. Carmignuola was made captain general of the league. So by this agreement the war was removed to Lombardy, where it was conducted very ably by Carmignuola. In a few months he took a number of towns from the Duke, including the city of Brescia, whose capture was considered remarkable for those times and those wars.

XIV

This war had lasted from 1422 to 1427, and the citizens of Florence were tired of the taxes imposed up till then. So they agreed to revise them. To make them equal according to wealth, it was laid down that property should be taxed and that a man with a hundred florins' worth of property would pay half a florin in tax. Since the law would impose the tax and not individuals, it weighed particularly heavily on the nobles, and it was opposed by them before it was decided upon. Only Giovanni de' Medici praised it openly, so much so that it was passed. In order to impose it, the value of everyone's property was added up, which the Florentines call *accatastare,* and because of this the tax was called the *Catasto.* By this means the tyranny of the powerful was partially checked, because they could no longer oppress the lower classes and silence them with threats in the councils, as they used to. So the common people welcomed this tax, while the powerful were greatly annoyed by it. But since men are never satisfied, and once they have got one thing they are not contented and want something more, the people were not content with the equality of the tax imposed by law, and they demanded that past records be gone into to see how much less the nobles had paid before, according to the new *Catasto* system. They asked for them to be forced to pay at the same rate as those who had had to sell their possessions in order to pay taxes they should never have paid. This demand frightened the nobles much more than the *Catasto,* and they never stopped objecting to it in order to protect themselves, saying that it was very unfair because it was levied on movable property too, which one may own one day and lose the next; and that many people have money hidden away that the *Catasto* cannot reach. They added that those who neglected their businesses to govern the republic should be less burdened by it, as it was enough that they labored for the republic with their persons. It was not fair for the city to enjoy both their property and their industry, while it only took money from others. The others who approved of the *Catasto* answered that if movable property changes, taxes can change too, and if they are changed often this difficulty can be overcome, and that there was no need to take into account those who had money hidden away, because it is not right to have to pay for money that is not making a profit, and if it makes a profit then the money must be disclosed. If they did not like giving their services to the republic, then they could stop doing so and not bother themselves, because the republic would find patriotic citizens who would have no difficulty in helping it with money and advice. A place in the government brings so many perquisites and honors, and these should be enough for them. They should not expect to be dispensed from responsibilities. But they did not say what their real objection was: They regretted that they could no longer declare war without hurting themselves, because they would have to contribute to the expenses like everybody else. If this tax had existed before, the war against King Ladislaus would not have been begun, nor would the present one against Duke Filippo. Both of them were started to keep the citizens busy, and not out of necessity. Giovanni de' Medici calmed the passions that had been roused by saying that it was unwise to go back over the past and much better to provide for the future. If the earlier taxes had been unfair, then they should thank God that a way had been found to make them fair. They should see to it that this method served to reunite the city and not to divide it, as would have happened if they had gone back over earlier taxes and tried to bring them into line with the present ones. The man who is satisfied with a mediocre victory will always do best, because those who want to win outright often lose. He calmed their feelings with words like these and put an end to talk of a comparison between taxes.

XV

As the war with the Duke was still going on, a peace treaty was signed at Ferrara with a papal Legate acting as intermediary. The Duke failed to observe its conditions from the start, so the league took up arms again and defeated him in a clash with his troops at Maclovio. After this defeat the Duke made new suggestions for an agreement, and the Venetians and Florentines consented, the former because they had seen Carmignuola going so slowly after the Duke's defeat that they felt they could no longer trust him, and the latter because they had grown suspicious of the Venetians, and felt they were

183

spending a great deal of money to increase someone else's power. So peace was concluded in 1428 by which the Florentines got back the cities they had lost in Romagna and the Venetians kept Brescia. The Duke also gave them Bergamo and its *contado*. The Florentines spent three million, five hundred thousand ducats on this war. It brought the Venetians power and greatness, but to Florence it brought nothing but poverty and disunity.

Once peace had been made abroad, the war at home began again. The nobles would not stand for the *Catasto*, and seeing no way of putting an end to it, they found ways of turning more people against it so that they would have more allies to help them break it. They persuaded the officers appointed to levy the tax that the law obliged them to add up all the property of people in the dependent communities as well, to see if it included the property of Florentine citizens. All the subjects were summoned to bring lists of their possessions by a certain date. The people of Volterra sent to the Signoria to complain, and the tax officers were annoyed and put eighteen of them in prison. This made the people of Volterra very angry, but they did nothing, out of consideration for their men in prison.

XVI

At this time Giovanni de' Medici fell ill, and knowing that he was going to die, he called his sons Cosimo and Lorenzo and said to them: "I believe that I have lived the span that God and Nature allotted to me at my birth. I shall die happy because I am leaving you rich, in good health and in a position to live honored and beloved by everyone in Florence if you follow in my footsteps. Nothing gives me so much happiness at my death as the memory that I have never harmed anyone but have done good to everyone, as far as I could. I advise you to do the same. As for politics, if you want security, take from the state what the law and men give you. This will not cause you envy or danger, because a man is hated for what he takes for himself, not for what he is given. You will always have more than those people who want someone else's share and so lose their own, and before they have lost it live under continual strain. By these methods I have not only kept but heightened my reputation in this city, despite so many enemies and disagreements. You, too, will keep and heighten yours if you follow in my footsteps. But if you do otherwise, reflect that your end will be no happier than that of those who within our memory have ruined themselves and destroyed their families." He died soon afterwards, and was very much missed by the common people of the city, as his excellent qualities deserved. Giovanni was a compassionate man, and he not only gave alms to anyone who asked but very often he gave help to the poor and needy without being asked. He loved everyone, and praised the good and pitied the wicked. He never asked for honors, yet he had them all. He never went to the Palace unless he was called for. He loved peace and shrank from war. He came to the rescue of men in adversity and helped them in prosperity. He would not be a party to robbery by the state, and he contributed to the public good. In office he was merciful —without great eloquence, but a man of very great prudence. In appearance he was melancholy, but then in conversation he could be witty and humorous. He died very rich in possessions but even more so in standing and in goodwill. This inheritance, both material and spiritual, Cosimo not only maintained but increased.

XVII

The men from Volterra were tired of being in prison, and in order to be set free, they promised to agree to what conditions were laid down. They were set free and returned to Volterra, and the time came for their new priors to take up office. Among them was drawn one Giusto, a worker respected by the working classes who was one of the men who had been imprisoned in Florence. He was full of hatred for the Florentines because of the public and private injury they had done to him, and he was further encouraged by Giovanni di Contugi, a nobleman who was a colleague of his in office, to incite the people to take the city from the Florentines and make himself ruler, using the authority of the priors and his own prestige. Giusto followed this advice, armed, and rode through the town. He arrested the captain who represented the Florentines and made himself Lord with the people's consent. This revolution in Volterra annoyed the Florentines greatly, but seeing that they had just made peace with the Duke and were in a mood for agreements, they felt there was time to win the town back again. In order not to lose it, they sent as commissioners Rinaldo degli Albizzi and Palla Strozzi. Meanwhile Giusto thought the Florentines would attack him, and so he asked the Sienese and Lucchese for help. The Sienese refused, saying they had an alliance with the Florentines. And Pagolo Guinigi, who was Lord of Lucca, in order to win back the favor of the people of Florence, which he felt he had lost during the war with the Duke by revealing himself as a friend of Filippo's, not only refused Giusto help, but sent prisoner to Florence the man who had come to ask for it. Meanwhile, hoping to attack the people of Volterra while they were unprepared, the commissioners collected all their men at arms together, raised a good number of infantry in the lower Arno Valley and the *contado* of Pisa, and set off for Volterra. Giusto did not give up hope after being deserted by his neighbors or because of the attack the Florentines were making. He put his faith in his good strategic position and in the fertility of the land, and prepared to defend himself.

There was in Volterra a man called Arcolano, the brother of the Giovanni who had persuaded Giusto to make himself Lord, and a person of standing among the nobility. He assembled some of his trusted friends and told them that God had come to the aid of their city in its need through this event. If they would like to arm, deprive Giusto of his position, and hand the city back to the Florentines, then they would be the chief citizens in the town, which would preserve all its ancient privileges. They agreed and went to the palace where the Lord was living. Some of them stayed downstairs while Arcolano went up into the great hall with three others. He found Giusto with some citizens, and he drew him to one side, as though he wanted to speak to him about something important. Going from one subject to another, he took Giusto into the bedroom. There he and those who were with him fell on Giusto with their swords. They were not quick enough to stop him from getting his hand on his own weapon, and before they killed him, Giusto wounded two of them seriously. But he could not stand up to so many in the end, and he was killed and thrown to the ground from the palace. Arcolano's party armed and gave the city to the Florentine commissioners who were close at hand with their army, and without making any other terms they entered the city. The result of this was that Volterra's conditions deteriorated, because among other things, they took most of her *contado* away and made it into a vicariate.

XVIII

After Volterra had been lost and won almost at the same time, there seemed no more reason for war, if men's ambition had not caused another one. Niccolò Fortebraccio, the son of a sister of Braccio da Perugia, had fought for the city of Florence for a long time during the wars with the Duke. When peace came he was dismissed by the Florentines, and when the Volterra affair happened he was still encamped at Fucecchio. So the commissioners for that campaign made use of him and his army. While Rinaldo was directing that operation with him, it was thought that he persuaded Niccolò to attack Lucca on some hidden pretext and that he told him that if he did he would arrange things in Florence so that there would be a campaign against Lucca and Niccolò would be put in charge of it. After they won Volterra, and Niccolò returned to his camp at Fucecchio, either because of Rinaldo's arguments or on his own initiative, in November 1429, he occupied the Lucchese castles of Ruoti and Compito with three hundred horse and three hundred foot. Then he went down into the plain and carried away a great deal of booty. When the news of this attack was made known in Florence, groups of all kinds of men gathered throughout the city, and most of them wanted an attack to be made on Lucca. Among the important citizens who favored it were the Medici party, and with them Rinaldo, who was prompted either by the idea that it would be a good thing for the republic, or by his own ambition, because he thought he would be given responsibility for the victory. Against the exploit were Niccolò da Uzano and his party. It seems incredible that there should have been such a diversity of opinion in one city about a declaration of war, because the same citizens and the same people who after ten years of peace had criticized the war against Duke Filippo, started in order to defend their liberty, now after the city had spent so much and had been so hard-pressed, were asking very effectively for war to be declared on Lucca so that they could take away the liberty of others. On the other hand, those who had wanted the earlier war were against this one. Opinions change so much with the times, the majority are so much readier to take other people's possessions than to guard their own, and men are so much more easily moved by the hope of gain than by the fear of loss: They only fear loss if it is threatened close at hand, whereas they can hope for gain that is a long way off. The people of Florence were full of hope because of the gains that Niccolò Fortebraccio had made and was still making, and the letters from the commanders near Lucca. The governors of Vico and Pescia wrote asking for permission to receive the castles that were surrendering to them because shortly the whole *contado* of Lucca would be won. Added to this, an ambassador was sent from the Lord of Lucca to Florence to complain about the attacks Niccolò had made and to ask the Signoria not to declare war on a neighbor and a city that had always been friendly. The ambassador's name was Iacopo Viviani. A short while before, he had been held prisoner by Pagolo because he had plotted against him, and although he had been found guilty, his life had been spared. Because Pagolo thought that Iacopo had forgiven him for the insult, he trusted

him. But Iacopo remembered the danger more than the
kindness, and in Florence he secretly urged the citizens
to carry out their campaign. These recommendations
together with their other hopes made the Signoria assemble the Council. Four hundred and ninety-eight citizens
met, and the question was debated in front of them by
the leading men of the city.

XIX

One of the foremost of those who favored the campaign, as we said above, was Rinaldo. He argued how
profitable the acquisition would be and how opportune
the moment was for an attack, since Lucca had been left
to them by the Venetians and the Duke, and the Pope
could not stop them as he was involved in the affairs of
the Kingdom. Added to this was the ease with which
Lucca could be captured, since it was in the grip of one
of its citizens and had lost its natural vigor and the old
care for the defense of its liberty. It would be surrendered either by the people in order to get rid of the despot
or by the despot out of fear of the people. He told of the
wrongs its Lord had done to our republic and of his evil
intentions toward us, and said how dangerous he would
be if either the Pope or the Duke made war on our city
again. Concluding, he said that the Florentine people
had never undertaken a campaign that was easier, more
profitable, or more just. Speaking against this view, Niccolò da Uzano said that the city of Florence had never
undertaken anything more unjust, more dangerous, or
so likely to give rise to more trouble. First they were
going to harm a Guelph city which had always been
friendly to the Florentine people, and at her own risk
had very often welcomed Guelphs when they could not
stay in their own country. In the records of our affairs
it will not be found that a free Lucca ever attacked
Florence, and if those who had enslaved Lucca, first
Castruccio and now the new man, had harmed Florence,
then the fault was not Lucca's but the despot's. If they
could make war on the despot and not the citizens, he

189

would not mind so much, but since this was impossible he could not consent to friendly citizens being deprived of their possessions. Because of the way men lived today very little attention was paid to the just and the unjust, therefore he would leave this matter aside and think only of the gain to the city. He thought that things could be called profitable if they could not easily do one harm. So he could not understand how anyone could call this campaign profitable when the disadvantages were certain and the advantages were doubtful. The certain disadvantages were the expense that it would entail, which was bound to be so great that it should frighten even a city that was rested, let alone one that was worn out by a long, bitter war as theirs was. The advantage that the campaign could bring was the acquisition of Lucca, which he admitted was great; but the doubtful elements had to be considered, and these seemed so numerous to him that he felt it could not be won. He begged them not to believe that the Venetians and Filippo would be happy about Florence acquiring Lucca. The Venetians only pretended to consent in order not to seem ungrateful because they had recently occupied so much territory using Florentine money. The Duke would be pleased to see them involved in a fresh war and in fresh expense, because he could attack them again when they were tired and weary on all fronts. He would not miss an opportunity, in the midst of the campaign and when hopes of victory were at their highest, of helping the Lucchese, either with money given secretly or by dismissing some of his troops and sending them to their aid as soldiers of fortune. So he urged them to give up the campaign and come to terms with the despot so that he made as many enemies at home as possible, because there was no easier way of subjugating Lucca than letting her live under the despot and allowing him to illtreat and weaken her. Then if things were managed prudently, the city would be reduced to a state where the despot could not hold her, and she would not know how, or be able, to rule herself, and would be bound to fall into their lap. He said he saw that feeling ran high, and his words were not being heeded. Yet, he wanted to prophesy this: They would wage a very costly war, they would run numerous dangers, and instead of occupying Lucca they would free her from the despot, and out of a friendly, oppressed, weak city they would make a free one, which would be opposed to them, and in time would stand in the way of their republic's greatness.

XX

When speeches had been made for and against the campaign, they came to the customary secret ballot to discover people's wishes, and only ninety-eight out of that large number voted against it. So the decision was taken, the Ten were appointed to conduct the war, and soldiers on foot and on horseback were hired. They appointed Astorre Gianni and Rinaldo degli Albizzi as commissioners and agreed with Niccolò Fortebraccio that he would hand over the towns he had taken, while he carried on the campaign in our pay. When the commissioners arrived with the army in Lucchese territory, they shared it between them. Astorre spread out over the plain toward Camaiore and Pietrasanta, and Rinaldo went up toward the mountains, thinking that once the city was deprived of its *contado* it would be easy enough to capture. They were both unsuccessful, not because they did not win a number of towns but because of the charges laid against both of them concerning their handling of the war. Certainly Astorre gave very clear cause for the charges brought against him. There is a valley near Pietrasanta, called Seravezza, which is rich and densely populated. When the people heard that the commissioner had come, they went out to meet him and asked him to accept them as faithful servants of the Florentine people. Astorre pretended to accept their offer. Then he had his troops occupy all the passes and strongholds in the valley, and he assembled all the men in their main church and took them all prisoner. He allowed his army to sack and destroy the whole area, and with great cruelty and greed spared neither holy places nor women, whether married

191

or virgins. When news of what had happened was learned in Florence not only the government but the whole city was distressed.

XXI

Some of the people of Seravezza who had escaped from the commissioner's grasp fled to Florence and told their troubles to everybody in every street. Since they were urged by many people who wanted to see the commissioner punished, either as a wicked man or because he was of the opposing party, they went to the Ten and asked for an audience. They were admitted, and one of them made this speech: "Magnificent Signori, we are certain that our words will meet with your trust and compassion when you know how your commissioner occupied our country and how we have been treated by him since. Our valley has always been Guelph, as must be fully shown in the records of your past history, and very often it was a safe refuge for your citizens who fled there when persecuted by the Ghibellines. We and our forefathers have always worshipped the name of this glorious republic as the head and leader of the Guelph party. While the people of Lucca were Guelph, we gladly owed them allegiance. But since they fell under the rule of a despot, who has left his old friends and followed Ghibelline policies, we have obeyed him more because we were forced to, not because we wanted to. God knows how often we have begged Him to give us a chance of showing our feelings toward the old party. How blind men are in their desires! What we desired as our salvation has been our ruin. When we first heard that your banners were coming toward us, we went out to meet your commissioner, not as if to an enemy but as if to our old overlords. We put the valley, our fortunes, and ourselves into his hands, and trusted ourselves to his keeping, thinking that he had the heart, if not of a Florentine, at least of a man. Your Lordships will pardon us, we have made so bold as to speak because we cannot tolerate worse than what we have suffered. This commissioner of yours has only the appearance of a man and only the name of a Florentine: as deadly a plague, as cruel a beast, as fearful a monster as ever any writer imagined. He assembled us in our church, making believe he wanted to speak to us, and he took us prisoner and scoured and burned the whole valley, while its inhabitants and their property were pillaged, plundered, sacked, beaten, and killed. He raped women and girls, and taking the girls from their mothers' arms, he handed them over to his soldiers. If we had deserved so much trouble because of some injury we had done him or the Florentine people, or if he had taken us while we were armed and putting up a fight, we would not mind so much. In fact we would think ourselves guilty and deserving of punishment because of our attacks and our arrogance. But we gave ourselves up to him freely, unarmed, and then he robbed and plundered us, doing so much damage and treating us so shamefully that we are forced to complain. Although we might have filled Lombardy with our grievances, and spread the story of our wrongs throughout Italy, to your city's cost, we did not want to do so, in order not to stain the reputation of such a good and merciful republic with the deceitfulness and cruelty of one wicked citizen. If we had known of his greed before our destruction, we would have tried to satisfy his voracious appetite, even though it is boundless, and in that way we would have saved a part of our substance by means of the rest. But since the time has now passed, we decided to turn to you and to beg you to help your subjects in their misfortune, so that our example does not frighten others from coming under your rule. If our unspeakable suffering does not move you, then may the fear of God's anger do so, for He has seen His churches sacked and burned, and our people betrayed in His bosom." After this speech they threw themselves to the ground shouting and begging for their property and their country to be restored to them, and for the wives to be returned to their husbands, and the daughters to their fathers (since honor could not be returned). The Ten were moved by the horror of the affair, which had been reported to them first of all, and then recounted in person by those who had suffered. Without delay Astorre was ordered home, and he was condemned and warned. A search was made for the property of the people of Seravezza, and what could be found was returned to them. The city compensated them for the rest in various ways as time went by.

XXII

As for Rinaldo degli Albizzi, he was said to be making war not for the sake of the Florentine people but for his own profit. Rumor had it that since he had become commissioner the desire to take Lucca had left him, and he was quite satisfied to plunder the *contado* and fill his farms with cattle and his houses with booty; that the booty that was found by his own hangers-on for his own needs was not enough; and that he bought his soldiers' loot, so that he had changed from a commissioner into a merchant. When these libels reached his ears they affected his proud and upright soul more than befitted a serious man. They upset him so much that he came back to Florence without waiting or asking for permission—he was so angry with the Ten and the citizens. He presented himself to the Ten and said that he knew very well how difficult and dangerous it was to serve a free people and a divided city. The people were swayed by every rumor; and the city condemned bad deeds, did not reward good ones, and brought charges in the case of those which were doubtful. So if you won, nobody praised you, if you made a mistake everyone blamed you, and if you lost everyone slandered you. You were attacked by your friends out of envy and by your enemies out of hatred. Yet he had never failed to carry out an undertaking that would have been of certain use to the city, for fear of a false charge. It was true that the falseness of the present slanders had exhausted his patience and had made him change his ways. But he begged the Ten to be quicker to defend their citizens in future so that they in turn could be more ready to do good for their country; and if it was not customary to be granted a triumph in Florence, at least they should defend their leaders against scurrilous untruths. They should remember that they, too, were citizens of that city, and at any time a charge might be brought against them and then they would know how hurtful false libels were to men of integrity. The Ten tried to mollify him as much as the times would allow, and they asked for Nero di Gino and Alamanno Salviati to take over the campaign. These two gave up the raids on the *contado* of Lucca and drew the army up near the town. Because it was still the cold season, it halted at Capannole, where the commissioners felt they were wasting time. They wanted to press closer to the town, but the soldiers would not agree because of the bad weather, even though the Ten were urging them to go into battle and were refusing to listen to excuses.

XXIII

At that time there was a very brilliant architect in Florence called Filippo, son of ser Brunellesco. Our city is full of his works, and after his death he was honored by having his image in marble placed in the principal church in Florence with an inscription at the foot that still bears witness to his abilities. He made out a case for flooding Lucca that took into account the city's situation and the course of the river Serchio, and he was so persuasive that the Ten ordered the experiment to be carried out. The only result was disorder in our camp and safety for the enemy, because the Lucchese threw up a dike in the area where we were directing the Serchio, and then one night they broke the dike along the canal where the water was being channeled. So the water found a high obstacle toward Lucca and a breach in the canal bank, and it spread out over the whole plain. The army was not only prevented from getting closer to the town, but it had to move farther off.

XXIV

As this attempt was unsuccessful, the Ten who took up office again sent Giovanni Guicciardini as commissioner. He besieged the town as soon as he could. The Lord, finding himself pressed, sent Salvestro Trenta and Lionardo Buonvisi to the Duke of Milan on the advice of one Antonio del Rosso of Siena, who was with him as representative of the Commune of Siena. They asked the Duke for help on the Lord's behalf, and getting a chilly reception they secretly begged him to let them have some troops, because on behalf of the people they promised him to give him their Lord as a prisoner and then to let the Duke take possession of their town. They warned him that if he did not fall in with this plan quickly, the Lord would give the town to the Florentines, who were trying to win it by making a great many promises. Fear of this made the Duke set his scruples aside, and he arranged for Count Francesco Sforza, who was in his pay, to ask leave of him publicly to go to the Kingdom. When the Count had received permission, he went to Lucca with his company, despite the fact that the Florentines sent his friend Boccaccino Alamanni to the Count to stop him, because they knew about this deal and feared what did in fact happen. When the Count came to Lucca, the Florentines withdrew their army to Librafatta, and the Count immediately went to besiege Pescia, where Pagolo da Diacceto was deputy governor. The latter fled to Pistoia, prompted more by fear than by any better plan; and if the town had not been defended by Giovanni Malavolti who was guarding it, it would have been lost. Not having been able to capture the town at the first assault, the Count went to Borgo a Buggiano and took it, and he burned Stigliano, a castle nearby. Seeing this destruction, the Florentines turned to remedies that had saved them often before. They knew how powerful bribery can be with mercenaries when force is not enough. So they offered the Count money if he would not only leave but give them the town. The

Count felt that he could get no more money from Lucca and was easily persuaded to accept it from people who had more. He made an agreement with the Florentines not to give them Lucca, which he would not consent to for shame, but to abandon it if he was given fifty thousand ducats. And so that the people of Lucca would excuse him to the Duke, he made a bargain with them that they should expel their Lord.

XXV

As we said above, Antonio del Rosso was in Lucca as Sienese ambassador. With the Count's authority, he plotted Pagolo's downfall with the citizens. The leaders of the conspiracy were Piero Cennami and Giovanni da Chivizzano. The Count was staying outside the town on the Serchio, and with him was Lanzilao, the Lord's son. The conspirators, forty in all, went one night to visit Pagolo, armed. At the sound of their approach he met them, astonished, and asked the reason for their visit. Piero Cennami replied that they had been ruled by him for some time and that he had reduced them to dying by the sword or because of hunger, surrounded by enemies. So they had decided that in future they wanted to rule themselves, and they asked him for the keys of the city and its funds. Pagolo replied that the funds were exhausted, and the keys and he were in their power. He made just one request, that they should allow his rule, which had begun and continued without bloodshed, to end without bloodshed, too. Count Francesco took Pagolo and his son to the Duke, and they died afterwards in prison.

The departure of the Count had freed Lucca from her despot and the Florentines from the fear of his army. The former prepared to defend itself while the latter returned to the offensive. They had chosen the Count of Urbino as their captain, and he pressed the town so hard that he forced the Lucchese to turn to the Duke again. The Duke sent Niccolò Piccino to their aid in the same way that he had sent the Count. As Niccolò was about to enter Lucca, our men went to meet him on the Serchio. The battle took place at the river crossing, and they were defeated. The commissioner and a few of our troops escaped to Pisa.

The whole city was saddened by this defeat. Because the campaign had been advocated by the common people, the *popolani* did not know whom to blame. They criticized those who had directed it, since they could not blame those who had made the decision, and they brought up the old charges against Rinaldo again. But the man who came off worst was Giovanni Guicciardini, who was accused of having been able to put an end to the war after Count Francesco left and of having received bribes and sent a pile of money home, and they named the men who had carried it and received it. These rumors and accusations reached such a pitch that the Captain of the People summonsed him because of the public outcry and pressure from the opposing party. Giovanni appeared, very angry indeed; and for the sake of their honor, his relatives managed to make the Captain give up his suit.

After the victory, the Lucchese not only took back their towns but occupied all those in the *contado* of Pisa, except Bientina, Calcinaia, Leghorn, and Librafatta. And if a conspiracy had not been discovered in Pisa, that city would have been lost too. The Florentines reorganized their army and made Micheletto, a pupil of Sforza's, their captain. On his side the Duke followed up the victory, and to get reinforcements with which to harry the Florentines he got the Genoese, the Sienese, and the Lord of Piombino to collaborate in the defense of Lucca and to hire Niccolò Piccino as their captain. This move gave him away completely. So the Venetians and the Florentines renewed their league, and war began to be waged openly in Lombardy and in Tuscany. In both provinces there were battles with various results. So in May 1443, when everyone was worn out, the parties reached an agreement whereby the Florentines, the Lucchese, and the Sienese, who had occupied several of each others' castles during the war, gave them all up, and each took back their original possessions.

XXVI

While this war was being waged, bitter party feeling was boiling up at home. After the death of Giovanni his father, Cosimo de' Medici behaved more boldly in politics and more carefully and generously to his friends than his father had done. Those who had been glad at Giovanni's death grew apprehensive when they saw what Cosimo was like. Cosimo was a very prudent man, with a grave, pleasant personality, all generosity and kindness. He never went against the party or the regime, but tried to do good to everyone and to win the support of a great many citizens by his generosity. His example showed up those in the government, and he reckoned that in this way he could either live in Florence as powerful and secure as anyone else, or, if a crisis was brought about by his enemies' ambition, he would be superior both in arms and in popularity.

Averardo de' Medici and Puccio Pucci were the chief instruments in laying the foundations for his power. They fostered his popularity and greatness, Averardo by his audacity, and Puccio by his prudence. Puccio's advice and judgment were so highly thought of, and recognized by everyone, that Cosimo's party was not named after him but after Puccio. The Lucchese campaign was carried on by a city divided in this way, and party feeling was mounting rather than dying down. Although Cosimo's party was the one that had favored the war, many men from the other party were sent to direct operations, as being men who had more political standing. Averardo de' Medici and the others could do nothing about this, and so they put all their energy and ingenuity into criticizing them. When there were losses, and there were many, it was not luck or the enemy's strength that was blamed, but the commissioners' lack of prudence. This is what increased the seriousness of Astorre Gianni's crimes; this is what angered Rinaldo degli Albizzi and made him give up his commission without leave; and this was why the Captain of the

People had Giovanni Guicciardini summonsed. This was the reason for all the other charges brought against members of the government and commissioners. The true charges were made more serious, those that were not true were invented, and both the true and the false were believed by the people, who hated them generally.

XXVII

Niccolò da Uzano and the other party leaders were very well aware of this strange procedure, and they had often discussed remedies together without finding any, because they felt that it was dangerous to allow it to continue, but that it was difficult to break it off. Niccolò da Uzano was the first to dislike extreme methods. While they were beset by war outside and these troubles at home, Niccolò Barbadoro, hoping to persuade Niccolò da Uzano to consent to Cosimo's downfall, went to see him at home, where he was sitting in his study deep in thought, and with the best arguments he could muster, he urged him to unite with Rinaldo in order to banish Cosimo. Niccolò da Uzano replied in these terms: "It would be better for you, your house, and our republic if you and those who think like you had silver beards rather than gold, as your name implies, because their advice would be wiser and more useful to everyone, if it came from a grey, experienced head. It seems to me that those who are thinking of banishing Cosimo from Florence must first of all size up their own strength and Cosimo's. You have christened our party the nobles' party and the opposition the proletarian party. If the name corresponded to the facts, victory would be doubtful in any case, and we would have more reason to fear than to hope, because of the examples of the ancient nobility of this city who were overthrown by the proletariat. But we have much more to fear because our party is split, while our enemies are united. First of all, Neri di Gino and Nerone di Nigi, two of our leading citizens, have never declared themselves so that we can say they are more friendly to us than to them. Many families, even many households, are divided; people side with them against us out of envy for brothers or kinsmen. I will remind you of some of the most important persons: You can think of the others for yourself. Of Maso degli Albizzi's sons, Luca has gone over to their party out of envy for Rinaldo; in the Guicciardini household, of the sons of Luigi, Piero opposes Giovanni and favors our enemies; Tommaso and Niccolò Soderini oppose us openly because of the hatred they bear their uncle, Francesco. So taking into consideration the character of both parties, I do not know why our party should deserve to be called noble any more than theirs does. If it is because they are followed by all the proletariat, they have the advantage over us; and if it comes to a fight, we will be in no position to resist. If we still have our privileges, it is because of the regime's long-standing reputation, which has been maintained for fifty years; but if it came to a test, and our weakness was discovered, then we would lose them. If you said that the justice of our cause would increase our standing and lessen theirs, I would reply that this justice would have to be understood and believed by other people as it is by us: Whereas the reverse is true, because our case is based on the suspicion that he is going to become ruler of this city; and if we have this suspicion others do not. On the contrary, and what is worse, they bring the same accusations against us as we bring against him. Cosimo's actions that make him suspect to us are: helping everyone with money, not only private persons but the public, and not only Florentines but soldiers of fortune; supporting various citizens who need favor with the officials; and trading on the goodwill he enjoys among the people to help various of his friends to higher ranks and honors. So the reasons we would have to give for expelling him would be that he was merciful, helpful, generous, and universally loved. Now tell me what law there is that forbids, or condemns and punishes, pity, generosity, and love in men? And although these are all methods used by men who are aiming at supreme power, they are still not seen as such, and we are not the right men to disabuse the people because our behavior has lost us their trust. The city which is naturally drawn to

201

divide along party lines, and which is corrupt because it has always lived with party feuds, will not be prepared to listen to such charges. But let us imagine that you managed to banish him—and you could easily do so with a favorable Signoria—how would you stop him returning, with so many friends left behind who would be longing for him to come back? It would be impossible, because you could never be sure of them. There would be so many and they would have the goodwill of the people; and however many of his more important known friends you expelled, you would make still more enemies. So he would come back after a little while, and all you would gain would be this: He would have been good when you expelled him, and he would come back wicked, because his nature would have been corrupted by those who asked him back, and being obliged to them, he could not oppose them. If you are planning to have him killed, you will never manage it through the magistracies, because his money and your bribability will always save him. But let us imagine that he dies, or that he does not return from exile, I do not see what our republic will gain by this. If it is freed from Cosimo, it becomes the tool of Rinaldo. For my part, I am one of those who wants no citizen to exceed another in power and influence, but if one of these two is going to get the upper hand, then I see no reason for preferring Rinaldo to Cosimo. I shall say no more to you, except God preserve this city from having any citizen as its ruler: But if our sins deserve it, may He preserve it from having to obey Rinaldo. So do not advise a course that would be harmful in all ways, and do not think that you can oppose the will of many with only a few on your side. All these citizens are ready to sell this republic partly out of ignorance, partly out of malice; and Fortune has been so good to them that they have found a buyer. So do as I advise: See that you live modestly, and as far as liberty is concerned, suspect those of our own party as much as those of the opposition. And if any trouble does arise, you will be in favor with both sides if you remain neutral; so you will do yourselves some good and not harm your country."

XXVIII

These words restrained Barbadoro's intention a little, and things remained quiet while the Lucca war lasted. But once peace was signed and after the death of Niccolò da Uzano, the city was left with no war and no restraining influence. Bad feeling grew out of all proportion, and Rinaldo, who felt that he had been left as the only leader of the party, never stopped begging and pestering all the citizens he thought might become Gonfalonier to arm and free their country from the man who was bound to reduce it to slavery, through the wickedness of a few and the ignorance of many. Rinaldo's behavior and that of the men of the opposing party kept the city in a state of apprehension. Whenever appointments to office were made, it was announced publicly how many of each party were included; and at the draw for the Signori, the whole city was agog. Every case that came before the officials, however trivial, became a struggle between them. Secrets were published, the good and the bad were both favored and discriminated against, both were equally slandered, and no official did his duty.

While Florence was in this state of confusion, and Rinaldo persisted in his desire to lessen Cosimo's power, he knew that Bernardo Guadagni might become Gonfalonier, so he paid his taxes so that he would not lose office because of a debt to the state. Then when the draw was made for the Signori, Fortune, who delights in our conflicts, had Bernardo drawn as Gonfalonier for September and October. Rinaldo went to visit him immediately. He told him how glad the nobles' party and all those who wanted to live quietly were that he had assumed that office and that it was up to him to act so that their rejoicings should not be in vain. Then he told him of the dangers of disunity and said that the only way to achieve unity was to overthrow Cosimo. It was Cosimo alone who kept them unstable because of the favors that he was able to do with his boundless wealth. He had reached such heights that, if they did not do something about it, he would become their ruler. It was the duty of a good citizen to take positive action, call the people into the square, and reform the regime to give the country back its liberty. He reminded Bernardo that Salvestro de' Medici had been able to check the power of the Guelphs unlawfully, because the government belonged to them by right because of the blood their forefathers had shed; what Salvestro had been able to do unjustly against so many, Bernardo could easily do justly against one man. He told him not to be afraid, because his friends would be ready to help him with arms. He should discount the working classes who adored Cosimo, because Cosimo would get no more support from them than Giorgio Scali had done. He was not to worry about Cosimo's wealth, because when he was in the Signori's power it would belong to them. And Rinaldo concluded that this would make the republic safe and united and that Bernardo himself would be famous. Bernardo replied in a few words that he thought what Rinaldo advised must be done, and since it was now time for action, he was to see that he was fully prepared with his men, once he had convinced his friends. When Bernardo had taken office, prepared his friends, and agreed with Rinaldo, he summonsed Cosimo. Although many friends advised him against it, Cosimo appeared, trusting more in his innocence than in the mercy of the Signori. Once Cosimo was at the Palace, and arrested, Rinaldo left home with numbers of armed men, and with the whole party following. They came into the square, and there the Signori had the people summoned: and they appointed two hundred men to a *Balìa* to reform the government of the city. In this *Balìa* they discussed reform as soon as they could, and also whether Cosimo should live or die. Many people wanted him sent into exile, many wanted him executed, and many others kept silent either out of pity for him or for fear of the others. These disagreements meant that nothing could be settled.

XXIX

In the Palace tower there is a room the width of the tower, called the Alberghettino. Cosimo was shut up in it and Federigo Malavolti was set to guard him. From this room Cosimo heard the popular assembly being called, and the noise of arms in the square, then the frequent ringing of the bell for the *Balìa*, and he started to fear for his life. But most of all he was afraid that his personal enemies might put him to death in some underhand way. So he refused to eat, and in four days he had eaten nothing but a little bread. Federigo noticed this and said: "Cosimo, you are afraid of being poisoned, and you are letting yourself die of hunger. You are doing me an injustice believing that I would have anything to do with such wickedness. I do not think you will lose your life; you have so many friends in the Palace and outside. But even if you were going to lose it, you can be sure that they would find other ways than to use me as a means of taking it, because I do not want to dirty my hands with anyone's blood, particularly not yours, for you never harmed me. So take heart, eat your food, and keep yourself alive for your friends and your country. I will eat the same things as you, so that you will be less suspicious." These words reassured Cosimo completely, and he embraced and kissed Federigo with tears in his eyes, thanked him warmly for such a kind and friendly service, and offered to show his gratitude if ever Fortune gave him the opportunity. So Cosimo was somewhat comforted. While the citizens were still debating Cosimo's case, to please him Federigo brought to dinner a friend of the Gonfalonier called Farganaccio, a very amusing and witty man. When they had almost finished eating, Cosimo, who wanted to take advantage of his coming, because he knew him very well, made a sign to Federigo to leave. Federigo understood why and pretended to fetch some things that were needed for the meal. They were left alone and Cosimo, after saying some friendly things to Farganaccio, gave him a check and told him to go to the Hospitaller of Santa Maria Nuova to fetch one thousand one hundred ducats. He was to keep one hundred for himself and take a thousand to the Gonfalonier, and ask him to find some honorable pretext for coming to visit Cosimo. Farganaccio accepted the job, the money was paid, and Bernardo became kinder, with the result that Cosimo was exiled to Padua, against the wishes of Rinaldo who wanted him done away with. Averardo and many others of the Medici family were also exiled, and with them Puccio and Giovanni Pucci. To frighten those who were annoyed by Cosimo's exile, the Signori gave the power of *balìa* to the *Otto di Guardia* and the Captain of the People. After these deliberations, on the third of October 1433, Cosimo came before the Signori, by whom he was declared exiled, and he was urged to obey unless he wanted them to proceed more harshly against his property and against himself. Cosimo seemed to accept his exile cheerfully, and he said that he would be glad to go wherever the Signoria sent him. He begged them that since they had spared him his life they should also defend it, because he heard there were many people in the square who were after his blood. Then he offered himself and his substance to the city, the people, and their Lordships, wherever he might be. The Gonfalonier set his mind at rest and he was kept in the Palace until nightfall. Then he took Cosimo home, gave him dinner, and had him accompanied to the border by a large number of armed men. Wherever he went, Cosimo was received with honor, and he was publicly visited by the Venetians and honored not as an exile but as someone of the highest rank.

XXX

With Florence bereft of such an important citizen and a man so universally loved, everyone was alarmed. Those who had won and those who had been beaten were equally afraid. Rinaldo was fearful of the trouble in store for him. In order not to fail himself or his party, he gathered together a number of citizens friendly to him and told them that he could see their end approaching because they had let themselves be overcome by their enemies' entreaties, tears, and money. But they did not realize that shortly it would be their turn to entreat and weep, their prayers would not be heard, and they would find no one to take pity on their tears. Of the money they had received, they would give back the capital and repay the interest with torture, death, and exile. It would have been better to have done nothing than to have left Cosimo alive and his friends still in Florence, because great men should either not be touched, or if they were touched they should be done away with. He saw nothing else for it but to gather their forces together in the city, so that when their enemies rallied, which they would do soon, they could expel them by force of arms, since orthodox methods had been of no use. The remedy was one that he had mentioned a long time before: to win the nobles over, giving them back all the privileges of government, and to join forces with this party, just as their enemies had done with the working classes. Their party would be more resilient if it had more life, more *virtù*, more spirit, and more prestige. And he said that if this last, sure remedy was not adopted, he saw no other way of maintaining the regime among so many enemies, and he prophesied the imminent ruin of their party and the city. Mariotto Baldovinetti, one of those assembled, opposed this view, pointing out the pride of the nobles and how intolerant they were, and he said it would be wrong to turn to certain despotism under them—in order to avoid the uncertain dangers of the proletariat. Seeing that his advice was not being taken, Rinaldo complained of his and the party's misfortunes, blaming everything on the heavens who wanted it so, rather than on men's ignorance and blindness. Things were at this stage without any of the necessary steps having been taken, when a letter written by Agnolo Acciaiuolo to Cosimo was found, which outlined the city's feelings toward him. The letter urged him to arrange for a war to be started and to win the friendship of Neri di Gino, because he judged that since the city needed money and no one could be found to provide it, Cosimo's memory would return fresh to the citizens' minds and with it the desire to have him back; and if Neri broke with Rinaldo, that party would be weakened so much that it would not be capable of defending itself. When this letter fell into the hands of the magistracies, it caused Agnolo to be arrested, tortured, and sent into exile. But this example did not in any way check the enthusiasm for Cosimo.

It was already almost a year since the day when Cosimo was banished, and at the end of August 1434, Niccolò di Cocco was drawn as Gonfalonier for the next two months, and with him eight Signori, all supporters of Cosimo. This Signoria frightened Rinaldo and all his party. Before the Signori take up office, they remain alone for three days. Rinaldo met with the leaders of his party again and pointed out how certain and how near danger was. He said that the answer was to take up arms and get Donato Velluti, who was then still Gonfalonier, to gather the people in the square, create a new *Balìa,* dismiss the new Signori from office, and appoint new ones for the sake of the regime, and to burn the voting bags and fill them with the names of friends after new electoral scrutinies. Many people thought this plan safe and essential, but many others found it too violent and too dishonest. Among those who disliked it was Palla Strozzi, who was a quiet man, kind and gentle, and more suited to literary studies than to restraining a party and opposing civic strife. He said that clever, bold plans can seem good at first, but then they can turn out to be difficult to put into effect and harmful to carry through. He thought that fear of new wars abroad, with the Duke's troops in Romagna on our borders, would make the Signori think more about them than about internal strife. But if they seemed to want change (and they could not start to make changes without it becoming known), then there would always be time to arm and do whatever was necessary for public safety. If this was done out of necessity, it would cause less surprise among the people, and they themselves would receive less blame. So it was concluded that they should let the new Signori take office and watch their movements closely. If they heard of anything being done against their party, they should all arm and gather in the Piazza di San Pulinari, a place near the Palace, from which they could go wherever they considered it necessary.

XXXI

They left after this decision, and the new Signori took up office. To win prestige and frighten those people who were thinking of opposing him, the Gonfalonier condemned his predecessor, Donato Velluti, to prison for having misappropriated public funds. Then he sounded his friends about getting Cosimo back, and finding them well disposed, he spoke to the people he considered to be leaders of the Medici party. With some persuasion from them, he summonsed Rinaldo, Ridolfo Peruzzi, and Niccolò Barbadoro as leaders of the opposing party. After this summons Rinaldo thought there was no time to lose, and he came out with a large number of armed men and was immediately joined by Ridolfo Peruzzi and Niccolò Barbadoro. There were many other citizens with them and several unemployed soldiers who were in Florence, and they all gathered in the Piazza di San Pulinari as agreed. Palla Strozzi did not come out, although he had collected a number of troops, and Giovanni Guicciardini did the same. Rinaldo sent to urge them on and reproach them for hesitating. Giovanni replied that he was doing enough damage to the enemy if by staying at home he stopped Piero, his brother, from going to the help of the Palace. After a number of representations had been made to him, Palla rode to San Pulinari, unarmed, accompanied by two men on foot. Rinaldo went to meet him and rebuked him harshly for letting them down, saying that his refusal to forgather with the others was a result either of lack of trust or lack of courage; both of which charges should be avoided by a man who wanted to be respected in the way he was. If he thought that by not doing his duty toward the party his enemies would spare him his life or fail to exile him when they won, then he was mistaken. As far as he himself was concerned, if anything untoward happened he could console himself with the thought that before the trouble he had not failed to give advice, and during the trouble he had not failed to give military support. But regrets would multiply for him and the others, when they thought that they had betrayed their country three times: once when they saved Cosimo, again when they did not take his advice, and now the third time when they refused to lend her the aid of their arms. In reply to these words Palla did not say anything that could be heard by those around him. He turned his horse away mumbling and went back home.

When they heard that Rinaldo and his party had armed, and saw themselves deserted, the Signori had the Palace locked, and being without advice did not know what to do. But as Rinaldo hesitated to come into the square because he was waiting for the reinforcements that did not come, he lost his chance of winning. This gave the Signori courage to defend themselves, while many citizens went to them to advise them to propose a truce. So some of the men who were least suspect went to Rinaldo on behalf of the Signori and said that the Signoria did not know the reason for these riots and that they had never meant to offend. If Cosimo had been discussed, they had not thought of reinstating him; and if this was the reason for their fear, then they could reassure him. They asked them to come to the Palace, where they would be welcomed and all their requests would be met. These words did not make Rinaldo change his mind, but he said he would be reassured if Cosimo and his followers were reduced to private citizens, and the city was then reformed to everybody's benefit. But it always happens that where power is equal and opinions differ things are very seldom resolved for the good. Ridolfo Peruzzi was affected by those citizens' words and said that as far as he was concerned he only wanted Cosimo not to come back, and that if they agreed about this then he felt it was victory enough. He did not want to bathe his city in blood in order to achieve a greater victory, and so he would obey the Signoria. He went to the palace with his men, where he was warmly welcomed. Rinaldo lost his chance of victory because he stopped at San Pulinari, because of Palla's lack of courage, and because of Ridolfo's desertion; and the enthusiasm of the citizens who supported him had begun to cool off as well. Added to this was the influence of the Pope.

XXXII

Pope Eugene was in Florence because he had been expelled from Rome by the people. When he heard of the riots, he felt that it was his duty to quell them, and he sent Giovanni Vitelleschi, the patriarch, and a great friend of Rinaldo's, to ask Rinaldo to come to him, because the Pope was in a position of authority and trust with the Signoria, and so could get what Rinaldo wanted without causing bloodshed or harming the citizens. Rinaldo was persuaded by his friend, and he went with all his armed followers to Santa Maria Novella, where the Pope was staying. Eugene told him of the promises the Signori had given him and that he was to settle all the differences. When they laid down their arms, things would be straightened out according to the Pope's advice. Rinaldo put himself entirely in the Pope's hands, having seen Palla's coldness and Ridolfo Peruzzi's unreliability, and having no better plan, but thinking that the Pope's authority would save him. The Pope sent word to Niccolò Barbadoro and the others who were waiting outside to go and disarm, because Rinaldo was staying with the Pope to draw up an agreement with the Signori. At this news everyone disbanded and disarmed.

XXXIII

Seeing that their enemies had disarmed, the Signori gave their attention to negotiating the agreement through the Pope. At the same time they sent secretly to the mountains near Pistoia for foot soldiers, and they arranged for them to come to Florence at night, together with all their men at arms; and when all the strong points were occupied, they called the people into the square and appointed a new *Balìa*. The first time this met it called Cosimo back to his country, together with the others who had been banished with him. Of the enemy party, they banished Rinaldo degli Albizzi, Ridolfo Peruzzi, Niccolò Barbadoro, and Palla Strozzi, with many other citizens. There were so many of them that there were few towns in Italy where some had not been sent into exile, and many outside Italy were full of them. Through this event Florence not only deprived herself of good men but also of wealth and industry. The Pope was very displeased to see such disasters befall those who had laid down their arms at his request. He commiserated with Rinaldo about the injustice he had suffered on account of his promise and urged him to be patient and hope for a change in fortune. He replied: "They trusted me as little as they should have done, and the excessive trust I placed in you destroyed me and my party. But I blame myself more than anyone else, since I believed that you, who had been expelled from your own country, could keep me in mine. I have had plenty of experience concerning the tricks of Fortune, and as I have put little trust in prosperity, so adversity will offend me less. I know that when she likes she can act more kindly toward me, but if she never does I will always think very little of living in a city where the laws have less power than the men. The ideal country is one where property and friends can be enjoyed in safety, not one where property can easily be taken from you and friends desert you in your greatest need for fear of their lives. Wise and good men always found it less bitter to hear about their country's troubles than to see them, and they think an honorable rebel a more praiseworthy man than a citizen who is a slave." He left the Pope and in a very angry mood went into exile complaining to himself about the Pope's advice and his friends' coldness. Cosimo returned to Florence when he heard that he had been reinstated. It must rarely have happened that a citizen returning in triumph from a victory was received by his country with such a gathering of people and such a great demonstration of affection as he received when he returned from exile. And of their own free will, everyone greeted him as a public benefactor and as the father of his country.

BOOK VII

Perhaps those who have read the previous book will feel that a writer concerned with Florentine affairs has spent too long on his account of the things that took place in Lombardy and in the Kingdom. But I have not omitted accounts of this kind and will not do so in future, because although I never promised to write about Italian affairs, I do not think I should leave out events worth noting in the province. If I did not mention them, our history would not be so easy to understand or so enjoyable, especially since most of the wars in which the Florentines are forced to become involved arise out of the actions of other Italian people and princes: For instance, the war between John of Anjou and King Ferrando gave rise to the antagonism and bitter enmity between Ferrando and the Florentines, particularly the Medici family. The King complained that in that war he had not only been given no help but favors had been shown to his enemy, and his anger was the cause of great troubles, as our account will show. In my description of foreign affairs I have reached 1463, now I must go back a number of years to tell of the troubles at home.

First however, following our usual procedure, I want to make the point that those who hope that a republic can be united are badly mistaken. It is true that some divisions harm republics and others do good. They do harm if they involve factions and partisans, but if they exist without factions or partisans they do good. So since the founder of a republic cannot guard against quarrels breaking out, at least he should see to it that there are no factions. Citizens make themselves a reputation in a city in two ways: either publicly or privately. Publicly a reputation can be acquired by winning a battle, taking a town, carrying out an embassy with care and prudence, or advising the republic wisely and successfully. Privately it may be acquired by doing good to various citizens, defending someone against the government officials, helping him with money, getting him undeserved honors, and winning over the lower classes with amusements and public benefactions. This sort of behavior gives rise to factions and partisans, and a reputation won in this way is as offensive as the other kind is valuable, if it does not involve factions, because it is based on a common good, not a private one. And although even among these citizens there is no way of guarding against bitter antagonisms, they cannot harm the republic because they have no hangers-on following them for their own gain. In fact, these citizens cannot help being useful to the republic because in order to accomplish their tasks they are bound to exalt the republic and to watch each other very closely to see that civic liberties are not infringed. The feuds in Florence always involved factions and they were always harmful. The winning side only remained united for as long as the opposing faction had life in it. As soon as the defeated side was broken, the reigning party was no longer restrained by fear or controlled by internal discipline, and it split up again. Cosimo de' Medici's party was the winner in 1434, but because the defeated party was large and full of very powerful men, Cosimo's party did remain united and benevolent for some time. They did not quarrel among themselves and did not earn the hatred of the people by any crooked behavior, so that whenever this regime needed the people in order to regain power, it always found them ready to grant the leaders all the authority and power they wanted. So from 1434 to 1455, that is, for twenty-one years, they were granted the special powers of *balìa* by the councils in the usual way.

II

As we have said several times, there were two very powerful citizens in Florence, Cosimo de' Medici and Neri Capponi. Neri was one of those who had won his reputation in public service, so that he had many friends and

few hangers-on. Cosimo, on the other hand, had found
both public and private openings to political power, and
he had plenty of friends and partisans. While they were
both alive they were friends, and they always got what
they wanted from the people without any difficulty because they mingled grace with power. But when 1455
came, Neri was dead, the enemy faction was broken,
and the regime had difficulty in resuming its authority.
Cosimo's own friends, who were very powerful in the
regime, were the cause, because they were no longer
afraid of the opposition which had died out, and they
aimed at lessening Cosimo's power. This desire gave
rise to the quarrels that took place later in 1466. In the
councils where public administration was discussed in
public, those who had charge of the government advised
that the power of *balìa* should not be assumed again,
that the voting bags should be closed, and that the officers
should be chosen by lot on the basis of past electoral
scrutinies. Cosimo had one of two ways to check this
aim. He could either regain power by force, using the
supporters who were left to him and alienating all the
others, or he could allow the affair to pass over and let
his friends see later that they were not taking power and
prestige from him but from themselves. It was the second
of these two remedies that he chose. He knew very well
that in that kind of government he ran no danger at
all because the voting bags were full of the names of his
friends and he could take power again when he liked.
Once the city had begun to appoint its officials by lot
again, the mass of the citizens felt that they had regained their liberty, and they were convinced that the
officers had been chosen not by the will of the powerful
citizens but according to their own judgment. Now one
friend of a powerful man was beaten, now another; and
those who had been used to seeing their houses full of
flatterers and presents found them empty of goods and
men. And they found that they had become the equals
of those whom they had thought far inferior, and those
who had once been their peers they saw had become their
superiors. They were not respected or honored, but often
even mocked and derided; and people spoke about them

and the republic in the streets and in the squares without any respect. So they very soon realized that they and not Cosimo had lost power. Cosimo pretended this was not so, and when there was any decision that pleased the people Cosimo was the first to support it. But what frightened the *Grandi* most, and gave Cosimo his greatest opportunity to make them pause, was that the system of the *Catasto* of 1427 was brought back, by which the taxes were imposed by law and not by men.

III

When this law had been passed and the board which was to execute it had been appointed, they all joined together and went to Cosimo to ask if he would rescue them and himself from the hands of the proletariat, and give back to the regime the reputation that brought power to him and honors to them. Cosimo replied that he would, but he wanted the law to be passed in the orthodox way, by the consent of the people and not by force, which was entirely out of the question. They tried to get the law for a new *Balìa* through the councils but failed. So the leading citizens went back to Cosimo and with all possible humility begged him to consent to a popular assembly. This Cosimo flatly refused to do, because he wanted to force them to recognize their mistake fully. Because Donato Cocchi, who was Gonfalonier of Justice, wanted to call an assembly without his consent, Cosimo caused him to be so ridiculed by the Signori who were sitting with him that he went mad and was sent home.

However, since it is not wise to let things reach a stage where they get out of hand, when Luca Pitti, a bold, courageous man, was Gonfalonier of Justice, Cosimo felt it was time to let him take matters in hand, so that if any blame was incurred it should fall on Luca and not on him. At the beginning of his period in office, Luca proposed several times to the people that a *Balìa* should be set up again; and when he failed, he threatened, in insulting and arrogant terms, those who were sitting in the councils. Shortly afterwards he followed this up with action, because on the eve of St. Lawrence in August 1458, after he had filled the Palace with armed men, he called the people into the square and by force of arms made them consent to something they had refused to agree to voluntarily. So the regime was in control again, a *Balìa* was set up, and the chief officers appointed according to the wishes of a few citizens. So that a regime that had been born in violence should begin with terror, they banished Girolamo Machiavelli and several others, and they deprived many more of their honors. This Girolamo was declared a rebel afterwards for having broken his bounds, and as he went around Italy inciting the princes against his country, he was arrested in Lunigiana through the bad faith of one of the Lords there; and he was brought to Florence where he died in prison.

IV

This type of government, which lasted eight years, was harsh and oppressive, because Cosimo was old, tired, and weakened by ill health now, and he could not pay as much attention to public affairs as he had before. So the city was at the mercy of a few citizens. As a reward for the good he had done the republic, Luca Pitti was knighted; and not to be outdone in gratitude, he ordered that those who before had been called the Priors of the Guilds should now be called the Priors of Liberty, so that they should at least have back the name of what they had lost. He also ordered that where before the Gonfalonier had sat at the right of the magistrates, in the future he should sit in their midst. So that God should seem to be taking part in their enterprise, they held public processions and solemn services to give thanks for the resumption of their privileges. Luca was very richly rewarded by the Signoria and by Cosimo, and the whole city competed with them, so that it was generally thought that the presents reached the sum of twenty thousand ducats. His acclaim reached such heights that it was not

Cosimo but Luca who ruled the city. He became so sure of himself that he began two buildings, one in Florence, and the other at Ruciano, about a mile from the city, both of them imposing and regal. The one in the city was much bigger than anything else built by a private citizen till then. To get these finished he did not fight shy of any extraordinary methods, for not only did citizens and private persons give him presents and supply him with things needed for the building work, but communes and whole peoples were subsidizing him. Besides this, all the exiles and anyone that had committed murder, larceny, or anything else that made him fear public punishment were sure of safety if they took refuge in those buildings, provided they could be useful in construction work. The other citizens, though they were not building like him, were no less cruel and greedy. So if Florence had no foreign wars to ruin her, her own citizens were bringing about her destruction.

During this time, as we have said, the wars of the Kingdom took place. The Pope made war in Romagna against the Malatesta, because he wanted to wrest Rimini and Cesena from them. Pope Pius spent his pontificate involved in these campaigns and in planning an attack on the Turks.

V

Florence persisted with her strife and troubles. The split in Cosimo's party began in 1455 for the reasons mentioned; and as we described, it was patched up thanks to his prudence. But in 1464 Cosimo became seriously ill and departed this life. Both his friends and his enemies regretted his death, because those who did not like him for political reasons saw how greedy the leading citizens had been while he was alive, when respect for him had made these citizens less intolerable; and they feared that once he had gone, they would be totally ruined. They did not have much faith in Piero his son, because, although he was a good man, they felt that being sickly too and new to power, he would be bound to show respect to those citizens, and that they, without any check, would be able to step up their extortions. So Cosimo was greatly missed by everyone.

Cosimo was the most famous and respected citizen— for a man who did not rely on force—who ever lived not only in Florence but in any other city of which there are records. Not only did he outdo all his contemporaries in power and wealth but also in liberality and prudence, because among all the other qualities that made him a ruler in his own country were his outstanding generosity and munificence. His generosity seemed much greater after his death, when Piero his son wanted to take stock of his assets: There was no citizen of any standing to whom Cosimo had not lent large sums of money; and often when he heard of some nobleman in need, he would help him without being asked. His munificence was apparent in the great number of buildings he erected, for he not only restored but completely rebuilt the monasteries and churches of San Marco and San Lorenzo and the convent of Santa Verdiana in Florence, and San Girolamo and the Abbey in the hills of Fiesole, and a Franciscan church in the Mugello. Besides this he had magnificent altars and chapels built in Santa Croce, in the Servi, the Angioli, and San Miniato, and he filled these churches and chapels with hangings and everything needed for the adornment of divine worship. Added to these sacred buildings were his own private houses: one in the city, which was of a suitable type for such a citizen, and four outside, at Careggi, Fiesole, Cafaggiuolo, and Trebbio—all of which were palaces fit not for private citizens but kings. It was not enough for him to be known in Italy for splendid buildings: He put up a hostel in Jerusalem for poor and sick pilgrims. He spent a very large sum of money on all these constructions. And although these residences and his other actions and achievements were princely, and he was the only ruler of Florence, nevertheless everything he did was so well tempered by his prudence that he never transgressed against civic modesty. In his conversation, the servants he had, the way he rode, his whole style of living, and the marriages he arranged for his family, he always behaved like any modest citizen. He knew that an excessive parade of wealth seen all the time causes much more envy than actual wealth hidden under a veneer of modesty. So when he had to find a wife for his sons he did not seek alliances with princes, but married Giovanni to Cornelia degli Alessandri and Piero to Lucrezia de' Tornabuoni; and of his granddaughters born to Piero, he married Bianca to Guglielmo de' Pazzi and Nannina to Bernardo Rucellai. No one either in the states ruled by princes or under free governments could touch him for intelligence during his lifetime. This was why he could maintain a regime for thirty-one years through such changes of fortune in such an unstable city with its restless populace. Being very prudent, he could recognize trouble a long way off, and then he had time either to stop it from growing or to prepare himself so that if it did grow it would not harm him. In this way he not only outdid private and civic ambitions but also outmaneuvered a number of princes so successfully and prudently that whoever made an alliance with him and his country ended up equal or superior to their enemies, and whoever opposed him wasted either their time and their money or lost their power. The Venetians can testify to this. With Cosimo they were always a match for Duke Filippo; without him they were always beaten first by Filippo then by Francesco. When they joined forces with Alfonso against the republic of Florence, Cosimo with his credit emptied Naples and Venice of money, so that they were forced to accept the terms that he agreed to offer them. So the difficulties that Cosimo experienced inside the city and out brought him honor and did his enemies harm. Civic feuds always increased his power in Florence, and foreign wars added to his strength and prestige. He brought under his republic's rule Borgo San Sepolcro, Montedoglio, the Casentino, and the Bagno Valley. So his *virtù* and his fortune destroyed all his enemies and added to the status of his friends.

VI

He was born in 1389, on the day of Saint Cosimo and Saint Damian. His early life was full of trials, as his exile, imprisonment, and the danger of death show. After the collapse of the Council of Constance, where he had gone with Pope John, he had to escape in disguise to save his life. But after he reached forty he lived very happily, and not only those who backed him up in public affairs, but also the men who looked after his interests throughout Europe, had a share in his success. The result was that many Florentine families became excessively rich, as happened in the case of the Tornabuoni, the Benci, the Portinari, and the Sassetti. Besides them, everybody who depended on his advice and his success became wealthy; and although he spent money continually on church buildings and on alms, he would sometimes complain to friends that he had never been able to spend so much for God's sake that he had been able to find Him down in his books as a debtor. He was of ordinary height and had olive coloring and a venerable appearance. He had no learning, but he was very eloquent and full of natural wisdom. He stood by his friends and showed compassion to the poor; and he was helpful in discussions, careful in his advice, swift to carry out promises, and shrewd and sensible in his sayings and repartee. Rinaldo degli Albizzi sent him a message at the beginning of his exile to say that the eggs were hatching out, to which Cosimo replied that they might not get on very well outside the nest. To other rebels who had let him know that they were not asleep, he said that he believed them because he had stopped them from sleeping. Of Pope Pius, when he was summoning the princes for the attack on the Turks, he said that he was an old man undertaking a young man's task. To the Venetian ambassadors, who came with the ambassadors of King Alfonso to complain about the republic, he showed his bare head and asked them what color it was. They replied: "White"; and he then added: "It will not be long before your senators have heads as white as mine." A few hours before he died, his wife asked him why he kept his eyes shut, and he answered: "To get them used to it." Some citizens said to him after he returned from exile that he was damaging the city and going against God's will by expelling so many upright men, and he replied that a damaged city was better than one that was lost: Two rods of rose-colored cloth made a man respectable, and governments were not kept in power by reciting the Lord's Prayer. These sayings gave his enemies a chance to accuse him of putting himself before his country and this world before the next. Many more of his sayings could be recorded, but we will leave them out as unnecessary. Cosimo was also a great lover and admirer of men of letters, and he brought Argyropoulos to Florence, who was of Greek birth, and one of the best-read men of those times, so that the young people of Florence could learn Greek and other subjects from him. Cosimo was particularly fond of Marsilio Ficino, the second father of Platonic philosophy, and brought him up in his household. So that Marsilio could pursue his study of literature more easily, and so that Cosimo himself could see him more conveniently, he gave him a house near his own at Careggi. His prudence, his wealth, his style of living, and his good fortune meant that he was feared and loved by the citizens in Florence, and extraordinarily respected by the princes not only of Italy but of the whole of Europe. Thus he left such a firm basis for his descendants that they were able to equal him in *virtù* and far surpass him in fortune, and they could achieve the power that Cosimo had in Florence not only in that city but throughout the whole of Christendom. However, during the last period of his life he had very serious troubles. Of his two sons, Piero and Giovanni, the latter, in whom he placed most of his hopes, died, and the other was an invalid and because of his physical weakness not very suited to politics or business. After the death of his son, he had himself carried around the house and said with a sigh: "This house is too big for such a small family." Then his proud soul was distressed by not having added any honorable ac-

223

quisitions to the Florentine dominions. He was all the more disappointed because he felt he had been let down by Francesco Sforza. While he was a Count, the latter had promised him that once he had won control of Milan he would conduct a Lucchese campaign on behalf of the Florentines. But this did not come about because the Count changed his mind when his luck turned, and once he had become Duke he wanted to enjoy in peace the state that he had won in war. So he did not want to keep the promises he had made about campaigns to Cosimo or to anyone else; and after he became Duke he did not go to war except when he was forced to defend himself. This annoyed Cosimo very much, because he felt that he had put himself out and had spent money to bring to power a man who was ungrateful and unreliable. Besides this, he felt that owing to ill health he could not put the same amount of work into public and private business; and he saw both deteriorating because the city was being harmed by its citizens and his property was being mismanaged by his executives and his sons. All this meant that the last period of his life was not peaceful. Nevertheless, he died covered with glory and with a very great reputation in the city and outside. On Cosimo's death, all the citizens and all the Christian princes sent their condolences to his son Piero, all the citizens followed his funeral procession, and he was buried with great pomp in the church of San Lorenzo. And by public decree he was named on his tomb "Father of the Country." If in describing the things Cosimo did I have imitated men who write the lives of princes rather than those who write universal histories, no one should be surprised. He was a man so rare in our city that I felt bound to praise him in an extraordinary way.

VII

During the time that Florence and Italy were in the state we have described, King Louis of France was subjected to a very fierce attack from his barons, aided by Francis, Duke of Brittany and Charles, Duke of Bur-

gundy. It was so severe that he could not think of helping Duke John of Anjou in his campaigns at Genoa and
in the Kingdom. And in fact, feeling that he needed
everybody's help, and since the city of Savona was in
French hands, he made Francesco, Duke of Milan, Lord
of the city, and let him understand that if he wanted
he could attack Genoa with his permission. Francesco
accepted this offer, and helped by the reputation he
acquired through the King's friendship and the favors the
Adorni did him, he gained control of Genoa. So as not to
seem ungrateful to the King for benefits received, he sent
fifteen hundred horse, captained by his eldest son Galeazzo, to help him in France.

Now that Ferrando of Aragon and Francesco Sforza
had become King of the whole Kingdom of Naples and
Duke of Lombardy and ruler of Genoa respectively, and
had become related by marriage, they began to think how
they could best establish their regimes so that while they
were alive they could enjoy them in safety and when
they died be free to leave them to their heirs. They
decided that the King must make sure of the barons who
had attacked him in the war with John of Anjou, and the
Duke must see to it that the Braccesque army was
crushed. They were natural enemies of his family, and
had won a very high reputation under Iacopo Piccinino
because he was now the leading captain in Italy, and
since he had no states, whoever was in control of a state
was bound to fear him, especially the Duke who, remembering his own example, did not feel that he could keep
his state or leave it safely to his son while Iacopo was
alive. The King made every effort to come to an agreement with his barons and tried every trick to make them
feel secure. He was successful because these princes saw
that if they remained at war with the King they would
clearly be ruined, but if they came to terms and trusted
him the outcome would be doubtful. Because men always
prefer to avoid certain evil, it follows that rulers can
more easily deceive lesser princes. Those princes trusted
the King's peace because they saw the obvious dangers
of war, and once they had put themselves into his hands
he did away with them in different ways on various

pretexts. This frightened Iacopo Piccinino who was at Sulmona with his army; and to stop the King from harming him, he negotiated with Duke Francesco through his friends so that the two of them could be reconciled. The Duke made him the biggest offers he could, and Iacopo decided to put himself in the Duke's hands; and accompanied by a hundred horse, he went to see him in Milan.

VIII

Iacopo had fought under his father and brother for a long time, first of all for Duke Filippo and then for the people of Milan, so because of this long acquaintance he had a number of friends in Milan and the goodwill of the common people. This was increased by the present state of affairs because the prosperity and new power of the Sforza had given rise to envy, whereas adversity and his long absence had encouraged the people to pity Iacopo and had also given them a strong desire to see him. All these things came out on his arrival, because there were few of the nobility who did not meet him. The streets he passed through were full of people who wanted to see him: His army's name was being shouted everywhere. These honors hastened his end, because as the Duke's fear grew so did his desire to do away with Iacopo. To do this more secretly, he ordered the celebration of Iacopo's marriage to his natural daughter Drusiana, which had been arranged some time before. Then he agreed with Ferrando that the latter should hire Iacopo and give him the title of captain of his army and a salary of a hundred thousand florins. After this agreement was concluded, Iacopo went to Naples with a ducal ambassador and his wife Drusiana; and he was welcomed there and honored, and entertained for a long time with all kinds of amusements. But when he asked permission to go to Sulmona where his army was, he was invited to the castle by the King. After the banquet, he was imprisoned with his son Francesco, and shortly afterwards he was put to death. So it was that our Italian princes feared in others the *virtù* they lacked themselves, and they crushed it, so that when nobody possessed it they exposed this province to the disasters that soon afterwards overtook it and destroyed it.

IX

At this time Pope Pius had settled the affairs of Romagna, and he felt it was time, seeing there was universal peace, to take the Christians into battle against the Turks. He followed the same procedure as his predecessors, and all the princes promised either money or troops; and in particular, King Matthew of Hungary and Duke Charles of Burgundy promised to accompany him personally, and they were put in charge of the campaign. The Pope let his hopes race on so far ahead that he left Rome and went to Ancona where the whole army had been ordered to muster. The Venetians had promised him ships to carry him over to the Balkans. After the Pope's arrival so many people gathered in the city that after a few days all the food there was in the town, or that could be brought in from places nearby, came to an end, so that everybody suffered from hunger. Besides this, there was no money to give to those who needed it, and no arms to equip those who were without. Matthew and Charles did not appear, and the Venetians sent one of their captains with a few galleys, more to display their pomp and show that they had kept their promise than to provide transport for the army. The Pope, who was old and ill, died in the midst of these troubles and disorders, and after his death everybody went back home. After the Pope's death, in the year 1465, Paul II, a Venetian by birth, was elected to the pontificate. And so that nearly all the states in Italy should change their rulers, in the following year Francesco Sforza, Duke of Milan, died after having held the dukedom for sixteen years, and his son Galeazzo was proclaimed Duke.

X

This ruler's death revived civic strife in Florence and made the factions more active. After Cosimo died, Piero his son, the heir to all his father's property and power, called Dietisalvi Neroni to him. He was a man of great influence and was highly respected by the other citizens. Cosimo trusted him so much that before he died he told Piero to be governed entirely by him in matters concerning his property and also concerning politics. Piero told Dietisalvi of the faith Cosimo had had in him and said that because he wanted to obey his father after his death as he had obeyed him in life, he wanted Dietisalvi's advice about his inheritance and the government of the city. To start with his own property, he would send for his accounts and put them into Dietisalvi's hands so that he could see if they were right or wrong, and when he had been through them he could advise Piero as he saw fit. Dietisalvi promised to be careful and honest in everything, but when the accounts came and he had examined them thoroughly, he saw that there were mistakes everywhere. Being a man who was ruled more by his own ambition than by love for Piero or the memory of earlier benefits received from Cosimo, he thought it would be easy to take away Piero's reputation and deprive him of the position that his father had left him as his inheritance. So Dietisalvi came to Piero with a piece of advice that seemed quite honest and reasonable, but beneath it disaster lay hidden. He explained to Piero that his affairs were in a bad state and told him how much money he would have to find if he did not want to lose his credit and with it the reputation of his wealth and power. And he told him that the most responsible way to straighten out his affairs would be to try to call in the money that his father was owed by many people, both foreigners and fellow citizens. Cosimo had been very generous in letting everyone have part of his wealth in order to win supporters in Florence and allies abroad, so that the amount he was owed for these reasons came to a sum of money that was neither small nor of little importance. This advice seemed good and sound to Piero who wanted to put his affairs straight with his own money, but as soon as he ordered this money to be recalled, the citizens took offense—as if he wanted to take away their property, not ask for his own back. They criticized him without mercy and blamed him for being ungrateful and mean.

XI

When Dietisalvi saw the general ill will which Piero had incurred because of his advice, he had a meeting with Luca Pitti, Agnolo Acciaiuoli, and Niccolò Soderini, and they decided to deprive Piero of his reputation and his power. Their motives were all different: Luca wanted to succeed to Cosimo's place because he had become so grand that he felt it beneath his dignity to have to acknowledge Piero; Dietisalvi, who knew that Luca was not a suitable head of the government, thought that with Piero out of the way his mantle would be bound to fall on him after a short while; Niccolò Soderini would have liked the city to enjoy greater freedom and be governed according to the wishes of the magistracies. Agnolo had a particular hatred for the Medici for the following reason: Raffaello his son had some time before taken as his wife Alessandra de' Bardi, who had a very big dowry. She was badly treated by her father-in-law and by her husband, either because of her own faults or the failings of others. Lorenzo di Larione, a relation of hers, took pity on the girl and one night, accompanied by several armed men, he took her from Agnolo's house. The Acciaiuoli complained about this wrong the Bardi had done them. The case was referred to Cosimo, and he judged that the Acciaiuoli should give back Alessandra's dowry and leave the girl to choose whether she went back to her husband. Agnolo did not feel that Cosimo had treated him like a friend in this judgment, and as he had not been able to get his revenge on Cosimo, he decided to have it on his son. Although the conspirators differed so much in their feelings, they put it about that there was only one reason.

They said that they wanted the city to be ruled by the magistracies, not by the advice of a small junta. Besides this, the bankruptcy of a number of merchants at this time increased the hatred of Piero and the reasons for attacking him. Piero was publicly blamed for this because by recalling his money so unexpectedly he had caused them to fail, much to the city's shame and loss. Added to this, the negotiations that were going on to marry Lorenzo, his eldest son, to Clarice degli Orsini, gave everyone more reason to criticize him. They said that it was obvious, since he refused a Florentine match for his son, that there was no longer room for him in the city as a citizen, and he was preparing to make himself sole ruler. He who does not want his fellow citizens for relatives wants them as servants, and so it is reasonable that he should not have them as friends. It seemed to the leaders of the revolt that they held victory in their hands, because most of the citizens sided with them, deceived by the word *liberty* which they had taken as their slogan to whitewash their purpose.

XII

While these feelings were coming to a head throughout the city, some of those who disliked civic strife felt that they should try to put an end to these feelings by some new kind of amusement, because it is most often an idle populace which is the tool of men who make revolutions. To put a stop to this idleness and to give people something to think about instead of politics, and since Cosimo had already been dead a year, they took advantage of the argument that it would be a good thing to liven the city up and arranged two holidays like the other solemn feast days that are observed in the city. One celebrated the coming of the three Kings from the East following the star that marked the birth of Christ, and this was so splendid and magnificent that the whole city was kept busy for several months preparing for it. The other was a tournament (this is the name for a display in which a battle between men on horseback is staged) in which the leading young men in the city tried their strength against the most famous knights in Italy. Among the young men of Florence the most famous was Lorenzo, Piero's eldest son, who won the highest honor not through favoritism but through his own valor.

After these displays were over, the citizens harked back to their old ideas, and each pursued his own views more purposefully than before. They caused great disagreements and troubles, which were greatly aggravated by two events: One was the loss of the full power of *balìa,* and the other was the death of Francesco, Duke of Milan. Because of this, Galeazzo, the new Duke, sent ambassadors to Florence to confirm the terms of the agreement that Francesco, his father, had with the city, in which it was agreed among other things that a certain sum of money should be paid to the Duke every year. The leaders of the opposition to the Medici took their cue from this request, and in the councils they opposed the decision publicly, pointing out that the alliance had been made not with Galeazzo but with Francesco; and now that Francesco was dead, the obligation no longer existed. They said there was no reason to resuscitate it because Galeazzo did not have Francesco's *virtù,* and consequently they should not and could not expect to gain the same from him. If they had had little enough from Francesco, they would get even less from Galeazzo; and if any citizen wanted to pay him for his power, it would be unworthy of a civilized society and against civic liberty. Piero, on the other hand, pointed out that it was not wise to end such an essential alliance out of niggardliness and that nothing had been better for the safety of the republic and the whole of Italy than their ties with the Duke. The Venetians, seeing them allied, could not hope to get the better of the Duchy either by feigned friendship or by open war. No sooner would they hear that the Florentines had broken with the Duke than they would take up arms against him, and finding him young, new to government, and without allies, they would easily win him over by deceit or force. In either case, this would mean the ruin of the republic.

XIII

These arguments were not accepted and the antagonisms began to come out into the open. Each of the
parties gathered at night in different groups, because the
friends of the Medici went to the Crocetta and their
adversaries to the Pietà. The latter, anxious to achieve
Piero's downfall, had enrolled many citizens favorable
to their cause. One particular night when they were
together they had a special discussion about the method
they should adopt. They wanted to lessen the Medici's
power but differed about how it should be done. One
group, which was the most moderate, wanted to concen-
trate on hindering the resumption of the powers of *balìa*
since they had come to an end; if they did this they
would achieve everybody's aim, because the councils and
the magistracies would govern the city, and in a very
short time Piero's authority would be broken. With the
loss of his political reputation his credit in business
would go too, because his affairs were in such a state
that if they saw to it that he could not make use of
public money he was bound to fail. If this happened,
there would be no more danger to fear from him, and
they would have regained their liberty without exile and
bloodshed; and every good citizen must desire this. But
if they tried to use force, they would be running all kinds
of risks, because some people will let a man fall who is
falling through his own fault, but if others push him,
then they will support him. Besides, if no extraordinary
measures were taken against him, he would have no
reason to arm or look for allies; and if he did, he would
come in for so much blame and would make everyone so
suspicious that he would hasten his downfall and give
others all the more reason for attacking him. Many
others at the meeting thought this method too slow and
said that time was on Piero's side and not theirs, because
if they decided to stick to orthodox methods, Piero was
in no danger and they would be running great risks; his
enemies among the government officials would let him

enjoy the city, and his friends would make him ruler by their own downfall, as happened in 1458. If the advice given had come from good men, this came from wise men; so while men were up in arms against Piero they must crush him. The way to do it was to arm at home, and abroad to hire the Marquis of Ferrara so as not to be defenseless; and if fate decided that they should have a friendly Signoria, they must be prepared to make sure of it. So they agreed on this decision to wait for the Signoria and to act according to its makeup. Niccolò Fedini was one of these conspirators and acted as chancellor to them. Moved by a more certain hope of reward, he revealed all his enemies' deliberations to Piero and brought him the list of the conspirators and the enrolled members. Piero was frightened when he saw the number and character of the citizens who were opposed to him, and when he had asked his friends' advice, he decided to make a list of his friends too. He gave the job to some of his most trusted men and found the minds of the citizens so unsettled and unstable that many of those enrolled against him had also enrolled on his side.

XIV

While these things were developing in this way, the time came for the chief magistracy to be renewed. Niccolò Soderini was appointed Gonfalonier of Justice. It was a wonderful thing to see what a crowd—not only of privileged citizens but everyone—accompanied him to the palace, and on the way a garland of olive leaves was placed on his head to show that the safety and liberty of the country depended on him. This and many other examples go to show that it is not desirable to take up an office or a princedom with an excessive reputation, because one's actions cannot come up to expectations since men want more than they can accomplish, and in the end the only result is dishonor and infamy. Tommaso Soderini and Niccolò were brothers: Niccolò was more wild and bold, Tommaso was wiser. Because the latter was a great friend of Piero's, and knew his brother's mind, and only wanted the city to be free and the regime to be stabilized without anyone being hurt, he advised Niccolò to hold a new electoral scrutiny in which the voting bags were to be filled with the names of citizens who favored free government: Once this was done the regime would be stable and sound, without riots and without harm to anyone, which was what he wanted. Niccolò easily accepted his brother's advice, and he spent his period in office on these empty concerns; and his friends, the leaders of the conspiracy, allowed him to spend it like that because they were so full of envy they did not want a revolution to come about under Niccolò's authority. They always thought that they would have time to achieve the same thing with another Gonfalonier. So the end of Niccolò's period of office arrived. He had started a number of projects and finished none, and the dishonor with which he left office was greater than the honor with which he had assumed it.

XV

This example brought new life to Piero's party, his friends felt that their hopes were justified, and those who had been neutral went over to Piero. Since the scores were now equal, several months went by without any further disturbances. Nevertheless, Piero's party was getting stronger and stronger, and his enemies reacted and came together with the idea of achieving by force what they had not been able or wanted to do easily through the government officers. They agreed to assassinate Piero, who was ill at Careggi, and to get the Marquis of Ferrara to approach the city with his army for this purpose. When Piero was dead they would get the army to come into the square armed and force the Signoria to set up a constitution which fitted in with their wishes. Although all the Signoria were not well disposed toward them, they still hoped to force the opposing group to yield out of fear. Dietisalvi visited Piero often to hide his intentions better, and he spoke to him about the unity of the city and gave him advice. All these plans had been revealed to Piero. Moreover, Domenico Martelli had informed him that Francesco Neroni, Dietisalvi's brother, had tried to persuade him to join with them, telling him that victory was certain and that the game was up. So Piero decided to be the first to arm, and he took as his reason the negotiations started by his enemies with the Marquis of Ferrara. He pretended to have received a letter from Giovanni Bentivogli, prince of Bologna, telling him that the Marquis of Ferrara was at the river Albo with an army, and that they were saying publicly that they were going to Florence. So on this advice Piero armed and came to Florence surrounded by a great throng of armed men. After that, all those who belonged to his party armed, and the enemy party did the same. But Piero's party was better organized, because it was prepared. The others were not yet organized according to their plans. Dietisalvi had his houses near Piero's and he did not feel safe there, consequently he spent his time between the palace, persuading the Signoria to get Piero to lay down his arms, and Luca, keeping him faithful to their cause. But the one who turned out to be the most active of all was Niccolò Soderini, who armed and was followed by nearly all the working class of his quarter. He went to Luca's house and begged him to get on his horse and ride to the square to help the Signoria, which was on their side. Victory was certain without a doubt, and he must not stay at home to be overcome dishonorably by unarmed men. He would soon repent not having done what he would be too late to do, and if he wanted to bring about Piero's fall by war, he could easily do so; if he wanted peace, it was much better to be in a position to dictate its terms, not to receive them. These words had no effect on Luca, because he had already made up his mind and had been won over by Piero with promises of new marriage ties and new conditions. They had arranged a marriage between one of his granddaughters and Giovanni Tornabuoni. So Luca advised Niccolò to put down his arms and go home, because it should be enough for him to have the city ruled by the magistracies. This would be the result: Everyone would disarm, and the Signori, among whom their party was the stron-

235

gest, would judge their differences. Since he could not change Luca's mind, Niccolò went home, but first he said to him: "I cannot do good to my city alone, but I can prophesy trouble for her. This decision you are taking will mean the loss of our country's liberty, the end of your power and wealth, and exile for me and the others."

XVI

During these riots the Signoria had shut the Palace and had withdrawn with its officials, favoring neither party. The citizens, especially those who had belonged to Luca's party, seeing Piero armed and his enemies unarmed, began to think not how they could harm Piero but how they could become his friends. The chief citizens who were leaders of factions met in the Palace in the presence of the Signoria, and they discussed the constitution of the city and the way in which the parties could be reconciled. Because Piero could not take part owing to his physical weakness, everyone except Niccolò Soderini agreed to visit him at home. Having first placed his children and his property in Tommaso's hands, he went to his villa to wait for the final outcome, which he thought would be unpleasant for him and harmful to his country. When the other citizens reached Piero's home, one of those who had been deputed to speak complained about the riots which had broken out in the city, pointing out that the man who had armed first was most to blame. Piero had been the first to arm, and as they did not know what he wanted, they had come to hear his wishes. If they were in line with the good of the city, then they would be met. Piero replied that the cause of trouble is not he who first takes up arms, but he who is the first to give cause for people to arm. If they thought more of their behavior toward him, they would be less surprised at what he had done to save himself, because they would see that nocturnal gatherings, enrollments, and plans to take the town from him and to take his life had forced him to arm. He had not moved these arms from his house and this was an obvious sign of his intentions,

236

because he had taken them to defend himself and not to attack anyone. He wanted nothing, and desired nothing, except his own peace and security, nor had he ever shown any signs of wanting anything else, because when the authority of the *Balìa* came to an end he had never contemplated any unorthodox way of getting it back. And he was very glad that the magistracies should rule the city, if they were happy doing so. They should remember that Cosimo and his sons had been able to live with honor both with the powers of *balìa* and without them. In 1458 they had been resumed not by his house but by them, and if they did not want them now, then he did not want them either. But this was not enough for them, because he had seen that they did not think they could stay in Florence if he was there. Really he would never have dreamed of this, let alone believed it, that his and his father's friends should believe they could not live in Florence with him, who had never shown any sign of being anything but quiet and peaceful. Then he turned his attention to Dietisalvi and his brothers who were present and upbraided them in solemn, angry tones, reminding them of the benefits they had received from Cosimo, the trust that had been placed in them, and their tremendous ingratitude. His words were so effective and moved some of those present so much that if Piero had not restrained them they would have done the men some injury with their weapons. Piero ended by saying that he would approve everything that they and the Signoria decided and that he asked nothing more than to live in peace and security. After this they discussed a number of things and for the time being no decisions were reached, except a general agreement that the city must be reformed and a new constitution drawn up.

XVII

The Gonfalonier of Justice at that time was Bernardo Lotti, who was not in Piero's trust. So Piero did not feel like making any move while he was in office. But he thought this would not matter much since his period of office was nearly over. At the election of the Signori for September and October 1466, Ruberto Lioni was appointed to the chief office. As soon as he had taken office and everything else was ready, he called the people into the square and created a new *Balìa* drawn entirely from Piero's party. Soon afterwards the *Balìa* appointed magistracies congenial to the new regime. These events frightened the leaders of the enemy faction. Agnolo Acciaiuoli fled to Naples, Dietisalvi Neroni and Niccolò Soderini to Venice, and Luca Pitti stayed in Florence, trusting in Piero's promises and their new marriage ties. Those who had fled were declared rebels and the whole of the Neroni family was dispersed; and Giovanni di Nerone, who was Archbishop of Florence at that time, chose a voluntary exile in Rome to escape worse trouble. Many other citizens who left immediately were exiled to various places. And this was not enough, because a procession was arranged to thank God for the preservation of the state and the reunification of the city. During the celebrations some citizens were arrested and tortured, and then some of them were put to death and some were sent into exile. There was no more remarkable example in this revolution than that of Luca Pitti, because he immediately learned the difference between victory and defeat, between dishonor and honor. An immense solitude reigned in his houses where before they had been visited by a great many citizens. In the street his friends and relations were afraid not only to accompany him but even to greet him, because some of them had lost their privileges and some their property, and all had been equally threatened. The proud buildings that he had begun were deserted by the builders. The favors that had been done to him in the past turned into insults, the honors into abuse. Many of those who had given him something of great value in return for a favor asked for it back, as if it had been lent, and others who used to praise him to the skies now blamed him for being ungrateful and cruel. He repented too late for not having believed Niccolò Soderini and sought rather to die an honorable death with his arms in his hand than to live dishonored among his victorious enemies.

XVIII

Those who had been expelled began to think up different ways of regaining control of the city they had managed to let slip from them. However, Agnolo Acciaiuoli, who was at Naples, wanted to sound Piero before he made any new moves, to see if he could hope to be reconciled with him. He wrote him a letter in these terms: "I laugh at the tricks of Fortune, and how she makes friends become enemies and enemies friends as she pleases. You will remember how, during your father's exile, I had more regard for the injury to him than the danger to myself and was deprived of my country and almost of my life. Never while I lived with Cosimo did I fail to honor and serve your house, and after his death I have not had any intention of harming you. It is true that your ill health and the youth of your children worried me so much that I thought the constitution should be reformed so that our country would not fall after your death. This was the reason for things that were done not against you but for the good of my country, and if I made mistakes my good intentions and my past actions should cancel them out. I cannot believe that since your house has found me so faithful for so long, you will not be merciful to me now, and that having deserved so well of you, all this should be obliterated by one mistake." When he received this letter, Piero replied: "Your laughing down there is the reason why I am not weeping, because if you had been laughing in Florence, I would be weeping in Naples. I admit you loved my father, and you will admit that you had benefits from him; so your obligation was greater than ours inasmuch as deeds carry more weight than words. Since you were rewarded for your good deeds, you should not be surprised if you are receiving a just reward for evil. Patriotism cannot excuse you, because no one will ever believe that this city was less loved and enhanced by the Medici than by the Acciaiuoli. So you may continue to live without honor

239

down there, since you did not manage to live here with honor."

XIX

Agnolo gave up trying to obtain pardon and came to Rome where he met the Archbishop and other exiles, and in the strongest terms they could they tried to discredit the Medici account in Rome. Piero had difficulty in preventing this, but he had help from his friends, and their plot failed. Dietisalvi and Niccolò Soderini, for their part, tried very hard to persuade the Venetian Senate to attack their country, reckoning that if the Florentines were faced with a new war they would not be able to stand up to it, because the government was new and unpopular. At Ferrara at that time was Giovan Francesco, the son of Palla Strozzi, who had been expelled with his father from Florence in the revolution of 1434. He had a great deal of credit, and the other merchants judged him to be very rich. These new rebels pointed out to Giovan Francesco how easy it would be to go back home if the Venetians made an attack. And they thought that they might easily do this if some contribution could be made to the expense; otherwise they thought it was unlikely. Giovan Francesco, who wanted to be revenged for the injuries he had received, easily believed their advice and promised to help the campaign with all the means at his disposal. So they went to the Doge and complained to him about their exile, which they said they were suffering for no other crime than that they wanted their country to live according to the laws and the magistracies to be honored rather than a few citizens. For this reason, Piero de' Medici and some of his followers, who were accustomed to living like despots, had armed by trickery, had made them disarm by trickery, and then by trickery had expelled them from their country. And not content with this, they used God as a means of oppressing many others who, trusting in a promise, had stayed behind in the city. They told how during public and holy ceremonies and solemn prayers, so that God should have a part in their betrayals, many citizens were imprisoned and put to death, which was an example of impiety and wickedness. They did not know where to turn with more hope of being able to take revenge than to the Senate, which, having always been free, must take pity on those who had lost their liberty. So they were setting free men against despots, and the pious against the impious. They reminded them how the Medici family had taken the dominion over Lombardy from them when Cosimo, against the will of the other citizens, had favored and aided Francesco against the Senate. So if they were not moved by their just cause, then they ought to be moved by their own just hatred and their just desire for vengeance.

XX

These last words moved the whole Senate, and they decided that Bartolomeo Colleoni, their captain, should attack Florentine territory. At the earliest possible date the army was assembled, and it was joined by Ercole da Este, sent by Borso, Marquis of Ferrara. On their first attack, before the Florentines were in battle order, they burned the village of Dovadola and did some damage in the surrounding country. But the Florentines, once the party opposed to Piero had been expelled, had made a new league with Galeazzo, Duke of Milan, and with King Ferrando, and had hired as their captain Federigo, Count of Urbino. So now that they were on good terms with their friends, they were less worried about their enemies. Ferrando sent his eldest son Alfonso, and Galeazzo came in person, both of them with a suitably large army. They made their headquarters at Castracaro, a Florentine castle at the foot of the mountains that go down from Tuscany to Romagna. Meanwhile, the enemy had retreated toward Imola, and so a few light skirmishes took place between the armies, as was the custom in those times. Neither of them attacked or fought for towns, nor was the enemy given a chance to do battle, but each

241

side kept to their tents and both behaved with amazing cowardice. This annoyed Florence, because she saw herself saddled with a fairly costly war from which she could hope for very little, and the officials complained to the citizens they had appointed as commissioners to direct the war. They replied that it was all the fault of Duke Galeazzo, who had a great deal of power and very little experience, and so could not make the right decisions, but did not trust those who could. It would be impossible to do anything right or useful while he stayed with the army. So the Florentines gave the Duke to understand that it had been very useful and convenient for them to have him come to their aid personally, because such a reputation as his was likely to frighten the enemy; nevertheless, they put his own safety and that of his state above their own convenience. If he were safe, then they hoped everything else would prosper; but if he were to suffer, then they could fear all kinds of trouble. They felt it was not very safe for him to be absent from Milan for very long, since he had recently come to power and had powerful, untrustworthy neighbors, and anyone who wanted to engage in intrigue against him could do so very easily. So they advised him to go back to his country and leave some of his troops to defend them. Galeazzo fell in with this advice and went back to Milan without worrying anymore. Left without this hindrance, the Florentine captains moved up closer to the enemy to show that they had been right in accusing him of being the cause of their slowness. And they held a pitched battle which lasted half a day without either side giving in. Nobody died in it, however; there were only some horses wounded and a few prisoners taken by either side. Winter had already come, when it was customary for the armies to go into barracks. Bartolomeo retreated toward Ravenna, the Florentine troops to Tuscany, and those of the King and Duke each returned to their masters' states. But as there had been no rising in Florence at the time of this attack, as the Florentine rebels had promised, and also as there was not enough money to pay the soldiers, an agreement was sought and concluded after only a few negotiations.

The Florentine rebels, entirely without hope, left for different places. Dietisalvi went to Ferrara where he was received and kept by the Marquis Borso; Niccolò Soderini went to Ravenna where, with a small pension from the Venetians, he grew old and died. He was considered a just and courageous man, who was hesitant and slow in making decisions, which meant that when he was Gonfalonier of Justice he lost the opportunity of success, which later as a private citizen he wanted to get back and could not.

XXI

Once peace had been made, those citizens who had got the upper hand in Florence did not feel that they had won unless they inflicted all kinds of injuries not only on their enemies but also on those who were suspect to their party. They arranged with Bardo Altoviti, who was Gonfalonier of Justice, to take privileges away from a great many citizens and to send many others into exile. This increased their power and added to the fears of the rest. They used this power unchecked and behaved in such a way that it looked as if God and Fortune had given the city over to them as a prize. Piero heard little of this and what he did hear he could do nothing about, because he was laboring under ill health. He was so paralyzed that he could use nothing but his tongue. The only thing he could do was warn them and ask them to conduct themselves in a civilized manner, to enjoy their country but keep her safe and not destroy her.

To amuse the city, he decided to put on a magnificent display for the wedding of his son, Lorenzo, whom he had betrothed to Clarice, of the Orsini family. The wedding was celebrated with the pomp and splendor fitting to such a man. Several days were spent in different kinds of balls, banquets, and performances of ancient plays. Added to these there were two military displays to demonstrate the greatness of the house of Medici and the regime. One was done by men on horseback who staged a battle skirmish, the other showed the storming of a city. Both were carried out with the greatest possible precision and *virtù*.

XXII

While these things were going on in Florence, the rest of Italy was living in peace but in great fear of the power of the Turk. The latter was making repeated attacks on the Christians and had taken Negroponte, much to the dishonor and hurt of Christendom. At this time, Borso, Marquis of Ferrara, died, and his brother Ercole succeeded him. Gismondo da Rimini, a lifelong enemy of the Church, died and his natural son Roberto was left as heir to his state. Later he was one of the most brilliant war leaders in Italy. Pope Paul died, and Sixtus IV was appointed his successor. He was called Francesco da Savona before, and was of very lowly and humble origins, but because of his qualities he had become general of the Order of St. Francis and then Cardinal. This Pope was the first to begin to show what a Pope could do, and how many things once considered wrong could be hidden under papal authority. He had in his household Piero and Girolamo, who were generally believed to be his sons. He disguised them under more respectable names, however. Piero, because he was a monk, he raised to the rank of Cardinal, with the title of San Sisto. He gave Girolamo the city of Forlì, taking it from Antonio Ordelaffi, whose forefathers had been rulers of the town for a long time. This ambitious behavior gained him the respect of the princes of Italy, and they each tried to win his friendship. The Duke of Milan gave Girolamo Catherine, his natural daughter, as his wife, and as her dowry the city of Imola, which he had taken from Taddeo degli Alidosi. Then the Duke and King Ferrando made new marriage ties between themselves, because Elisabella, the daughter of the King's eldest son Alfonso, was betrothed to the Duke's eldest son Giovan Galeazzo.

XXIII

So Italy was living fairly peacefully, and the princes' major preoccupation was to watch each other and to tie each other down by marriages, new friendships, and alliances. However, despite the peace, Florence was torn apart by her citizens, and Piero, hampered by his illness, could not stand up to their ambitions. Nevertheless, to ease his conscience and to see if he could shame them, he called them all to his house and made this speech to them: "I would never have believed that a time would come when my friends' methods and behavior would make me long for my enemies and that victory would make me desire defeat. I thought I had with me men who knew how to control their greed, and for whom it would be enough to live safe and honored in their own country and to be revenged on their enemies. But now I know that I was very much mistaken, and I had little idea of men's natural ambitions, and even less of yours. Because it is not enough for you to be rulers of such a great city and to share among the few of you the honors, dignities, and profits that once belonged to many more citizens. It is not enough for you to share your enemies' property among yourselves. It is not enough for you to be able to inflict the burdens of the state on all the others, while you are free of them and enjoy all its amenities. You deprive your neighbor of his goods, you sell justice, you avoid civic judgments, you oppress peaceful men and exalt the aggressive. I do not believe that there are so many instances of violence and greed in the whole of Italy as there are in this city. Has our country given us life for us to take life from her? Has she made us victorious for us to destroy her? Has she honored us for us to put her to shame? I promise you by the faith that good men give and receive, that if you continue to act so that I repent of having won, I too will act so that you repent of having misused your victory." The citizens gave a reply suitable to the time and place, but they did not give up their evil ways. So Piero had Agnolo Acciaiuoli come secretly to Cafaggiuolo, and he spoke to him at length about the state of the city. And there is no doubt that if he had not been interrupted by death, he would have repatriated all the exiles to check the ravages of those at home. But death thwarted his good intentions, and he died in the fifty-third year of life, weighed down with physical illness and mental worries. His country could not fully recognize his *virtù* and goodness because he had been with Cosimo his father until almost the very end of his life, and those few years by which he survived him were spent in illness and civic strife. Piero was buried in the church of San Lorenzo near his father; and his funeral was celebrated with the pomp that so great a citizen deserved. He left two sons, Lorenzo and Giuliano, who, although they both roused hopes of being of great service to the republic, nevertheless frightened everyone because of their youth.

XXIV

One of the chief citizens in the government of Florence, and by far superior to the rest, was Tommaso Soderini, whose prudence and influence were known not only in Florence but to all the princes of Italy. After Piero's death the whole city looked to him; and many citizens visited him at home as if he were head of the town, and many princes wrote to him. Being wise, and knowing his own fortune and that of the Medici very well, he did not reply to the princes' letters, and he gave the citizens to understand that they should be visiting the Medici house and not his. To give force to his recommendations, he assembled all the heads of the noble families in the monastery of Sant' Antonio and arranged for Lorenzo and Giuliano de' Medici to be there. He made a long, serious speech about the state of the city and of Italy, and about the policies of the Italian rulers. He concluded that if they wanted to live together peacefully in Florence, free from internal divisions and foreign wars, then they must honor these young men and maintain the reputation of their house. Men never complain at having to do things they are used to, but new ways are given up as quickly as they are accepted. It was always more simple to maintain a regime, which because it had lasted a long time had put an end to envy, than to establish a new one which could easily be overthrown for all kinds of reasons. Lorenzo spoke after Tommaso, and although he was young, he spoke with so much good sense and modesty that he roused hopes that he would become what in fact he did become later. And before they left, those citizens swore they would treat them as sons, and the young men would consider them as fathers. Once this decision was made Lorenzo and Giuliano were honored as rulers of the state. And they did nothing without Tommaso's advice.

XXV

Life went on fairly quietly at home and abroad, as there was no war to disturb the general peace. Then an unexpected disturbance arose which was a kind of harbinger of the trouble to come. Among the families which had fallen with Luca Pitti's party were the Nardi. Salvestro and his brothers, the heads of the family, were first exiled and then declared rebels because of the war started by Bartolomeo Colleoni. Among them was Bernardo, Salvestro's brother, a lively, bold young man. He could not bear exile because of his poverty, and seeing no way of returning because of the peace that had been made, he decided to start something that might give rise to a new war. Very often a small beginning brings about effective results, because men are more prepared to fall in with something that has already been started than to start something themselves. Bernardo had a lot of friends in Prato and even more in the *contado* of Pistoia, particularly among the Palandra, a family with many men, although they were from the *contado,* who like the other Pistoians were brought up amid fighting and bloodshed. He knew they were dissatisfied because they had been badly treated by the Florentine officials in their disagreements. Besides this, he knew the feelings of the Pratese: how they believed they had been treated high-handedly and exploited, and he knew that some of them were ill-disposed toward the regime. All this made him hope that he could kindle a fire in Tuscany by making Prato rebel, and that so many others would then join to fan the flames that there would not be enough people to put it out. Bernardo communicated his plan to Dietisalvi and asked him, if he managed to occupy Prato, what help Dietisalvi might be able to get him from the Italian princes. Dietisalvi thought the enterprise most dangerous and almost impossible to bring off. However, seeing that he could try his luck again at others' risk, he urged him on, promising him definite help from Bologna and Ferrara, if he managed to hold and defend Prato for fifteen days at least. This promise filled Bernardo with high hopes and he went secretly to Prato, divulged his plans to some of his friends, and found them very willing to join in. He found the same spirit and will among the Palandra, and when they had agreed on the time and the method, Bernardo let Dietisalvi know exactly how things stood.

XXVI

Cesare Petrucci was Podestà of Prato on behalf of the people of Florence. These governors of towns have the habit of keeping the keys of the gates about them, and, particularly at times when there is no fear of danger, they give them to any of the townsfolk who ask for them so that they can come and go at night. Bernardo, who knew this habit, presented himself shortly before daylight, with the Palandra and about a hundred armed men, at the gate that looks toward Pistoia. Those inside who were in the know armed too, and one of them asked the Podestà for the keys, pretending that someone from the town was asking for them to get in. The Podestà, who could have no suspicions of anything like this, sent one of his servants with the keys, and when the man was some way from the Palace the keys were taken from him by the conspirators, the gate was opened, and Bernardo and his soldiers were let in. They joined and divided into two parties: One of them was guided by Salvestro Pratese and occupied the citadel, and the other under Bernardo took the Palace. And Cesare with all his household were given to some of them to guard. Then they raised a riot by going through the town and shouting the name of liberty. It was already light and at the noise many *popolani* ran into the square, and hearing how the citadel and Palace had been occupied and the Podestà and his men taken, they wondered how such a thing could have happened. The eight citizens who hold the chief office in the town met in their palace to take counsel as to what should be done. But Bernardo, having ridden through the town with his men for some time and seeing that no one was following him, went to the Eight, whom he heard were meeting, and told them that the aim of his attack was to free them and his country from slavery. He told them how much glory they would earn if they took up arms and accompanied him in this glorious campaign in which they would gain perpetual peace and eternal fame. He reminded them of their ancient liberty and their present state, and he explained that help was certain if they resisted, for a very few days, such forces as the Florentines could manage to get together. He said that he was in touch with friends in Florence who would come out into the open as soon as they heard this town was united behind him. These words had no effect on the Eight and they replied that they did not know whether Florence lived in freedom or in servitude, as it was none of their business, but they knew very well that they had never wanted any other liberty than to serve the magistracies that ruled Florence. The magistracies had never subjected them to any injustice that would warrant their taking up arms against them. So they advised him to set the Podestà free and to relieve the town of his troops, and get himself quickly out of the danger his lack of prudence had got him into. These words did not frighten Bernardo, but he decided to see if the Pratese would be affected by fear, since requests had had no effect. To frighten them, he decided to put

Cesare to death. He brought him out of prison and ordered him to be hanged at the palace windows. Cesare was already near the windows with the rope around his neck when he saw Bernardo, who was trying to hurry on his execution. He turned to him and said: "Bernardo, you are putting me to death because you think that afterwards the Pratese will follow you, but the opposite will happen; these people so revere the magistrates that the people of Florence send, that when they see the wrong you are doing me, they will stir up so much hatred against you that it will end in your downfall. Not my death but my life might cause your victory, because if I order them to do whatever you want, they will obey me rather than you; and if I follow your orders you will achieve your ambition." Bernardo who was short of ideas felt that this was good advice, and he ordered Cesare to go out onto a balcony overlooking the square and command the people to obey him. When Cesare had done this, he was sent back to prison.

XXVII

The conspirators' weakness was already laid bare, and many Florentines who lived in the town had formed a group, among whom was Giorgio Ginori, a knight of Rhodes. He was the first to start a fight with them, and he attacked Bernardo who was riding around the square —now entreating, now threatening the people—to make them follow and obey him. He was set upon by many of Giorgio's followers, wounded, and taken prisoner. Once this was done it was easy enough to free the Podestà and overcome the others, and they were nearly all captured or killed since they were few in number and split into several groups. Meanwhile, news of these events had reached Florence, much magnified, so that they heard Prato had been taken, the Podestà and his family were put to death, and the town was full of enemies. Pistoia was said to be up in arms and many of its citizens a party to the plot. The Palace immediately filled with citizens, and they met to take counsel with the Signoria.

In Florence at that time was Roberto da San Severino, a very famous general. It was decided to send him to Prato with the largest number of men he could muster, and they ordered him to approach the city and send back a full report on the situation, taking what measures he considered to be necessary. Roberto had gone little further than the castle of Campi when he was met by a messenger from Cesare, who told him that Bernardo had been taken and his companions put to flight or killed, and that all the fighting was over. So he returned to Florence, and soon afterwards Bernardo was brought there. When the government asked him the reason for his exploit and found it unconvincing, he said that he had done it because he had decided to die in Florence rather than live in exile, and he wanted his death at least to be distinguished by some memorable deed.

XXVIII

After this revolt, which had broken out and been quelled almost at the same time, the citizens went back to their normal way of living, thinking that they could enjoy without responsibilities the regime they had established. For the city this gave rise to the troubles which usually arise during peacetime, because the young men, who were freer than usual, spent excessive amounts on clothes, banquets, and other such luxuries, and because they were idle they squandered their time and money on games and women. Their chief care was to appear magnificently dressed and be wise and witty in conversation, and the one who was best at scoring off the others was the cleverest and the most admired. This sort of behavior was aggravated by the courtiers of the Duke of Milan, who came to Florence with his wife and all the ducal court to fulfil a vow, as he said. He was received with the pomp befitting such a prince and such a friend of the city. Then something was seen in our city which had not been seen before. It was Lent, when the Church commands that no meat shall be eaten, but the Duke's court ate nothing but meat, showing respect neither for the

Church nor God. Many plays were given in his honor, among them a representation in the church of Santo Spirito of the gift of the Holy Spirit to the Apostles. Because of the number of fires that are lit for this kind of solemn celebration, the whole church caught fire, and many people thought that God was angry with us and had wanted to show this sign of His anger. If the Duke found the city of Florence full of courtly frivolities and customs contrary to all well-ordered societies, he left it even more so. And good citizens felt that they must put a stop to this, and by a new law they put an end to showy fashions, burial feasts, and banquets.

XXIX

In the middle of this period of peace a new and un-looked-for disturbance broke out in Tuscany. In the *contado* of Volterra some of the citizens found beds of alum. They realized their importance and approached some Florentine citizens for financial help and backing, and allowed them a share in the profits. To begin with, as very often happens with new enterprises, the affair did not interest the people of Volterra, but as time went on and they realized how profitable it was, they tried to make up for their neglect. But they were too late and had no success, whereas they would have been successful earlier on. The affair began to exercise their councils, where it was said that it was not right for an industry based on public land to be put to private profit. They sent ambassadors to Florence to present this point of view. The case was entrusted to some citizens who, either because they had been bribed by the party or because they felt it was right, reported that the people of Volterra were asking for something unjust, when they wanted to deprive the citizens of Florence of the fruits of their labors; therefore the alum works belonged to private owners and not to the people, but it would be right for the citizens to pay a certain sum of money each year as a sign that they recognized the people of Volterra as the landlord. This reply had the effect of increasing rather than calming the riots and the antagonism in Volterra, and nothing else was discussed throughout the whole city and in the councils. The common people wanted to get back what they felt had been taken from them, and the private citizens wanted to keep what they had first acquired and then had had confirmed as theirs by the Florentine verdict. Things reached such a pitch that a well-known citizen of the town, called Pecorino, was killed, and after him many others who had sided with him, and their houses were plundered and burned. Filled with the same urge, the rioters barely stopped short of murdering the magistrates who represented the Florentine people in Volterra.

XXX

After this first insult, they decided first of all to send ambassadors to Florence. These ambassadors gave the Signori to understand that if they wanted to keep the old agreements, then they would also maintain the city in her old subjection. Tommaso Soderini advised that the Volterrans should be welcomed whatever way they chose to come back, as he did not feel that it was a good time to kindle a flame so near home that it could burn our house down. He was afraid of the Pope's temperament and the power of the King. And he did not trust the alliance with the Venetians or the Duke, not knowing how much faith existed in the one or how much *virtù* in the other. He recalled the old saying: "Better a thin agreement than a fat victory." On the other hand, Lorenzo de' Medici felt this was a chance to show what he could do by relying on his own counsel and prudence, particularly as he was urged to do this by those who envied Tommaso his power, and he decided to start a campaign and punish the arrogance of the Volterrans by using force. He said that if he did not make an example of them, others would lose all respect and reverence and would not be afraid to do the same thing for the slightest reason. Once war had been decided upon, a reply was sent to Volterra, saying that they could not demand the observance of the agreements they themselves had broken, and they should either put their case into the hands of the Signoria or expect war. When the Volterran ambassadors had returned with this reply, they prepared to defend the town by fortifying it and by sending to all the Italian rulers to get help. They were heard by very few, and only the Sienese and the Lord of Piombino held out any hope of help. For their part, the Florentines felt that their hope of victory lay in speed, and they collected ten thousand foot soldiers and two thousand horse, under the command of Federigo, Lord of Urbino; and they arrived at the *contado* of Volterra and occupied it easily. Then they laid siege to the city. Because it is on a hill and cut off on almost every side, they could only fight on the side where the church of Sant' Alessandro is. The Volterrans had hired about a thousand soldiers for their defense. When these men saw the brisk attack the Florentines were making, they gave up hope of being able to defend the town, and they were slow in their defense but swift to injure the Volterrans every day. So those poor citizens were fighting the enemy outside, and they were being bullied by their friends at home. They gave up hope of success and began to think of coming to terms, but they found this no better and therefore put themselves in the commissioners' hands. The commissioners had the gates opened and let most of the army in, and they went to the Palace where their Priors were. They ordered the Priors to go back to their homes, and on the way one of them was robbed and insulted by one of the soldiers. The destruction and sack of the city grew from this beginning, since men are more prone to evil than to good. The city was plundered and overrun for one whole day; women and holy places were not spared; and the soldiers, both those who had failed to defend the town and those who had besieged it, emptied it of its wealth. News of this victory was received with immense joy by the Florentines, and because it had been Lorenzo's idea entirely, his reputation increased enormously. One of Tommaso Soderini's most intimate friends reproached him for his advice and said: "What have you to say now that we have got Volterra?" Tommaso replied: "I feel that Volterra is lost; because if you had won it by agreement you would have got both profit and security; but since you must hold it by force, in difficult times it will bring you weakness and trouble, and in peacetime difficulty and expense."

XXXI

At this time the Pope, who was anxious to keep the states of the Church in subjection, had had Spoleto sacked after it had rebelled because of its internal factions. Later he had besieged Città di Castello because it was in the same state of insubordination. The ruler of the town was Niccolò Vitelli. He was very friendly with Lorenzo de' Medici, who did not fail to send him aid. It was not enough to defend Niccolò, however, but it was sufficient to sow the first seeds of enmity between Sixtus and the Medici; and very shortly they bore very evil fruit. This fruit would not have been long in appearing if the death of Friar Piero, Cardinal of Santo Sisto, had not taken place. This Cardinal had gone around Italy and had been to Venice and Milan with the excuse of honoring the wedding of Ercole, Marquis of Ferrara, and he had sounded the rulers to see how they were disposed toward the Florentines. But he died when he got back to Rome, and there was some suspicion that he had been poisoned by the Venetians, because they feared the power Sixtus would have if he was allowed to make use of Friar Piero's intelligence and ability. Although Nature had made Piero of humble birth and he had been brought up modestly within the walls of a monastery, no sooner had he been made a Cardinal than he showed so much pride and ambition that not only the cardinalate but the pontificate itself was not big enough for him. He had no qualms about holding a banquet in Rome that would have been considered extravagant for a king: He spent more than twenty thousand florins on it. After Sixtus had lost this minister he went on more slowly with his plans. Nevertheless, when the Florentines, the Duke, and the Venetians had renewed the alliance and had left an opportunity for the Pope and the King to join it, Sixtus and the King made an agreement too, leaving the other princes free to take part in that. Already one could see Italy divided into two camps, because every day something happened to stir up hatred between these two alliances. It happened over the island of Cyprus, to which King Ferrando had aspirations, and which the Venetians occupied. This brought the Pope and the King closer together. In Italy at that time Federigo, Prince of Urbino, was considered an outstanding soldier, and he had campaigned for the Florentine people for a long time. The King and the Pope decided to win Federigo over so that the enemy alliance would be without his leadership. The Pope advised him, and the King asked him to visit him in Naples. Federigo obeyed, much to the Florentines' surprise and annoyance, for they thought that the same thing would happen to him as had happened to Iacopo Piccinino. But, in fact, the opposite happened. Federigo came back from Naples and Rome laden with honors, having been made general of their league. Nor did the King and the Pope fail to try to win over the Lords of Romagna and the people of Siena to become allies so that they could do more harm to the Florentines with their help. The Florentines realized this and armed themselves with every possible defense against their ambition. Having lost Federigo da Urbino, they hired Roberto da Rimini. They renewed their alliance with the Perugians and made an agreement with the Lord of Fienza. The Pope and the King gave as the reason for their hatred of the Florentines the fact that they wanted the Florentines to break their alliance with the Venetians and join theirs instead. The Pope thought that the Church could not maintain its standing, nor Count Girolamo keep his states in Romagna, if the Florentines and the Venetians were united. On the other hand, the Florentines were afraid that the Pope and the King wanted to turn them against the Venetians, not because they wanted their friendship but in order to attack them more easily. These fears and contrasting aims persisted in Italy for two years before any trouble arose. But the first to arise, although it was slight, was in Tuscany.

XXXII

Braccio da Perugia, a man who was very famous in war, as we have often explained, left two sons: Oddo and Carlo. The latter was very young, the other had been killed by the men of the Lamona Valley, as we mentioned earlier. When Carlo had reached military age he was taken on by the Venetians as one of the generals of the republic because of his father's memory and the promise he showed. At that time he came to the end of a period of service, and he did not want it renewed by the Senate for the time being. Instead, he decided to see if with his name and his father's reputation he could get back his state of Perugia. The Venetians easily consented, as they knew that revolutions always increased their power. Carlo entered Tuscany, and finding the Perugia venture difficult because of the alliance with the Florentines, and yet wanting his move to produce some memorable achievement, he attacked the Sienese, saying that they owed him money for services his father had done them in the affairs of their republic, and that he wanted satisfaction. He attacked them with such force that he turned nearly all their territory upside down. As the Sienese readily believe ill of the Florentines, when they saw the damage, they were convinced that everything had been done with their consent, and they showered the Pope and the King with complaints. They also sent ambassadors to Florence, who complained of the injustice and proved skillfully that Carlo could not have attacked them in such safety if he had not been helped. The Florentines made their excuses, saying that they would do everything they could to prevent Carlo from troubling them, and ordered Carlo to stop attacking Siena as the ambassadors asked. Carlo complained at this, saying that the Florentines had lost a great conquest by not helping him and that they had deprived him of great glory. He promised them they would have taken possession of the town in a very short time, as he had found it so cowardly and so badly organized for defense. So Carlo left and went back

257

to his old position with the Venetians. The Sienese were still very angry with the Florentines, although they had been freed from danger by them. But the Sienese did not feel that they owed anything to people who had rescued them from trouble which they had caused.

XXXIII

While these affairs we have described above were taking place between the King and the Pope, and in Tuscany, an event of greater importance occurred in Lombardy, and one that heralded greater trouble. In Milan, teaching Latin to the young noblemen of the city, was Cola Montano, an ambitious man of letters. Either because he hated the life the Duke was leading, or for some other reason, in all his lectures he criticized life under a bad prince and called glorious and happy those whom Nature and Fortune had allowed to be born in a republic. He argued that all famous men had been brought up in republics and not under princes; because the former encourage virtuous men, while the latter do away with them; republics make use of men's *virtù*, princes fear it. The young men with whom he was most friendly were Giovannandrea Lampognano, Carlo Visconti, and Girolamo Olgiato. He spoke to them several times about the ruler's evil nature and the wretchedness of those who were ruled by him. And he gained such a hold over the minds and wills of those youths that he made them swear that when they were of an age they would free their country from the tyranny of that prince. So the young men were fired with this ambition which grew with the years, and the Duke's behavior and the personal injuries directed against them made them hasten to put it into effect. Galeazzo was lecherous and cruel; frequent examples of both vices had earned him a great deal of hatred. It was not enough for him to seduce noblewomen, he also enjoyed broadcasting the fact; added to this he was not happy having men put to death unless they were killed in some cruel way. He was not above suspicion of having killed his mother. He did not feel that he was prince while she was there, so he treated her so badly that she began to want to retire to her dower house at Cremona. On the journey she died of a sudden illness, and many people thought that her death had been arranged by her son. The Duke had humiliated Carlo and Girolamo over some women, and he had refused to let Giovannandrea have possession of the Abbey of Miramondo, which the Pope had assigned to a relative of his. These personal insults increased these young men's desire to free their country from such ills by taking their revenge, and they hoped that whenever they succeeded in killing him they would be followed not only by many of the nobles but by all the people. Once they had decided to undertake the task, they often met together, but they aroused no suspicion because of their old friendship. They talked about nothing but their plot, and to keep up their courage they struck each other on the legs and chest with the sheaths of the swords they had destined for the deed. They discussed the time and the place: In the Castle it did not seem safe; out hunting it was risky and dangerous; while the Duke was out in the town it would be impossibly difficult; and at a banquet uncertain. So they decided to assassinate him on some public ceremonial occasion where they would be sure he was coming, and they would be able to muster their friends on various pretexts. They also agreed that if any of them was held for any reason by someone from the Court, then the others would kill him by the sword and with the help of the armed enemies.

XXXIV

It was 1476 and the Christmas celebrations were near. On St. Stephen's Day the prince used to visit the church of the martyr in great pomp, so they decided this was the right time and place to carry out their plot. On the morning of that day they armed some of their most trusted friends and servants, telling them that they were to go to help Giovannandrea, who wanted to build an aqueduct on his land against the wishes of some of his rivals. They took them to the church armed, saying that they wanted to take leave of the prince before they left. They also got several of their other friends and relations to be there on different pretexts, hoping that once the deed was done they would all follow them in the rest of their plot. Once the prince was dead, their idea was to go with the armed men to the part of the city where they thought they could most easily rouse the populace and arm them against the Duchess and the heads of the government. They reckoned the people would follow them easily because of the hunger they suffered, and they planned to give them the houses of Cecco Simonetta, Giovanni Botti, and Francesco Lucani to plunder, all of whom were leaders of the government. In this way they hoped to ensure their own safety and give the people their liberty. This was the plan; they confirmed their intentions of carrying it out, then Giovannandrea and the others went to the church early. They heard Mass together, and then Giovannandrea turned to a statue of St. Ambrose and said, "O patron of our city, you know our minds and the reason why we are running so many risks, smile upon our plans; and show how much you hate injustice by favoring justice." Meanwhile, the Duke received many signs of his impending death before he reached the church. When it was light he put on a breastplate, as he often used to do, but he took it off again right away, as if it was annoying or hurting him. Then he wanted to hear Mass at the castle and found that his chaplain had gone to Santo Stefano with all his chapel furnishings. Then he wanted the Bishop of Como to celebrate Mass instead, but the latter put forward several reasonable objections. So he was almost forced to decide to go to the church. Before he left he called for Giovangaleazzo and Ermes his sons and embraced and kissed them over and over again, and did not seem able to tear himself away from them. However, in the end he decided to go, left the castle, and went to the church between the ambassadors of Ferrara and Mantua. Meanwhile, the conspirators had withdrawn into a room belonging to the chief priest of the church, a friend of theirs, in order to arouse less suspicion and to get out of the bitter cold. Hearing that the Duke was coming, they went into the church. Giovan-nandrea and Girolamo stationed themselves on the right of the entrance to the church and Carlo on the left. Those who preceded the Duke were already coming into the church; then he entered surrounded by a vast throng, as befitted the ducal splendor in that ceremony. The first to move were Lampognano and Girolamo. Pretending to make way for the Duke, they got closer to him, gripped their weapons which were short and sharp, and had been hidden in their sleeves, and fell upon him. Lampognano wounded him twice, once in the stomach and once in the throat; Girolamo also stabbed him in the throat and in the chest. Carlo Visconti, because he had been nearer the door and the Duke had passed beyond him, could not strike him in front when the Duke was attacked by his companions, but he stabbed him twice, in the back and in the shoulder. These six wounds were so swift and sud-den that the Duke was on the ground before anybody realized what was happening. He could not do or say anything, except that as he fell he called out the name of Our Lady once. When the Duke fell, there was uproar. Swords were drawn, and as happens in sudden crises some people fled from the church, others ran toward the trouble without knowing anything about it. Nevertheless, those who had been nearest to the Duke, having seen him killed and recognizing the assassins, followed them. Of the conspirators, Giovannandrea tried to escape from the church and hid among the women. There were a great many of them, sitting on the ground as they usually do. He was held up by being entangled in their clothing, and a Moor, the Duke's groom, caught up with him and killed him. Carlo was also killed by some bystanders. But Giro-lamo Olgiato got out of the church in the throng, and seeing his comrades dead and not knowing where else to go he went to his own home, where his father and brothers refused to admit him. Only his mother took pity on her son and recommended him to a priest who was an old friend of the family. He dressed Girolamo up in some of his clothes and took him home. He stayed there for two days, hoping there would be a revolution in Milan that would save him. But this did not happen, and

261

fearing that he might be discovered there he tried to escape incognito. But he was recognized and taken into custody, and he revealed the entire structure of the plot. Girolamo was twenty-three, and he was no less courageous in death than he had been in action. Naked, facing the executioner who had the knife in his hand ready to strike him, he said these words, in Latin because he was an educated man: *"Mors acerba, fama perpetua, stabit vetus memoria facti."*

These unfortunate young men's plot was secretly laid and boldly executed. They came to grief when those they hoped would follow and defend them neither defended them nor followed them. Let princes learn to live so that they are honored and loved and so that no one hopes to save themselves by killing them. And may the rest realize how futile it is to trust too much in a mob to follow and help them, however discontented it may be. This affair frightened all Italy, but still more frightening was what happened in Florence shortly afterwards. It broke the peace that had lasted for twelve years in Italy, as we will explain in the following book, which, if it has a sad and tragic ending, has a bloody and fearful beginning.

BOOK VIII

Since this eighth book begins in the midst of two conspiracies—one already described, which took place in Milan, the other about to be described, which took place in Florence—it might seem right, if we wanted to follow our custom, to discuss the nature and importance of conspiracies. I would be pleased to do this if I had not already spoken about them elsewhere, and if it was a subject that could be dismissed briefly. But as it is something that needs a great deal of consideration and has already been discussed elsewhere, we will leave it alone. Passing on to another subject, we will describe how once the Medici regime had repulsed all the attacks to which it had been subjected openly, it had also to get the better of those who were plotting against it secretly, if it wanted the family to have supreme power in the city and stand out above the others for good citizenship. Because while the Medici were on an equal footing with some of the other families they were opposing, the citizens who envied their power could openly oppose them without fear of being suppressed in the early stages of their opposition. Since the magistracies were now free, neither of the parties had any reason to fear until after they had lost. But after the victory of 1466, the government was so restricted in favor of the Medici who took so much power that those who were dissatisfied either had to tolerate that way of living patiently, or if they wanted to put an end to it they had to try to do so by plotting in secret. Because conspiracies rarely succeed, they most often bring about the ruin of those who plan them, and they bring greatness to those against whom they are directed. The ruler of a city who is conspired against in this way, if he is not assassinated like the Duke of Milan, which seldom happens, almost always achieves greater power, and very often if he was good previously he be-

263

comes bad. By their example, conspiracies give him a reason for fear: Fear makes him protect himself, and this protection in turn leads to injustice. This gives rise to hatred and very often his downfall is the result. Thus these conspiracies destroy their organizers immediately, and in the long run harm the man against whom they are first directed.

II

As we have explained above, Italy was divided into two camps; the Pope and the King on one side, the Venetians, the Duke, and the Florentines on the other. Although they were not yet in a state of open war, new reasons for opening hostilities arose between them every day. The Pope especially tried to harm Florence in everything he did. On the death of Filippo de' Medici, Archbishop of Pisa, the Pope, against the wishes of the Signoria of Florence, invested Francesco Salviati with the bishopric, a man he knew to be unfriendly to the Medici. The Signoria did not want to let him have possession, and new disputes arose between them and the Pope in the handling of this affair. Besides this, the Pope was doing the Pazzi family great favors in Rome and undermining the Medici in everything he did.

The Pazzi outshone all the other Florentine families at that time, both in their wealth and in their nobility. Their head was Iacopo, who had been made a knight by the people because of his wealth and nobility. He had no children except a natural daughter. He did have a great many nephews, the children of his brothers Piero and Antonio. The first of these were Guglielmo, Francesco, Rinato, Giovanni, and then Andrea, Niccolò, and Galeotto. Cosimo de' Medici, seeing their wealth and nobility, had married Bianca, his granddaughter, to Guglielmo, hoping that the match would make the families more united and would do away with feuds and hatreds, which most often are caused by fear. However, men's plans are so unreliable that things turned out otherwise. Lorenzo's advisers told him how dangerous to him and detrimental to his authority it was to allow citizens to have both riches and power. This meant that Iacopo and his nephews were not allowed the degree of honor that the other citizens considered they deserved. This gave rise to the first feeling of anger on the part of the Pazzi and the first fear among the Medici, and as the one grew it gave reason for the other to grow. So in any affair where other citizens were involved, the Pazzi were frowned upon by the government. While Francesco de' Pazzi was in Rome, the Eight forced him to come back to Florence for a trivial reason, without paying him the respect due to important citizens. The Pazzi complained everywhere in angry, abusive terms, and this added to the general fear and thus to the attacks upon the Pazzi. Giovanni de' Pazzi's wife was the daughter of Giovanni Buonromei, a very rich man, whose property all went to his daughter when he died, as he had no other children. However, his nephew Carlo took over some of the property, and when the case came to be disputed, a law was passed by which Giovanni de' Pazzi's wife was deprived of her father's inheritance, and it was given to Carlo. The Pazzi blamed this injustice on the Medici. Giuliano de' Medici complained to his brother Lorenzo about this often, saying he was afraid that because they wanted too much they would lose everything.

III

However, Lorenzo, urged on by youth and power, wanted to be responsible for everything and to have everybody recognize it. The Pazzi could not tolerate so many insults to their nobility and wealth, and they began to think of a way of revenge. The first to start plotting against the Medici was Francesco. He was bolder and more sensitive than the others, and he decided either to get what he wanted or lose what he already had. Because he hated the way Florence was governed, he lived almost all the time in Rome, where he managed a large sum of money as is the custom of Florentine merchants. He was very friendly with Count Girolamo, and they often complained to each other about the Medici. After they had grumbled a great deal, they started to discuss the need for a revolution in Florence, if the one was to live safely in his states and the other in his city. They did not think this could be achieved without killing Giuliano and Lorenzo. They thought that the Pope and the King would easily give their consent, as long as they were both persuaded that it would be easy. Once they had agreed on this idea, they let Francesco Salviati, Archbishop of Pisa, know all about it. He was willing to join in because he was ambitious and had recently been insulted by the Medici. They discussed what they should do, and so that the plot would have a better chance of succeeding, they decided to win Iacopo de' Pazzi over to their point of view, as they thought that they would not be able to do anything without him. They felt that Francesco de' Pazzi should go to Florence to do this, and the Archbishop and the Count should remain in Rome to be with the Pope when the right time came to let him know about it. Francesco found Iacopo more respectful to the Medici and more obstinate than he would have wished. When he reported this to Rome, it was felt that Iacopo needed more authority to convince him: So the Archbishop and the Count put everything before Giovan Battista da Montesecco, the Pope's general. He had a high reputation in military matters and was under obligations to the Pope and the Count. Nevertheless, he pointed out how difficult and dangerous the plan was. The Archbishop tried to minimize these dangers and difficulties by referring to the help the Pope and the King would give them, as well as to the hatred the citizens of Florence felt for the Medici, the relatives the Salviati and the Pazzi would bring with them, and the ease with which the Medici could be assassinated because they went about the town unaccompanied and unsuspecting. Once they were dead, it would be easy to start a revolution. Giovan Battista did not entirely believe all this, because he had heard many other Florentines speak quite differently.

IV

While these discussions and plots were going on, Carlo, Lord of Faenza, happened to fall ill, and it was feared that he would die. The Archbishop and the Count felt that it was a good time to send Giovan Battista to Florence and from there to Romagna with the excuse of winning back some towns that the Lord of Faenza had taken from him. The Count asked Giovan Battista to talk to Lorenzo and to ask on his behalf how the Count should act in the internal politics of Romagna. Then he was to speak to Francesco de' Pazzi, and together they were to try to get Iacopo de' Pazzi to fall in with their wishes. So that they could use the Pope's authority to convince him, they arranged for Giovan Battista to speak to the Pope before he left. The Pope offered all possible help in the undertaking. Giovan Battista arrived in Florence, spoke to Lorenzo, who received him very kindly and gave him wise and friendly advice on the matters on which he was consulted. Giovan Battista was very impressed by him, and felt he had found someone quite different from what he had been led to expect, and judged him to be all kindness and wisdom, and very friendly to the Count. Nevertheless, he wanted to speak to Francesco, and not finding him at home because he had gone to Lucca, he spoke to Iacopo. At the beginning he found him very ill-disposed toward the plot, but before he left, the Pope's authority moved Iacopo a little. So he told Giovan Battista to go to Romagna and come back, then Francesco would be in Florence and they would discuss things in more detail at that time. Giovan Battista went and returned, and continued his pretended discussion of the Count's affairs with Lorenzo de' Medici. Then he had a meeting with Iacopo and Francesco de' Pazzi, and they managed things so well that Iacopo gave his consent to the plot. They talked about ways and means. Iacopo felt that they had no chance of success if both brothers were in Florence, and so they should wait until Lorenzo went to Rome, as it was rumored that he was going, and then put the plot into effect. Francesco liked the idea of Lorenzo being in Rome, but if it did not work out all right, he said that both brothers could be murdered either at a wedding, during some sporting event, or in church. About outside help, he thought that the Pope could get some troops together to attack the castle of Montone, since he had just cause to take it from Count Carlo, who had been responsible for the trouble around Siena and Perugia. Nevertheless, they reached no conclusion except that Francesco de' Pazzi and Giovan Battista should go to Rome and there settle everything with the Count and the Pope. The matter was gone into again in Rome, and in the end, after the attack on Montone was decided on, it was agreed that Giovanfrancesco da Tolentino, a soldier in the Pope's service, should go to Romagna, and Lorenzo da Castello to his own town. With the men of the district, both were to keep their companies in readiness to do what they were ordered by Archbishop Salviati and Francesco de' Pazzi. They were to go to Florence with Giovan Battista da Montesecco and to prepare whatever was needed to carry out the plot. Through his ambassador, King Ferrando promised whatever help was needed. When the Archbishop and Francesco de' Pazzi came to Florence, they won Poggio's son Iacopo over to their side. He was an educated young man, but ambitious and something of a revolutionary. They also attracted two Iacopo Salviatis, one a brother and the other a relative of the Archbishop's; and they brought in Bernardo Bandini and Napoleone Franzesi, daring young men who were under obligations to the Pazzi family. The foreigners who took part, besides those already mentioned, were Antonio da Volterra, and a priest named Stefano who taught Latin to Iacopo's daughter at home. Rinato de' Pazzi, who was a serious, wise man, and knew very well the trouble that these plots give rise to, did not agree to the conspiracy. In fact, he abhorred it and did what he could honorably do to stop it.

V

The Pope had sent Raffaello de' Riario, Count Girolamo's nephew, to the University of Pisa to study canon
law, and while he was still there the Pope raised him to
the rank of Cardinal. The conspirators felt that it would
be a good idea to bring this Cardinal to Florence so that
his arrival could cover up the conspiracy, since they
could hide the conspirators they needed in his entourage
and make this the reason for carrying it out then. So
the Cardinal came and was received by Iacopo de' Pazzi
at Montughi, his villa near Florence. The conspirators
wanted to use him to get Giuliano and Lorenzo together,
and kill them as soon as this happened. They arranged
to give a banquet for the Cardinal in their villa at Fiesole,
to which Giuliano did not come, either by chance or on
purpose. When this plan came to nothing, they reckoned
that if they invited them in Florence both would be
bound to come. So arrangements were made and Sunday,
the twenty-sixth of April, 1478, was the day appointed for
this banquet. Thinking that they would be able to kill
the brothers during the banquet, they met on Saturday
night and planned everything they had to do the next
morning. When the day came, Francesco received a
message to say that Giuliano would not be coming to the
banquet. So the leaders of the conspiracy met again and
agreed that it could not be postponed any longer. It was
known to so many people, it could not possibly remain
a secret. They decided to assassinate them in the cathedral church of Santa Reparata. Since the Cardinal would
be there, the two brothers would attend, as was the custom. They wanted Giovan Battista to be responsible for
killing Lorenzo, and Francesco de' Pazzi and Bernardo
Bandini, Giuliano. Giovan Battista refused to do it. Either
the friendly relations he had had with Lorenzo had made
him soft, or else he was prompted by some other reason,
but he said he would never have the heart to commit
such a crime in church and add sacrilege to treachery.
This marked the beginning of the failure of their plan.

With time pressing, they were forced to give this job to Antonio da Volterra and the priest Stefano, both of whom were completely unsuited to such a task by their way of life and their temperaments. Because if ever any task requires a strong and firm resolve, hardened by long experience in life and death, then it is this one. On such occasions men expert in warfare and steeped in blood have often been known to lose heart. Having reached this decision, they arranged that the signal to begin should be the moment when the priest who was celebrating the principal Mass in the church took Communion. At that time Archbishop Salviati with his men and Poggio's son Iacopo were to occupy the public Palace so that once the two young men were dead the Signoria would be favorable toward the conspirators either voluntarily or under duress.

VI

Once this decision was taken, they went into the church where the Cardinal had already gone with Lorenzo de' Medici. The church was full of people, divine service had begun, and Giuliano de' Medici was still not in church. So Francesco de' Pazzi and Bernardo, his appointed murderers, went to his home and brought him to church with skillful persuasion. It really is worth recording how Francesco and Bernardo could disguise such hatred and the plans for such an outrage so wholeheartedly and so obstinately. Because on the way to the church, and once there, they entertained him with jokes and youthful conversation. Francesco even ran his hands over him, pretending to embrace him, to see if he was wearing a corselet or any similar protection. Giuliano and Lorenzo knew how bitter the Pazzi were against them and how they wanted to deprive them of their power in the government. But they did not fear for their lives, thinking that even if the Pazzi did try something, they would do it constitutionally and not by force. So they also pretended to be friendly, having no thought for their own personal safety. The murderers were ready.

Some were beside Lorenzo, where they could easily stay without fear because of the crowd in the church, and the others were with Giuliano; and the appointed hour arrived. Bernardo Bandini stabbed Giuliano in the chest with a short weapon that was specially prepared for the purpose, and after a few steps he fell to the ground. Francesco de' Pazzi fell on him and wounded him over and over again. He was so intent on striking him that he was blinded by his fury and wounded himself seriously in the leg. Antonio and Stefano attacked Lorenzo, and aimed several blows at him, wounding him slightly in the throat. But all their efforts were frustrated either by their own incompetence, or by the help Lorenzo's companions gave him, or by the courage of Lorenzo himself, who seeing the attack coming defended himself with his own sword. So those two fled terrified and went into hiding. But they were found later, and they died a shameful death and were dragged around the whole city. Lorenzo was surrounded by the friends who were with him, and he shut himself up in the sacristy of the church. When Bernardo Bandini saw that Giuliano was dead, he also killed Francesco Nori, a great friend of the Medici, either because of an old feud or because Francesco had tried to help Giuliano. Not content with these two murders, he ran to look for Lorenzo, so that by his courage and speed he could put to rights the mistake that the others had made with their slowness and weakness. But he could do nothing because he found that Lorenzo had escaped into the sacristy. During these grave revolutionary events which were so violent that the church seemed about to collapse, the Cardinal clung to the altar, and two priests managed to save him so that the Signoria could take him back to their Palace when the disturbance was over. And he stayed there very much afraid until he was set free.

VII

During this time, there were some Perugian political exiles in Florence, whom the Pazzi had persuaded to join them by promising to restore them to their country. Archbishop Salviati, who had gone to occupy the Palace with Poggio's son Iacopo and Salviati and his friends, had taken them with him. When they reached the Palace, he left some of his men down below with orders that if they heard a noise they were to hold the door, and he went up with most of the Perugians. He found the Signoria at dinner, as it was late, but he was soon received by Cesare Petrucci, the Gonfalonier of Justice. The Archbishop took some of his men in with him but left the rest outside, and most of them locked themselves in the chancery, because the door was so made that if it was shut it could not be opened from inside or out except by key. Meanwhile, the Archbishop, who had obtained an interview with the Gonfalonier on the pretext of bringing him a message from the Pope, began to speak to him so hesitatingly and showed such emotion in his face and in his speech that the Gonfalonier grew suspicious, and he suddenly dashed out of the room shouting. He found Poggio's son Iacopo and took him by the hair and handed him over to his guards. The alarm was raised among the Signori and they took whatever weapons chance offered. All the men who had come up with the Archbishop, part of whom were locked in and part of whom had lost heart, were either killed on the spot or thrown out of the Palace windows alive. Among those put to death were the Archbishop, the two Iacopo Salviatis, and Poggio's son Iacopo, who were all hanged. Those who had stayed downstairs in the palace had overwhelmed the guards and had taken over the door and all the ground floor, so that the citizens who ran to the Palace at the alarm could give the Signoria no help if they were armed and no advice if they were unarmed.

VIII

Meanwhile, Francesco de' Pazzi and Bernardo Bandini panicked when they saw that Lorenzo had escaped and that one of them, on whom the whole plan depended, was seriously wounded. Bernardo thought of his own

safety with the same wholeheartedness with which he
had planned to bring down the Medici, and realizing
that the game was up he escaped to safety. Francesco
went home wounded and tried to see if he could sit a
horse, because the arrangement was to surround the town
with soldiers and call the people to liberty and arms.
But the wound was so deep, and he had lost so much
blood, that he could not manage it. So he undressed,
threw himself on his bed naked, and begged Iacopo to
do what he himself could not do. Although he was old
and unused to such rioting, Iacopo rode out with perhaps
a hundred men who had been prepared for this job, to
make this last trial of their fortune, and he went to the
Palace square calling the people and liberty to his aid.
But the first had been deafened by Fortune and the
liberality of the Medici, and the second was unknown in
Florence, so there was no response, except that the
Signori who were in control of the upper floors of the
Palace greeted him with stones and tried to frighten him
with threats. Iacopo hesitated and was met by Giovanni
Serristori, his brother-in-law, who first took him to task
for the upheaval they were causing, and then advised
him to go back home, telling him that the people and
liberty were as dear to the hearts of the other citizens as
to him. Iacopo lost all hope when he found the Palace
against him, Lorenzo alive, Francesco wounded, and
nobody following him. Not knowing what else to do, he
decided to save his life, if he could, by escaping. And he
left Florence for Romagna with the following that had
gone to the square with him.

IX

By this time the whole city was up in arms, and
Lorenzo had gone home accompanied by a great many
armed men. The Palace had been retaken by the people,
and those who had occupied it were all either imprisoned
or put to death. The name of the Medici was already
being shouted throughout the city, and the dead men's
limbs could be seen stuck on the points of weapons or

being dragged around the city. Everybody attacked the Pazzi either with angry words or cruel deeds. Their houses had already been occupied by the people, and Francesco was dragged out naked as he was, taken to the Palace, and hanged next to the Archbishop and the rest. However much abuse he suffered on the way and later by words or deeds, nobody managed to make him speak. He stared at people, sighing silently, but did not complain otherwise. Guglielmo de' Pazzi, Lorenzo's brother-in-law, escaped to Lorenzo's house and was saved with the help of his wife, Bianca, and because he was innocent. There was not one citizen who did not go to Lorenzo's house, armed or unarmed, in that time of need, and each one offered his service and his possessions: The family had earned itself so much good fortune and good-will by its prudence and liberality. Rinato de' Pazzi had retired to his villa when the affair took place. Hearing how things had gone, he tried to escape in disguise, but he was recognized on the way, arrested, and brought to Florence. Iacopo was also captured crossing the mountains. The mountain people had heard what had happened in Florence, and when they saw him escaping, they attacked him and brought him to Florence. Although he begged them several times, he could not persuade them to kill him on the way. Iacopo and Rinato were condemned to death four days after the affair took place; and of so many deaths that occurred in those days, filling the streets with men's limbs, the only one that was looked on with pity was Rinato's death. He was thought of as wise and good and was not accused of pride like the other members of that family. So that the affair should not lack any extraordinary feature, Iacopo was first buried in his ancestors' tomb. Then, because he was excommunicated, he was exhumed and buried along the city walls. Then he was dug up again and dragged naked around the whole city by the rope with which he had been hanged. Since he had found no burial place in the earth, the men who had been dragging him threw him into the river Arno, whose waters were very high at that time. This was a truly great example of Fortune, to see a man fall from so much affluence and prosperity into such misery, so shamefully and disastrously! They say his vices were gambling and swearing more than was fitting for any sinner, but he made up for these vices by generous alms-giving, because he helped many needy people and religious houses. It can also be said in his favor that on the Saturday before the Sunday appointed for the murder, he paid all his debts, and very carefully delivered to its owners all the merchandise that he had been holding in bond or at home, so that nobody else should share in his ill fortune. Giovan Battista da Montesecco had his head cut off after a long examination. Napoleone Franzesi escaped punishment by flight. Guglielmo de' Pazzi was exiled and his cousins who were still alive were imprisoned in the depths of the fortress of Volterra. When all the riots had died down and the conspirators had been punished, Giuliano's funeral was held. All the citizens followed him in tears because he had as much generosity and humanity as could be wished for in anyone born in his estate. He left a natural son who was born a few months after he was killed, and he was called Giulio. He was full of the *virtù* and good fortune that the whole world now recognizes, and which we will describe fully when we come to current events, if God grants us life. The troops that were commanded by Lorenzo da Castello in the Tiber valley and those under Giovan Francesco da Tolentino in Romagna had moved on toward Florence together in order to bring support to the Pazzi, but they turned back when they heard that the plot had failed.

X

Since the revolution that the Pope and the King were hoping for in Florence had not occurred, they decided to achieve their object by war, having failed by conspiracy. With very great speed, they both collected their armies together in order to attack the state of Florence, giving it out that all they wanted from the city was that it should get rid of Lorenzo de' Medici who was their only enemy among all the Florentines. The King's troops had already

crossed the Tronto and the Pope's were in Perugian territory. The Pope excommunicated the Florentines and
cursed them so that they would have spiritual as well as
temporal wounds. Seeing so many armies ranged against
them, the Florentines prepared their defense with the
utmost care. Before everything else, Lorenzo chose to
assemble all the qualified citizens, more than three hundred of them, with the Signori in the Palace, and he
spoke to them in these terms: "Noble Signori, and gracious citizens, I do not know whether I should grieve with
you or congratulate you on what has happened. Certainly
when I think how treacherously and bitterly I have been
attacked and how my brother has been killed, I cannot
help my heart sorrowing and my soul mourning. Then
when I think how my brother was revenged and myself
defended so swiftly and carefully, with such love and
such unanimous agreement from the whole city, I am
bound not only to congratulate you but to rejoice and
glory in it. If experience has made me realize that I had
more enemies in this town than I thought, it has also
proved that I had more ardent and warmhearted friends
than I believed. So I am obliged to complain to you
about the injuries done by others and to rejoice at your
goodness. But I do feel bound to complain all the more
about the injuries in that they are so rare, so unparal-
lelled, and so undeserved. Gracious citizens, consider
how low ill fortune had brought our house: It was not
safe among friends and relatives, or in church. Those
who are in fear of death usually look to their friends for
help, or they go to their relatives, but we found them
armed to destroy us. Those who are being attacked for
public or private reasons usually take refuge in churches.
So we are killed by those who defend others. Where parricides and assassins are safe, the Medici found their
murderers. But God, Who never has abandoned our
house in the past, has saved us again, and He took up
the defense of our just cause. What injustice have we
ever done anyone, that deserved such a desire for vengeance? We never made any personal attacks on these
men who have shown themselves to be such enemies of
ours; because if we had attacked them, they would have

276

had no chance to attack us. If they attribute public injuries to us, if any have been done to them, which I do not know, then they offend you more than us, and this Palace and the dignity of this government more than our house, by thinking that you injure your citizens without cause because of us. This is very far from the truth, because if we had ever been able to do so, or if we had asked you to, neither you nor we would have made such an attack. Anyone trying to get at the truth will find that our house has always been looked up to by you by common consent only because it has tried to outdo everybody in kindness, liberality, and generosity. If we have honored strangers, how could we have harmed our relations? If desire for power was their motive, as the occupation of the Palace and their coming into the square with armed men prove, then this reason stands revealed and condemned as ugly, ambitious, and damnable. If they did it out of hatred and envy of our power, they are attacking you not us, since you gave power to us. Certainly power that is usurped should be hated, but not that which men gain through liberality, kindness, and munificence. You know that our house never took upon itself any rank that was not thrust upon it by this Palace with your unanimous consent. My grandfather Cosimo did not return from exile by force or under arms but by your general agreement. My father, when he was old and sick, did not defend the state against so many enemies, it was you who defended it with your authority and benevolence. As for me, after my father's death, when I can be said to have been still a child, I would not have kept up my house's standing if it had not been for your advice and help. My house would not have been able, nor would it now be able, to support this republic if you had not supported it with her and did not still do so. So I do not know what can be the reason for their hatred of us or, if there is any just cause, for their envy. Let them hate their ancestors, who by their pride and greed lost the kind of reputation that our family managed to earn with the opposite kind of behavior. But if we allow that they did suffer great injustice at our hands, and that they were right in aiming to destroy us, why come to attack this Palace? Why make an alliance with the Pope and the King against the liberty of this republic? Why break the long period of peace in Italy? They have no excuse for this: They ought to have attacked those who had harmed them, and not confused private feuds with public affronts. This means that now that they are out of the way our trouble is greater, because the Pope and the King are coming against us to back up their cause with force; and they say that this war is directed against me and my house. Would to God this were true, because the answer would be swift and sure. I would not be such a bad citizen as to put my safety before your danger; in fact, I would be glad to put out your fire by my own fall. But the wrongs the powerful do always bear some less shameful disguise, and they have used this as a way of disguising their shamefully unjust attack on us. Nevertheless, if you believe differently, I am in your hands. It is up to you to support me or leave me, you, my fathers and my defenders. Whatever you order me to do I will always do gladly, and I will never refuse, if you see fit, to end this war with my own blood, as it was begun with my brother's." The citizens could not restrain their tears while Lorenzo was speaking, and the same compassion with which he was heard was felt in the reply which one of them was charged to make. He said that the city was grateful for so many benefits received from Lorenzo and his family and that he should take heart, for they would preserve his reputation and his position with the same readiness with which they had revenged his brother's death and preserved his own life; and he would not lose his power before they lost their country. And to fit the deed to the word, they provided him, at public expense, with a bodyguard of a number of armed men to defend him from surprise attacks on his own person.

XI

After this they prepared for war, collecting as much money and troops as they could. They sent for help, because of the league, to the Duke of Milan and the Venetians. Since the Pope had shown himself a wolf and not a shepherd, they justified their cause in every way they could in order to avoid being devoured as sinners. They broadcast throughout Italy the story of the treachery against their regime, stressing the evil and injustice of the Pope and his misuse of the papal power which he had taken wrongly. He had sent men he had raised to the highest dignities of the Church, with traitors and parricides, to commit this treachery in church, during divine service and the celebration of the sacrament. Then because he had not managed to murder some citizens, start a revolution in their city, and sack it as he pleased, he had placed an interdict upon it and menaced and attacked it with papal curses. But if God is just and hates violence, then He must have hated the violence of His Vicar, and been pleased that the men under attack turned to Him when they found no mercy from the Pope. Not that the Florentines accepted the interdict or obeyed it: They forced the priests to celebrate divine service. They called a council in Florence of all the Tuscan prelates that obeyed their jurisdiction and at it they made an appeal to the future Council about the Pope's injustice. The Pope was still not without reasons to justify his cause, and he said it was up to a Pope to do away with tyranny, to overcome the wicked and raise up the good. He must do these things in whatever way seemed appropriate, but it was not the place of secular princes to detain cardinals, hang bishops, kill and dismember priests and have them dragged around the city, or murder the innocent and the guilty indiscriminately.

XII

Despite these charges and accusations, the Florentines handed the Cardinal, whom they were still holding, back to the Pope; with the result that the Pope attacked them mercilessly with all his own forces and the King's. The two armies, commanded by Alfonso, Ferrando's eldest son and Duke of Calabria, under the guidance of Federigo, Count of Urbino, were allowed passage into the Chianti by Siena, which was on the enemy side, and occupied Radda and several other castles and laid waste the whole district. Then they laid siege to Castellina. The Florentines were very afraid after seeing these attacks, because they had no army and their friends' aid was slow in coming. Even though the Duke had sent help, the Venetians had said they were under no obligation to help the Florentines in cases involving private persons; and since the war was directed against private persons, they were not obliged to come to their aid, because individual quarrels should not be disputed publicly. So the Florentines sent Tommaso Soderini as ambassador to the Venetian Senate to persuade the Venetians to a healthier point of view. Meantime, they hired troops and made Ercole, Marquis of Ferrara, commander of their armies. While these preparations were being made, the enemy army pressed Castellina so hard that the inhabitants gave up hope of help and surrendered after withstanding a forty days' siege. The enemy turned from there to Arezzo and besieged Monte a San Sovino. The Florentine army was already in battle order and had gone out to meet the enemy, positioning itself at three miles from them, and was harassing them so much that Federigo of Urbino asked for a few days' truce. It was granted to him, though it was so much to the Florentines' disadvantage that those who asked for it were surprised to be allowed it. If they had not got it they would have had to retreat with dishonor, but with those few days in which to reorganize themselves, they occupied the castle on our troops' front when the truce expired. But winter had already come, and the enemy retired to spend it in comfort in Sienese territory. The Florentine troops also withdrew to better quarters, and the Marquis of Ferrara went back to his own country, having done himself little good and others even less.

XIII

During this time, Genoa rebelled against the Milanese regime for the following reasons: After Galeazzo's death, when Giovan Galeazzo his son was still too young to rule, a quarrel broke out between the Sforzas, Ludovico, Ottaviano, and Ascanio, his uncles, and Bona, his mother, because they all wanted to have charge of the little Duke. Bona, the old Duchess, got the upper hand through the advice of Tommaso Soderini, who was Florentine ambassador to that state at the time, and Cecco Simonetta, who had been Galeazzo's secretary. So the Sforzas fled from Milan and Ottaviano was drowned crossing the Adda. The others were exiled to different places and so was Roberto da San Severino, who had deserted the Duchess in the dispute and had sided with them. When the disturbances in Tuscany took place, these princes hoped for a change in their luck with the new events and they broke their bounds, and each tried new ways of getting back his former power.

King Ferrando saw that the Florentines had only received help from the Milanese government in their need, and ordered the Duchess to be given so much to think about at home that she could not provide aid for the Florentines, so that they would lose that help, too. With the help of Prospero Adorno, Roberto, and the Sforza rebels, he made Genoa revolt against the Duke. Only the Castelletto remained in his power, and relying upon this the Duchess sent a number of men to retake the city; but they were defeated. Seeing the danger that threatened her son's rule and herself while the war lasted, she decided to have Genoa as an ally if she could not have it as a subject, since Tuscany also was in turmoil and the Florentines, who were her only hope, were themselves in difficulties. She made an agreement with Batistino Fregoso, an enemy of Prospero Adorno, that she would give him the Castelletto and make him the ruler of Genoa if he expelled Prospero and gave no help to the Sforza rebels. After this agreement Batistino took control of

281

Genoa with the help of the Castle and his party, and made himself Doge according to their custom. The Sforzas and Roberto were expelled from Genoese territory and came into Lunigiana with the troops who were following them. The Pope and the King, seeing that the troubles in Lombardy were over, made use of these men expelled from Genoa to stir up Tuscany around Pisa, so that the Florentines would be weakened by having to divide their forces. When winter was over, they arranged for Roberto to leave Lunigiana with his army and attack Pisan territory. Roberto created havoc and took and sacked a number of castles in Pisan territory and carried out raids as far as Pisa itself.

XIV

At this time ambassadors came to Florence from the Emperor, the King of France, and the King of Hungary, who had been sent to the Pope by their princes. They persuaded the Florentines to send ambassadors to the Pope and promised to do everything they could to persuade the Pope to put an end to this war with a satisfactory peace treaty. The Florentines did not refuse to make the experiment, so that everyone would see they were not guilty, because for their part they were peace-lovers. So the ambassadors went, and they came back without achieving anything. Then the Florentines, who had been either attacked or deserted by Italians, decided to make use of the reputation of the King of France, and they sent as ambassador to him Donato Acciaiuoli, a very great Greek and Latin scholar whose ancestors had always held high office in the city. But he died on the way, at Milan. His country buried him at public expense with full honors, to reward the family he left behind and to honor his memory, and they granted his sons exemption from taxes and gave his daughters dowries. Instead of him they sent Guid' Antonio Vespucci as ambassador to the King, an expert in canon and imperial law. The attack Roberto had made on Pisan territory worried the Florentines greatly, as unexpected things do. With a very

serious war in the Siena sector they did not see how to
protect the country toward Pisa. Yet they did send aid
to the city of Pisa by seconding troops to that front and
by making similar provisions. To keep the Lucchese
friendly and to stop them from helping the enemy with
money or food, they sent Piero, son of Gino and grandson
of Neri Capponi, as ambassador. They received him with
such suspicion because of the way Lucca hates the people
of Florence for the old wrongs and the continued threat,
that he was very often in danger of being killed by the
people. In fact, his arrival gave rise to more anger instead of creating a new friendship. The Florentines called
back the Marquis of Ferrara, hired the Marquis of Mantua, and with much insistence asked the Venetians for
Count Carlo, Braccio's son, and Deifebo, Count Iacopo's
son. Finally, after much quibbling, the Venetians allowed
them these men. The Venetians had made a truce with
the Turk and so they had no excuse, and were ashamed
not to keep faith with the league. Count Carlo and
Deifebo came with a large number of men at arms, and
they added to them all the men at arms that could be
spared from the army that was fighting the Duke of
Calabria's troops under the Marquis of Ferrara. They went
toward Pisa to look for Roberto, who had his army near
the river Serchio. Although he had pretended to be waiting for our army, he did not wait, but retreated into
Lunigiana to the camp he had left when he entered
Pisan territory. After his departure Count Carlo retook all
the towns that had been occupied by the enemy in Pisan
territory.

XV

Once the Florentines were free of the attack from the
direction of Pisa, they made all their forces gather between Colle and San Gimignano. But as the army contained both Sforzeschi and Bracceschi since the arrival
of Count Carlo, their old quarrels broke out again immediately. And it was feared they might come to blows if
they had to be together for long. To take the lesser of

two evils, it was decided to divide the army, and send one part into Perugian territory under Count Carlo and keep the rest at Poggibonsi to set up a strong camp to stop the enemy from entering Florentine territory. They also expected to force the enemy to divide his army by this strategy, because they believed that either Count Carlo would occupy Perugia, where they thought he had plenty of supporters, or that the Pope would be obliged to send a vast army to defend it. Besides this, to press the Pope still harder, they ordered Niccolò Vitelli, who had left Città di Castello under the rule of his enemy Lorenzo, to approach the town with troops to attempt to expel his enemy and remove the town from papal jurisdiction. At the beginning, Fortune seemed to be favoring the Florentine side, because Count Carlo could be seen making good progress in Perugian territory. Although Niccolò Vitelli had not been able to enter Castello, he and his army had the upper hand in the countryside, and his raids around the town met with no opposition. Again, the troops that had remained at Poggibonsi carried out raids as far as the walls of Siena every day. Yet in the end, all these hopes came to nothing. First of all, Count Carlo died at the height of his hopes of victory. Yet his death would have improved the Florentines' position if the victory that resulted from it had been properly followed up. Once they heard of the Count's death, the army of the Church, which was already gathered at Perugia, grew hopeful of beating the Florentine army, and they went out into the country and pitched their camp by the lake three miles from the enemy. On the advice of Roberto of Rimini, who, after the death of Count Carlo, was now left as chief of the army and its most respected member, Iacopo Guicciardini, the Commissioner for the Florentine army, decided to wait for them, having realized the reason for the enemy's pride. They clashed by the lake, where Hannibal of Carthage inflicted that memorable defeat on the Romans, and the Church's army was routed. The news of this victory was received in Florence with general rejoicing and much praise for the leaders, and it would have helped the campaign and made it famous if the irregularities that took place in the army at Poggibonsi had not

284

upset everything. So the good that one army did was completely cancelled out by the other. That army had collected booty in Sienese territory, and when they came to divide it up a quarrel broke out between the Marquis of Ferrara and the Marquis of Mantua. They fought over it and attacked each other with every means available. The Florentines felt they could no longer employ both of them, and they agreed to let the Marquis of Ferrara go back home with his army.

XVI

The army was weakened and without a commander, and irregularities were occurring very frequently. The Duke of Calabria, who was near Siena with his army, felt encouraged to go out and meet it. He did so, and the Florentine army seeing themselves attacked lost faith in their arms, in their numbers, which were superior to the enemy's, and in the very strong position they held, and they fled at the sight of the dust without even waiting to see the enemy, leaving behind their ammunition, their transport, and their artillery. The armies of that period were full of this sort of cowardice and indiscipline, where the success or failure of a campaign could depend on a horse turning its head or its hindquarters. This defeat brought a great deal of booty to the King's soldiers and terror to the Florentines, because their city was stricken not only by war but by a very severe plague as well. This had taken such a hold on the city that all the citizens had retired to their villas to escape death. This meant that the defeat was even more terrible, because the citizens who had fled to property in the Pesa and Elsa valleys, came back to Florence as soon after the defeat as they could, bringing not only their children and their possessions but also their workers. It looked as if there was fear of the enemy arriving in the town at any moment. Those who were in charge of the direction of the war saw the trouble and ordered the troops who had been victorious near Perugia to stop attacking the Perugians and go to the Elsa valley to resist the enemy who was carrying out raids on the countryside and meeting no opposition. Although those troops had reduced Perugia to such a state that victory was expected at any moment, the Florentines still wanted to defend their own before they tried to occupy another's land. So the army was taken from the scene of its successes and brought to San Casciano, a castle eight miles from Florence, as it was thought they could not be based anywhere else, until the remains of the defeated army were put together again. As for the enemy, those at Perugia who had been freed by the departure of the Florentine troops took heart and plundered the country around Arezzo and Cortona every day. The others, who had won at Poggibonsi under Alfonso, Duke of Calabria, had taken over Poggibonsi first, then Vico, and then sacked Certaldo. After these assaults and sacks, they laid siege to the castle of Colle, which was considered very strong at that time. It was manned by troops faithful to the Florentine regime, and it was able to keep the enemy at bay until the troops had been gathered together. When the Florentines had mustered all their troops at San Casciano, and the enemy was besieging Colle with all their might, the Florentines decided to approach them in order to encourage the people of Colle to defend themselves. So that the enemy would think twice about attacking them when their adversaries were near, once the decision was made they moved their camp from San Casciano to San Gimignano, five miles from Colle, and from there they harried the Duke's camp every day with light cavalry and other fast-moving troops. However, this aid was not enough for the people of Colle. They had run out of essential supplies and they surrendered on the thirteenth of November, much to the Florentines' annoyance and to the great joy of the enemies, especially the Sienese, who had a particular hatred for the people of Colle, apart from the general hatred they felt for the city of Florence.

XVII

It was already deep winter and a bad time for waging war, and the Pope and the King offered the Florentines a three months' truce either because they wanted to raise their hopes of peace or else because they wanted to enjoy their own victories more peacefully, and they gave them ten days to reply. The offer was immediately accepted. But just as everybody finds that wounds are more painful when the blood has cooled than when they were first made, this short breathing space made the Florentines realize more fully the wrongs they had suffered. The citizens accused each other without restraint or respect, and pointed out the mistakes that had been made during the war. They pointed to the useless expenditure, the taxes that had been unfairly imposed, and these things were discussed not only in private circles but were the subject of lively debates in the public councils. One person grew so bold that he turned to Lorenzo de' Medici and said: "This city is tired and wants no more war"; and that it was time to think of peace. Lorenzo realized the need and got advice from those friends he thought wisest and most trustworthy. Their first decision was that they should seek new fortune with new friends, realizing that the Venetians were cold and unreliable, and the Duke was a minor and involved in civic strife. But they were uncertain whether to put themselves in the hands of the Pope or the King. They considered everything and settled on an alliance with the King, this being more stable and secure. A secular prince cannot have complete confidence in a Pope or throw in his lot with him safely, because of the shortness of a Pope's life, the changes in succession, the little respect the Church shows princes, and the lack of consideration she shows in taking decisions. The man who is an ally of the Pope through wars and dangers will have his company in his victories, but in defeat he will be alone, because the Pontiff is supported and defended by his spiritual power. Once they had decided it would be a better proposition to earn the King's friendship, they judged this could not be done better or more safely than by Lorenzo in person. They believed that the more generously they behaved toward the King, the easier it would be to make up for the quarrels of the past. Lorenzo had quite made up his mind to go. He put the city and the government in the care of Tommaso Soderini, who was Gonfalonier of Justice at the time, and he left Florence at the beginning of December. When he reached Pisa he wrote to the Signoria giving the reason for his journey. The Signori, both to honor him and to give him more standing in his peace negotiations with the King, made him ambassador of the Florentine people and gave him authority to draw up the alliance with the King in the way he considered best for the republic.

XVIII

At this same time Roberto da San Severino, accompanied by Lodovico and Ascanio Sforza only, because their brother had died, attacked the state of Milan again in order to return to power. They had occupied Tortona, and Milan and the whole country was up in arms. Duchess Bona was advised to receive the Sforzeschi back and restore them to their position to put an end to this civil war. The chief man behind this advice was Antonio Tassino, a Ferrarese of lowly origin, who when he came to Milan had entered the service of Duke Galeazzo, who had given him to his wife the Duchess as a servant. Because he was handsome or because he had some other secret virtue, he acquired such standing with the Duchess after the Duke's death that he almost ruled the state. Cecco, who was an outsanding man both for his prudence and his long experience, was very annoyed by this, and he tried to undermine Tassino's influence when he could, both with the Duchess and with the others in the government. When Tassino realized this he advised the Duchess to receive the Sforza back, in order to be revenged and to have someone near him who would protect him from Cecco. The Duchess followed his advice, and without discussing anything with Cecco she allowed them to return. Cecco told her: "You have taken a decision which will cost me my life and you your state." Both of which things happened soon afterwards. Cecco was put to death by Lodovico, and some time later when Tassino had been expelled from the Duchy, the Duchess was so angry that she left Milan and handed over the charge of her son to Lodovico. So Lodovico remained sole governor of the Duchy of Milan, and as will be shown, he was the cause of the destruction of Italy. Lorenzo de' Medici had left for Naples and the truce was in force between the two sides, when quite unexpectedly Lodovico Fregoso, having come to some agreement with some people in Serezana, entered the town secretly with troops, occupied it, and took prisoner the representative of the Florentine people. This affair greatly annoyed the leaders of the Florentine regime, because they were convinced that everything had been done on orders from King Ferrando. They complained to the Duke of Calabria, who was at Siena with his army, that they had been attacked on a new front during the truce. He did his best to prove both by letters and ambassadors that this had happened without the consent of his father or himself. Nevertheless, the Florentines felt that they were in a most serious position, having to cope by themselves, without money and with the head of the republic in the King's hands, with an old war with the King and the Pope, and a new one with the Genoese, and also finding themselves without allies. They hoped for nothing from the Venetians and they tended rather to be afraid of the Milanese government because of its instability. The Florentines' only hope was in Lorenzo's negotiations with the King.

XIX

Lorenzo had arrived in Naples by sea, and he was received with much honor and great expectations not only by the King but by the whole city. Because the war had been directed wholly against him, the greatness of the enemies he had had made him very famous. When he was in the King's presence, he discussed the state of Italy and the feeling of its rulers and peoples, and what might be hoped from peace and feared from war. When he heard him, the King was even more surprised by Lorenzo's great spirit, his sharp intelligence and sound judgment, than he had been earlier by his solitary resistance to such a war. He doubled the honors shown to Lorenzo and began to think that he should let him go as a friend rather than hold him as an enemy. Nevertheless, he did detain him with different excuses from December to March, to make doubly sure not only of him but also of the city. Lorenzo was not without enemies in Florence who would have liked the King to have held Lorenzo and treated him like Iacopo Piccinino. They pretended to complain and spoke about it all over the city, and in the public debates they opposed those who were in favor of Lorenzo. In this way they spread the rumor that if the King kept him in Naples for long, there would be a revolution in Florence. This made the King postpone sending him back for that amount of time to see whether any trouble did break out in Florence. But when he saw that things went on peacefully there, he bade him farewell on the sixth of March 1479, having first won his friendship with all kinds of gifts and demonstrations of affection. And they made a perpetual agreement for the defense of both their states. If Lorenzo was great when he left Florence, on his return he was very great indeed, and the city welcomed him with the joy that his great qualities and recent triumphs deserved, for he had risked his own life to bring peace to his country. Two days after his arrival the agreement between the republic of Florence and the King was published. By it they each committed themselves to the preservation of both their states. It was to be up to the King to restore the towns taken from the Florentines in the war; the Pazzi imprisoned in the tower at Volterra were to be set free; and a certain sum of money was to be paid to the Duke of Calabria for some time. As soon as this treaty was published, the Pope and the Venetians were very angry. The Pope felt that he had been treated disrespectfully by the King, and the Venetians felt the same about the Florentines. They had both been allies in the war, and they were annoyed at not having a part in the peace negotiations. When they heard about their annoyance in Florence, everybody was afraid that a greater war might arise because of the peace treaty. The leaders of the regime decided to take a firmer hold on the government and reduce the number of people present at important discussions. They set up a council of seventy citizens with the greatest possible authority in all important matters. This new institution made those who had been thinking of revolution change their minds. And to gain prestige, the first thing the council did was to welcome the peace Lorenzo had made with the King. They appointed Antonio Ridolfi and Piero Nasi as ambassadors to the Pope and the King. Despite the treaty, however, Alfonso, Duke of Calabria, did not leave Siena with his army, but said that he was detained by the quarrels among the citizens. They were so bad that when he was residing outside the city they brought him inside and made him settle their differences. The Duke used this as an opportunity to fine many of the citizens, condemn a good many to prison, others to exile, and some to death. Because of this behavior, not only the Sienese but the Florentines began to suspect that he wanted to become the ruler of the city. They could think of no remedy, as Florence had a new alliance with the King and was at enmity with the Pope and the Venetians. This suspicion was felt not only among the common people of Florence, a subtle interpreter of every event, but also among the leaders of the regime. Everybody agrees that our city was never in such danger of losing its liberty. But God, Who has always taken particular care of it in such crises, brought about an unexpected event which gave the King, the Pope, and the Venetians more important things to think about than the affairs of Tuscany.

XX

Mahomet, the Grand Turk, had besieged Rhodes with a vast army, and fighting had gone on for many months.

But although he had large forces and had carried on the siege most obstinately, the obstinacy of the beleaguered was even greater. In fact, they defended themselves against his onslaught with such *virtù* that Mahomet was forced to raise the siege, much to his own discredit. After he left Rhodes, part of his army, under Pasha Keduk Ahmed, came toward Valona and as it passed the Italian coast he suddenly landed four thousand soldiers, either because he saw what an easy thing it would be or because his master had ordered him to. They attacked the city of Otranto, took it immediately, sacked it and killed all the inhabitants. He built up fortifications inside the city and in the port in the best way he could, brought in some good cavalry, and raided and plundered the surrounding countryside. When the King had news of this attack and heard what a great prince was responsible for it, he sent messengers everywhere with the news, asking for aid against the common enemy, and called the Duke of Calabria and his army back from Siena with great urgency.

XXI

So the attack pleased Florence and Siena as much as it disturbed the Duke and the rest of Italy. Siena felt that she had regained her liberty, and Florence that she had escaped the dangers that had made her afraid of losing hers. These feelings were confirmed by the Duke's complaints when he left Siena that Fortune had deprived him of dominion over Tuscany by an unexpected and illogical accident. This same affair made the Pope change his mind, and where before he had never agreed to listen to any Florentine ambassador, he became so much milder that he would hear anybody who would talk to him about world peace. The Florentines were assured that if they bowed down and asked the Pope's forgiveness it would be granted. They felt that they should not let this opportunity go by, and they sent to the Pope twelve ambassadors who, when they reached Rome, were held up by the Pope for different negotiations before he gave them an audience. In the end, however, the two parties agreed on a *modus vivendi* for the future and on how much each should contribute in peace and in war. Then the ambassadors came up to the feet of the Pope, who was waiting for them in excessive pomp surrounded by his cardinals. They apologized for what had happened. They blamed necessity and the ill will of others and the people's anger and their righteous indignation, and they said how unhappy are those men who are forced either to fight or to die. Since anything is better than death, they had put up with war, the interdicts, and the other discomforts that the past events had brought with them, so that their republic would escape slavery, which is death to free cities. Nevertheless, if they had committed any sin out of necessity, they were ready to make amends, and they trusted in the clemency of the Pope who like the Redeemer would receive them into his merciful arms. The Pope replied to these apologies with words full of pride and anger, reproaching them with every sin they had committed against the Church in the past. However, to keep God's commandments, he was content to grant them the pardon they were asking. But he would have them understand that they must obey. And if they failed to obey, they would lose the liberty they had been about to lose, and justly, because those who perform good deeds and not bad deserve to be free, and because liberty misused harms itself and others. To respect God little and the Church less is not the sign of a free but a dissolute man, more inclined to evil than to good, whose correction is the duty not only of princes but of every Christian. They themselves were to blame for what had happened, for they had caused the war by their bad deeds and kept it going by even worse deeds. The war had ended more because of the kindness of others than because of anything they had done. The text of the agreement was then read, and the blessing, to which the Pope added, besides the clauses that had been negotiated and agreed on, one which stated that if the Florentines wanted to enjoy the benefits of the blessing, they must supply the money to keep fifteen galleys armed for as long as the Turk was fighting the Kingdom. The ambassadors complained bitterly about this burden laid on them over and above the agreement that had been made, but they could not lessen it at all by any means, not by favors or by complaints. When they got back to Florence, the Signoria sent as ambassador to the Pope Guidantonio Vespucci, who had recently returned from France. By his prudence he brought everything within tolerable limits and received many favors from the Pope, which were signs of a greater reconciliation.

XXII

Now that the Florentines had settled their accounts with the Pope and they and Siena were free of their fear of the King, because of the Duke of Calabria's departure from Tuscany, and with the Turkish war still going on, they pressed the King in every way to return the castles that the Duke of Calabria had left in Sienese hands. The King feared that the Florentines might desert him in his great need, and by declaring war on Siena might stop him from getting the aid he hoped for from the Pope and the other Italians. So he agreed to return them, and he put the Florentines under fresh obligations to him. So it is force and necessity, not promises and obligations, that make princes keep faith. Once the castles had been received back and this new alliance was firmly established, Lorenzo de' Medici won back the reputation that had been undermined first by the war, then by the peace treaty, because of doubts about the King. At the time there was no shortage of people who slandered him openly. They said that he had sold his country to save himself and that during the war the towns had been lost and by the peace treaty they would lose their liberty. But when the towns were returned, and an honorable agreement was signed with the King, and the city had won back her old reputation, there was a change of heart in Florence, a city which loves to talk and judges policies by their results and not by the reasoning behind them. Lorenzo was praised to the skies. It was said that by his wisdom he had been able to win in peace what ill fortune

had taken from him in war and that he had done more
by his advice and judgment than the arms and forces of
the enemy. The attacks of the Turk had postponed the
war that had been about to break out because of the
Pope's and the Venetians' anger at the peace that had
been signed. But just as the beginning of that attack had
been unexpected and had caused a great deal of good,
its end was unforeseen and it caused very great trouble.
Mahomet the Grand Turk died, very unexpectedly, and
a quarrel broke out among his children. This meant that
the men who were in Apulia were abandoned by their
commander, and they agreed to give Otranto up to the
King. Everyone was afraid of new trouble once this fear
was removed, for it had given a firm purpose to the Pope
and the Venetians. On one side was the alliance of the
Pope with the Venetians, and with them were the Genoese, the Sienese, and other less powerful states. On the
other side were the Florentines, the King and the Duke,
and with them the Bolognese and a number of other
rulers. The Venetians wanted to take Ferrara, and they
felt that they had good cause to attack it and a definite
hope of success. The cause was that the Marquis said
he was no longer under an obligation to receive the
Vicedominus and salt from the Venetians since it had
been agreed that after seventy years the city would be
freed from both liabilities. To this the Venetians replied
that as long as the Ferrarese held the Polesine they would
have to receive the Vicedominus and the salt. Since the
Marquis would not agree, the Venetians felt that they
were justified in arming, and thought it was a good time
to do so while the Pope was very angry with the Florentines and the King. Count Girolamo had gone to Venice,
and the Venetians welcomed him with great honor. In
order to curry favor with the Pope, they gave him the
freedom of the city and made him a member of their
nobility, which is always a mark of very great honor for
whoever receives it. To prepare for the war, they had
imposed new taxes and made Roberto da San Severino
commander of their armies. He had broken with Lodovico, ruler of Milan, and had fled to Tortona, where he

had caused some rioting, and then had gone to Genoa. He was called in from there by the Venetians and was put in charge of their military affairs.

XXIII

When the enemy alliance learned of these preparations for fresh attacks, they too prepared for war. The Duke of Milan chose Federigo, Lord of Urbino, as his general; the Florentines chose Lord Costanzo of Pesaro. To find out the Pope's intentions and to see whether the Venetians were threatening Ferrara with the Pope's consent, King Ferrando sent Duke Alfonso of Calabria and his army over the Tronto and asked the Pope for permission to pass through into Lombardy to help the Marquis. This the Pope flatly refused. The King and the Florentines felt that they now knew his mind, and they decided to harass him so much that he would be forced to become their friend, or at least to put so many obstacles in his way that he would not be able to send aid to the Venetians. The Venetians had already started their campaign and had launched an attack on the Marquis; they raided his territory and then laid siege to Ficheruolo, a very important castle in the defense of his state. Since the King and the Florentines had decided to attack the Pope, Duke Alfonso of Calabria carried out raids toward Rome, and with the help of the Colonna, who had allied themselves to him because the Orsini had sided with the Pope, he did a good deal of damage in the countryside. At the same time the Florentine troops attacked Città di Castello with Niccolò Vitelli, and took the town, expelling Lorenzo who was holding it for the Pope, and making Niccolò its ruler. The Pope was in great difficulties because Rome was divided by party differences at home, and outside her countryside was being overrun by enemy raiders. However, as he was a brave man who intended to win and not surrender to the enemy, he appointed as his military commander the illustrious Roberto of Rimini. The Pope invited Roberto to Rome where the papal men at arms were all gathered, and he told him what an honor it would be for him if, against a King's army, he could free the Church from the difficulties she was in, and what an obligation not only he but all his successors would feel toward Roberto, and how not only men but God would be grateful to him. Roberto first inspected the Pope's troops and all his preparations, and advised him to get as much infantry as possible. This advice was acted upon with all care and speed. The Duke of Calabria was near Rome, and every day he carried out plundering raids as far as the city gates. The Roman people were so annoyed by this that they volunteered to help Roberto with the liberation of the city, and he thanked them and welcomed them all. When the Duke heard about these preparations, he moved some distance from the city, thinking that if he was farther off Roberto would not have the courage to go out and look for him. Partly, too, he was waiting for his brother Federigo, whom his father had sent with reinforcements. Realizing that his men at arms were almost equal in number to those of the Duke, and that his infantry outnumbered the Duke's, Roberto left Rome in battle array and pitched camp two miles from the enemy. When he saw the enemy was upon him so unexpectedly, the Duke decided that he must fight or flee in defeat. He was almost forced to decide to fight in order not to do something unworthy of a King's son. They each turned their faces to the enemy, positioned their troops in the way that was customary at the time, and went into battle. It lasted until midday. The battle was fought with more *virtù* than any other that had taken place in Italy for fifty years, because more than a thousand men died in all. It ended in glory for the Church because the weight of the papal infantry struck the ducal cavalry so hard that the Duke was forced to turn tail. He would have been taken prisoner if he had not been saved by some Turks who had been at Otranto and who were now fighting with him. After he had won this victory, Roberto returned to Rome in triumph. However, he was only able to enjoy it briefly, for he had drunk a great deal of water because of the heat of battle and fell ill with diarrhea, which killed him in a few days. His body was honored by the Pope in every possible way. As soon as the Pope had won this victory, he sent the Count toward Città di Castello to try to reinstate Lorenzo there, and also to make an attempt on the city of Rimini. After Roberto's death, there was only a small boy left in his wife's care, and the Pope thought it would be easy to occupy the city. He would have managed this easily if the lady had not been defended by the Florentines, who put up such a strong resistance that he failed both at Castello and at Rimini.

XXIV

While these things were taking place in Romagna and in Rome, the Venetians had taken Ficheruolo and their troops had crossed the Po. The army under the command of the Duke of Milan and the Marquis was in disarray because Federigo, Count of Urbino, had fallen ill. He had arranged to be taken to Bologna for treatment, and he died there. So the Marquis's fortunes were declining, and every day the Venetians' hopes of taking Ferrara grew. Meanwhile, the King and the Florentines did everything they could to make the Pope comply with their wishes. Having been unsuccessful in making him yield to force, they threatened him with a Council that the Emperor had already called at Basle. It was by means of the Emperor's ambassadors who were in Rome, and the chief cardinals who wanted peace, that the Pope was persuaded and made to think of peace and the unity of Italy. The Pope turned to an agreement with the league out of fear, and because he saw how a too powerful Venice would be the ruin of the Church and Italy. He sent nuncios to Naples; and the Pope, the King, the Duke of Milan, and the Florentines made a five-year alliance there, leaving the Venetians free to agree to it. After this, the Pope gave the Venetians to understand that they must give up the war with Ferrara. The Venetians refused and, in fact, prepared to put larger forces into the war. They defeated the army of the Duke and the Marquis at Argenta, and were so close to Ferrara that they had pitched their camp in the Marquis's garden.

XXV

The league felt that they could no longer postpone offering strong reinforcements to the Marquis, so they sent the Duke of Calabria to Ferrara with his own and the Pope's troops; and the Florentines also sent all their troops. In order to direct operations better, the league called a diet at Cremona to which the papal legate came with Count Girolamo, the Duke of Calabria, Lodovico, Lorenzo de' Medici, and many other Italian princes. At the diet the rulers laid all the plans for the coming war. They judged that they could not help Ferrara better than by creating a strong diversion, and they wanted Lodovico to agree to launch an attack on the Venetians through the Duke of Milan's state. Lodovico would not agree to this, for fear of starting a war he could not stop when he wanted to. So they decided to collect all the troops at Ferrara, and with four thousand men at arms and eight thousand foot soldiers they went out to meet the Venetians who had two thousand two hundred men at arms and six thousand foot. The league felt that the first thing to do was to attack the navy the Venetians had on the Po. They attacked it near Bondeno and broke it up, sinking more than two hundred ships, and taking prisoner Antonio Iustiniano, superintendent of the navy. When the Venetians saw all Italy united against them, they tried to enhance their prestige by hiring the Duke of Lorraine with two hundred men at arms. After they had suffered this naval setback, they sent him with some of their army to keep the enemy at bay. They ordered Roberto da San Severino to cross the Adda with the rest of their army and make toward Milan shouting the name of the Duke and the Lady Bona, his mother. They hoped to cause a revolution in Milan in this way, as they believed that Lodovico and his government were hated in the city. This invasion caused a great deal of fear to begin with, and the city armed. However, the result was the opposite of what the Venetians had planned, because this affront caused Lodovico to agree to the course he had refused earlier on. Leaving the Marquis of Ferrara to defend his own territory with four thousand horse and two thousand foot soldiers, the Duke of Calabria, with twelve thousand horse and five thousand foot, entered the territory of Bergamo, then Brescia, and then Verona, and almost entirely deprived those three towns of their *contadi*, without the Venetians being able to do anything to prevent it. Roberto and his troops were hard put to it to save the cities themselves. As for the Marquis of Ferrara, he had won back most of his land, since the Duke of Lorraine could not resist him, as he only had two thousand horse and a thousand foot. So the league fought successfully all that summer of 1483.

XXVI

The winter passed quietly and when spring came the next year the armies returned to the campaign, and the league had pooled all its armies in order to conquer the Venetians more speedily. If the war had proceeded as it had the year before, the Venetians would have lost all the land they held in Lombardy. The Duke of Lorraine had gone home at the end of his year's service, and they had been left with six thousand horse and five thousand foot, and against them were thirteen thousand horse and six thousand foot. But it often happens that when several people with equal authority come together, their disagreements give the victory to the enemy. Federigo Gonzaga, Marquis of Mantua, had died, and he had kept the Duke of Calabria and Lodovico true to their word by his authority. Now disagreements began to arise between them, and these led to jealousy, because Giovangaleazzo, Duke of Milan, was already old enough to take over the government of his duchy, and since his wife was the Duke of Calabria's daughter, the latter wanted his son-in-law and not Lodovico to rule the state. Lodovico knew the Duke's feelings, and he decided to deprive him of the means of acting upon them. The Venetians realized Lodovico's fear and played on it. They thought that since they had lost by using warlike methods, they could win by peaceful means. A secret agreement was negotiated between them and Lodovico and signed in August 1484. When the other allies heard the news, they were very annoyed, particularly when they saw that the towns taken from Venice were to be returned, and Rovigo and the Polesine, which the Venetians had taken from the Marquis of Ferrara, were to be left with them, and that they were to have all the claims to the city of Ferrara that they had had before. Everyone felt they had fought a war which had been costly and which had brought them honor while it lasted but shame by its end, since the towns captured had been surrendered, and those that had been lost had not been recovered. But the allies were forced to accept the peace because they were drained of resources and did not want to test their fortune any longer for the sake of the faults and ambitions of others.

XXVII

While things were being settled in Lombardy in this way the Pope had got Lorenzo to harass Città di Castello in order to oust Niccolò Vitelli, who had been deserted by the league because they hoped to win the Pope over to their side. During the siege of the town, those inside who were supporters of Niccolò came out, and when they clashed with the enemy they beat them. The Pope recalled Count Girolamo from Lombardy and ordered him back to Rome to reinforce his troops and return to that campaign. Later he decided it would be better to win Niccolò over by peaceful means than to attack him again, and he came to an agreement with him. The Pope reconciled him to his enemy Lorenzo as best he could. He was forced to this conclusion more by fear of new disturbances than by a love of peace, because he could see bad feeling growing up between the Colonna and the Orsini. In the war between the Pope and the King of Naples, the latter had taken the *contado* of Tagliacozzo from the Orsini and had given it to the Colonna, who were on his side. Then when the peace was made between the King and the Pope, the Orsini asked to have it back because of the agreements. The Pope repeatedly told the Colonna that they must give it back, but they would not agree despite the Orsini again carrying out plundering raids and similar attacks. The Pope could not tolerate this, and he mobilized all his forces and those of the Orsini against the Colonna, and he sacked the houses they possessed in Rome, and killed or captured anyone who tried to defend them. He deprived them of most of their castles; and in the end the unrest died down, not because peace had been restored but because one of the parties had been destroyed.

XXVIII

Things were still not quiet in Genoa or in Tuscany, because the Florentines were keeping Count Antonio da Marciano and his army on the frontiers of Serezana, and while the war lasted in Lombardy they pestered the Serezanese with raids and other slight attacks. At Genoa, Batistino Fregoso, Doge of the city, and his wife and children were taken prisoner by Archbishop Pagolo Fregoso, whom he had trusted; and the latter made himself ruler of the city. Again the Venetian fleet had attacked the Kingdom, occupied Gallipoli, and was ravaging the places nearby.

However, once peace was signed in Lombardy, all the unrest died down except in Tuscany and in Rome. The Pope died five days after peace was proclaimed, either because the end of his life had arrived or because the sorrow of having to make peace killed him, since he was an enemy to it. But this Pope left Italy at peace, having kept it in a continual state of war while he was alive. On his death Rome immediately rose. Count Girolamo withdrew with his troops close to the Castle, the Orsini were afraid the Colonna would want revenge for their recent attacks, and the Colonna were asking for their houses and castles back. This resulted in murders, robbery, and arson in many parts of the city in a few days. But the cardinals persuaded the Count to return the Castle to the College, go back to his own states, and free Rome from his army. He obeyed, wanting the new Pope to be well-disposed toward him. He restored the Castle to the College and went off to Imola. So the cardinals were relieved of fear, and the barons of the help from the Count that they had hoped for in their differences. They came to the creation of the new Pope. After some disagreement Giovanbattista Cibò, Cardinal of Malfetta, a Genoese, was elected and took the name of Innocent VIII. With his easygoing nature, for he was a quiet, kind man, he made everyone disarm and brought peace to Rome for the time being.

XXIX

After the peace of Lombardy the Florentines could not rest, because they felt that it was shamefully and disgracefully bad for a private gentleman to have deprived them of the Castle of Serezana. The clauses of the treaty said not only that what had been lost in battle could be demanded back, but that war could be made on anyone who hindered its restoration, so they immediately prepared men and money for such an attack. Agostino Fregoso, who had occupied Serezana, did not feel that he could withstand such an attack with his own forces, and he gave the town to St. George. Since I shall have to mention St. George and the Genoese several times, I feel it is not out of place to explain the government and customs of that city, as it is one of the most important in Italy. When the Genoese had made peace with the Venetians after the great war that had taken place between them many years earlier, their republic could not repay those citizens who had lent large sums of money, and they granted them the revenue from the customs, and laid it down that each one should have a share of this revenue, according to the original amount lent, until they had been fully repaid by the Commune. So that these people could meet together, they gave them the palace over the customs house. These creditors set up a form of government among themselves, appointed a council of a hundred of them which debated public affairs, and created a board of eight citizens which was the governing body and which executed the decisions. They divided their credits into parts which they called "Places" and they gave the name of St. George to their company. Once their internal government had been established in this way, the Commune of the city found itself in need again, and it turned to the Company of St. George for more help. They were rich and well organized, and they were able to help. Just as the Commune had given them the customs before, it now began to give them land as a surety for the money it was borrowing. Things have gone on in this way because of the Commune's need and the help the Company of St. George has given, so that the Company now has under its administration most of the towns and cities under Genoese rule. It rules and defends them and sends its magistrates to them every year by public suffrage, without the Commune worrying at all. The result of this is that the citizens have switched their affections from the Commune, which they regard as being ruled despotically, to St. George, which is well and fairly administered. This is the reason for the frequent, easy revolutions: For they pay allegiance now to one of their citizens, now to a foreigner, because it is not St. George that changes its government but the Commune. When there was a fight for power between the Fregoso and the Adorni, because the government of the Commune was at stake, most of the citizens stood aside and left it to the winner. When someone has taken power, all the office of St. George does is to make him swear to observe its laws. These have not been altered to this day; because with arms, money, and power on their side, the laws cannot be altered without the certain risk of a dangerous rebellion. This is a truly unique example and one never found in the real or imaginary republics of the philosophers: liberty and tyranny, citizenship and debauchery, justice and license side by side within the same circle of walls and among the same citizens. It is that institution alone that keeps the city true to its ancient and venerable traditions. If it happened, as it will do in time, that the Company of

St. George took over the whole city, then that republic would be more worthy of memory than the republic of Venice.

XXX

It was to the Company of St. George that Agostino Fregoso surrendered Serezana. They received it gladly and undertook to defend it, put a fleet to sea immediately, and sent soldiers to Pietrasanta to stop anyone from getting to the Florentine army, which was already near Serezana. Meanwhile, the Florentines wanted to occupy Pietrasanta, for if they did not possess this town, Serezana would be less useful to them, as it lay between there and Pisa. But they could not reasonably besiege it if the people of Pietrasanta, or whoever controlled it, had not stopped them from taking Serezana. To provoke them they sent a large quantity of munitions and supplies to the army from Pisa, with a small escort, so that the people in Pietrasanta would be encouraged by the small guard and would want to attack it more because of the considerable booty. Things went according to plan; the men at Pietrasanta were dazzled by so much plunder and carried it off. This gave the Florentines a legitimate excuse for making an attack; and leaving Serezana on one side, they laid siege to Pietrasanta, which was well garrisoned and put up a very brave defense. The Florentines placed their artillery on the plain and built a fort on the hill to attack it from that side as well. The commissioner for the army was Iacopo Guicciardini. While they were fighting at Pietrasanta, the Genoese fleet took and burned the fortress of Vada, and landed an army which was raiding and plundering the nearby country. Bongianni Gianfigliazzi was sent to oppose them with foot soldiers and cavalry, and he checked their arrogance a little, so that they did not carry out their raids so freely. But the fleet went on worrying the Florentines, and it went to Leghorn, and using pontoons and other devices approached the new tower and attacked it for several days with its artillery. But they saw they were having no success, and made a dishonorable retreat.

XXXI

During this time the fighting at Pietrasanta was slow, so the enemy felt encouraged to attack the fort, and they took it. They won such prestige by this, and the Florentine army was so afraid that it almost broke up of its own accord. It retreated four miles from the town, and the leaders reckoned that since it was already October it was time to retire to winter quarters and save the capture of the city for the new season. When news of this mishap reached Florence, the leaders of the government were very angry, and they immediately elected Antonio Pucci and Bernardo del Nero as new commissioners, to restore the army's reputation and its strength. They arrived in the camp with large sums of money and told the captains how angry the Signoria, the regime, and the whole city would be if they did not take the army back to the walls, and what would be their disgrace if such great captains, with such an army, could not take such a small, weak town with only a small garrison to resist them. They pointed out the immediate usefulness of this gain and what it could mean in the future, and in the end the troops were fired with courage to return to the walls. First of all, they decided to take the fort. Its capture demonstrated how effective kindness, affability, and friendly words and behavior are with soldiers. Antonio Pucci, by comforting one soldier, making promises to another, giving his hand to some and embracing others, made them go into the attack with such dash that they took the fort in no time. It was not captured without loss, because Count Antonio da Marciano was killed by a cannonball. This victory so terrified the people in the town that they began to talk about surrendering. In order to bring things to a dignified conclusion, Lorenzo de' Medici felt that he should join the army, and not many days after he arrived the castle was won. It was already winter, and the captains felt that they should not carry on with the campaign but wait for the new season, especially because that autumn the army was sickly because of the unhealthy climate, and many of the commanders were seriously ill. Among these were Antonio Pucci and Bongianni Gianfigliazzi, and the latter not only fell ill but died, much to everyone's sorrow. Antonio had won great popularity because of what he had done at Pietrasanta. Since the Florentines had won Pietrasanta, the Lucchese sent ambassadors to Florence to ask for it, as it was a town that had once belonged to their republic, and they asserted that it was one of the treaty obligations to return to their first lord all those towns that were recovered. The Florentines did not deny the terms of the agreement, but they replied that they did not know whether it would have to be returned to the Genoese under the peace treaty that was being negotiated between them and Genoa. Therefore they could not make a decision about it until then, and if they did not have to return it, the Lucchese would have to compensate them for their expenses and the losses suffered through the deaths of so many of their citizens. If they did this, they could safely hope to get it back. All that winter was spent in peace negotiations between the Genoese and the Florentines, which were carried on in Rome with the mediation of the Pope. But as no conclusion was reached, the Florentines would have attacked Serezana when spring came, if they had not been stopped by Lorenzo de' Medici's illness and the war that broke out between the Pope and King Ferrando. Lorenzo was attacked not only by gout, which he had inherited from his father, but by very bad stomach pains, and he was forced to go to a watering place for treatment.

XXXII

The most important reason, however, was the war. And this was the cause of the war: The city of Aquila was subject to Naples, but in such a way that it was almost a free city. A person of great importance in the city was the Count of Montorio. The Duke of Calabria was near the Tronto with his men at arms on the pretext of quelling some riots which had broken out among the country people in that area, but he was planning to bring Aquila into complete subjection to the King. He sent for the Count of Montorio, pretending to need his help in the business he was dealing with at the time. The Count obeyed without suspecting anything, and when he reached the Duke he was taken prisoner by him and sent to Naples. When news of this was heard in Aquila, the whole city was angry and the people took up arms. Antonio Concinello, the King's commissioner, was killed, and with him some citizens who were known as supporters of his majesty. To have somebody to defend them in their rebellion, the people of Aquila raised the banner of the Church and sent ambassadors to the Pope to give him their city. They begged him to help them against the tyranny of the King as if they were his own subjects. The Pope sprang to their defense, for he hated the King for public and private reasons; and as Roberto da San Severino had quarrelled with the government of Milan and was without a commission, he took him as his general and made him come to Rome with all possible speed. Besides this, he incited all the friends and relations of the Count of Montorio to rebel against the King. The Princes of Altamira, Salerno, and Bisignano took up arms against the King. Seeing himself attacked so suddenly, the King turned to the Florentines and the Duke of Milan for help. The Florentines hesitated as to what they should do, because they felt that they could hardly leave their own battles for someone else's, and it seemed dangerous to take up arms against the Church again. Nevertheless, because of the alliance, they put their promises before expediency and their own danger, hired the Orsini, and sent all their soldiers, under the Count of Pitigliano, toward Rome to help the King. The King drew up two armies: One under the Duke of Calabria he sent toward Rome, and with the Florentine troops they faced the army of the Church; he took on the barons with the other one under his own command. The war was fought out with varying fortunes on both sides. In the end as the King had the upper hand everywhere, peace was made in August 1486 with the help of the King of Spain's ambassadors. The Pope agreed to it, because he had been beaten by Fortune and he no longer wanted to tempt it. All the Italian powers joined in, except for the Genoese, who were left out as rebels against the government of Milan and as usurpers of Florentine territory. Once peace was made, Roberto da San Severino, who had been an unfaithful friend to the Pope in the war and not a very formidable enemy to the others, was expelled from Rome by the Pope and pursued by the soldiers of the Duke and the Florentines. He saw he was being overtaken when he had passed Cesena, and he fled and reached Ravenna with less than a hundred horse. Part of the rest of his army were taken on by the Duke and part were set upon by the country people. After the peace treaty and his reconciliation with the barons, the King had Iacopo Coppola and Antonello d'Anversa put to death with their children, because they had betrayed his secrets to the Pope during the war.

XXXIII

This war had taught the Pope how swiftly and carefully the Florentines stand by their alliances. And where he had hated them before, because of his friendship with the Genoese and because of the help the Florentines had given the King, he now began to love them and do their ambassadors greater favors than usual. When Lorenzo de' Medici realized this tendency, he did everything he could to encourage it because he felt it would be greatly to his credit if he could add an alliance with the Pope to the one he had with the King. The Pope had a son called Francesco, whom he had wanted to honor with lands and allies so that after his death he would be able to keep them. The Pope knew of no one in Italy who would make a safer ally than Lorenzo, and so he arranged for Lorenzo to give Francesco one of his daughters as his wife. After this match was made, the Pope asked the Genoese to agree to give Serezana up to the Florentines, telling them that they could not keep what Agostino had sold, and Agostino could not give the Company of St. George something that was not his. But

he could never make any headway and, in fact, while
discussions were going on in Rome, the Genoese armed a
number of their ships, and without Florence getting wind
of it, they landed three thousand foot soldiers and attacked Serezanello, a fortress owned by the Florentines
above Serezana. They sacked and burned the village
next to it, and then trained their artillery on the fortress
and attacked it with great persistence. To the Florentines
this attack was quite unexpected. They immediately mustered their troops under Virginio Orsino at Pisa. They
complained to the Pope that while he had been negotiating for peace, the Genoese had made war on them.
Then they sent Piero Corsini to Lucca to keep that city
faithful, and Pagolantonio Soderini to Venice to find out
the republic's intentions. And they asked for help from
the King and Lodovico, but got it from neither, because
the King said he was afraid of the Turkish fleet, and
Lodovico postponed sending help because of other quib-
bles. In this way the Florentines are almost always alone
in their wars, and they never find anyone to help them
with the same spirit with which they help others. But they
were not afraid because their allies had deserted them
this time, as this was nothing new to them. They put a
large army under Iacopo Guicciardini and Piero Vettori
and sent it against the enemy. The latter pitched camp
on the river Magra. Meantime, Serezanello was being
hard pressed by the enemy, who were trying to capture
it by quarrying underneath it and by using every other
means. The commissioners decided to go to its aid. The
enemy did not refuse to fight, and in the clash the
Genoese were defeated. Luigi dal Fiesco was taken prisoner with many other leaders of the enemy army. This
victory did not frighten the Serezanese enough to make
them give in. They prepared to defend themselves obstinately, and the Florentine commissioners prepared to
attack. Both the attack and the defense were spirited.
Since the operation was taking a long time, Lorenzo de'
Medici felt that he should visit the camp. When he arrived the morale of our soldiers went up, and the Serezanese lost theirs. They saw the persistence of the Florentine attack and the Genoese rebuffs when they were

asked for help, and freely and unconditionally they placed themselves in Lorenzo's hands. Once they had come under Florentine rule they were treated with kindness, except for a few who had been responsible for the rebellion. During the siege, Lodovico had sent his men at arms to Pontremoli to make a show of coming to our aid. But he had an understanding with some people in Genoa, and the party which opposed the government there rose, and with the help of these troops they handed the city over to the Duke of Milan.

XXXIV

At this time the Germans had made an attack on the Venetians, and Boccolino from Osimo in the Marches had caused Osimo to rebel against the Pope, and he made himself its sole ruler. Eventually Lorenzo persuaded him to surrender the city to the Pope, and he came to Florence, where he lived and was honored under Lorenzo's protection for some time. Afterwards he went to Milan, where he did not find the same trust, and was put to death by Lodovico. The Venetians were attacked and beaten by the Germans near the city of Trent, and Roberto da San Severino, their general, was killed. After the defeat, the Venetians made an agreement with the Germans that was more worthy of conquerors than losers. Their luck ran true to form and the republic received honor because of it.

Also at this time there was very serious trouble in Romagna. Francesco d'Orso was a man of great power in the city of Forlì. Count Girolamo grew suspicious of him and threatened him several times. Since Francesco was living in great fear, his friends and relations advised him to prevent trouble, and if he was afraid of being killed by Girolamo to kill him first and end his own danger by another's death. The decision was taken and their minds were made up. They chose the day which was to be market day in Forlì. As many of their friends came into the town from the country on that day, they thought they would be able to make use of them without having to call them in. It was May, and most Italians have the custom of dining during the day. The conspirators thought the best time to kill him would be after his dinner, at which time his household would be dining and he would be almost alone in his room. With this plan in mind, Francesco went to the Count's home at the appointed hour, and leaving his companions in the anterooms, he reached the room where the Count was. He told one of the Count's servants to tell him that he wanted to speak to him. Francesco was admitted, and finding the Count alone, he killed him after a few words of pretended discussion. Then he called his friends, and they killed the servant. By chance the captain of the town came to talk to the Count, and when he arrived in the room with a few of his men, he too was killed by the Count's murderers. After these murders, there was a great uproar, and the Count's head was thrown out of the window. They shouted Church and Liberty and made all the people arm. They had hated the Count's greed and cruelty, and they sacked his house and captured the Countess Catherine and all her children. The fortress was the only thing left for them to take if their plan was to be successful. As the commandant would not agree, they begged the Countess to persuade him to give it up. She promised to do this if they would let her go inside, and they could keep her children as hostages for her good behavior. The conspirators believed her and allowed her to go in. Once she was inside she threatened them with death and all kinds of torture in revenge for her husband. They threatened to kill her children, and she answered that she had with her the means of having more. The conspirators were frightened when they realized the Pope had not supported them, and they heard that Lodovico, the Countess's uncle, was sending troops to help her. They took what they could of their property and went to Città di Castello. The Countess took over the government and revenged her husband's death with all kinds of cruelty. When the Florentines heard of the Count's death, they took the opportunity to recover the fortress of Piancaldoli, which the Count had taken from them in the past. They sent their troops there and retook it, causing the death of Cecca, the famous architect.

XXXV

To this trouble in Romagna was added more of no less importance in the same province. Galeotto, Lord of Faenza, was married to the daughter of Giovanni Bentivoglio, ruler of Bologna. She hated her husband either through jealousy or because he ill-treated her, or because she had a wicked nature; and she hated him so much that she decided to deprive him of his power and his life. She pretended to be ill and went to bed, and she ordered that when Galeotto came to see her he was to be killed by some of her trusted friends whom she had hidden in her room for that purpose. She had communicated her plan to her father, who was hoping to become Lord of Faenza after his son-in-law's death. When the appointed time came for the murder, Galeotto went into his wife's room as usual, and after he had been with her talking for some time, his murderers came out of their hiding places in the bedroom and killed him before he could put up any resistance. After his death there was chaos. His wife and a small baby named Astorre escaped to the castle, the people took up arms, and Giovanni Bentivoglio entered Faenza with a certain Bergamino, the Duke of Milan's captain, and a number of armed men he had waiting. Antonio Boscoli, the Florentine commissioner, was still in the town. While all these leaders were gathered together amid this confusion, discussing the government of the town, the men of the Lamona valley who had all flocked in to the riots, turned their forces against Giovanni and Bergamino. They killed Bergamino and took Giovanni prisoner, and shouting the name of Astorre and the Florentines, they placed the city in the hands of the Florentine commissioner. Everyone in Florence was sorry to hear of this affair. But they had Giovanni and his daughter set free, and took charge of the city and Astorre with the consent of all the people.

Besides these riots, there were several others in Romagna, the Marches, and at Siena for many years, after the major wars between the chief rulers came to an end. But they were of little importance, and I believe it would be superfluous to describe them. It is true that those in Siena were more frequent after the Duke of Calabria left at the end of the 1478 war. There were a great many changes, with the people in control sometimes, and sometimes the nobles, and in the end the nobles won. Of these, Pandolfo and Iacobo Petrucci had more power than the others, and they became as good as rulers of the city, one by his prudence and the other by his courage.

XXXVI

When the Serezana war was over, however, the Florentines lived through a period of great prosperity until 1492, when Lorenzo died. After Italy's disarmament, which had been brought about through his good sense and authority, Lorenzo turned his attention to accomplishing his own and his city's greatness. He married Piero, his eldest son, to Alfonsina, the daughter of the knight Orsino. Then he raised his second son, Giovanni, to the rank of cardinal. This was all the more remarkable in that he was invested with the dignity before he was fourteen, for which there was no precedent. This was a ladder that could lead his house up to heaven, as did in fact happen later on. For Giuliano, his third son, Lorenzo could provide little out of the ordinary because he was so young and because Lorenzo himself lived such a short time. Of his daughters he married the first to Iacopo Salviati, the second to Francesco Cibo, and the third to Piero Ridolfi. The fourth, whom he had married to Giovanni de' Medici to keep the family together, died. In his other private affairs he was very unlucky as far as commerce was concerned. Much of his movable property was lost through the mismanagement of his executives, who handled his affairs not like private persons but like princes. His country was forced to subsidize him with a large sum of money. So he gave up commercial enterprises to avoid tempting Fortune and turned to property as being a more stable and reliable form of wealth. He bought property near Prato, Pisa, and in the Pesa Valley which was worthy not of a private citizen but of a King in its profitability and the quality and the impressive appearance of the buildings.

After this he turned to making the city more beautiful and even greater. As there were many open spaces in it he ordered 'new streets to be built and filled with new buildings. And the city did become more beautiful and greater. And so that people could live more safely and peacefully in the state, and fight and resist their enemies farther away, he fortified the castle of Firenzuola in the mountains toward Bologna. Toward Siena he laid the foundations of Poggio Imperiale, which was to be made very strong. Toward Genoa he closed the way to the enemy by the acquisition of Pietrasanta and Serezana. Then by dispensing pensions and aid he kept the Baglioni of Perugia and the Vitelli of Città di Castello friendly. He was in charge of the government of Faenza. All these were like firm bulwarks for his city. Then during this peaceful period he kept the town in a continual state of holiday. Tournaments and pageants of historical events and triumphs were often to be seen, and his aim was to keep the city prosperous, the people united, and the nobility honored. He was particularly fond of anyone who excelled in any form of art, and he helped men of letters: Agnolo da Montepulciano, Cristofano Landini, and Demetrius the Greek can all bear witness to this. This was why Count Giovanni della Mirandola, a man who was almost divine, was influenced by Lorenzo's generosity to leave the other parts of Europe that he had visited and make his home in Florence. Lorenzo had an extraordinary love of architecture, music, and poetry, and many pieces of poetry exist which were not only written but also commented on by him. He opened a University in Pisa to which he brought the best men then in Italy, so that the youth of Florence could be educated in the study of literature. He built a monastery near Florence for Friar Mariano da Ghinazzano, of the order of St. Augustine, because he was such a fine preacher.

He was particularly beloved by Fortune and by God, and all his enterprises were successful while those of his enemies were unsuccessful. Besides the Pazzi, Battista Frescobaldi tried to kill him in the Carmine and Badinotto di Pistoia tried at his villa. Both of them, with those who had been a party to their secrets, suffered just punishment for their wicked plots. His style of living, his prudence, and fortune were recognized and admired not only by the Italian princes but by those farther afield. Matthew, King of Hungary, gave many tokens of the love he bore him, the Sultan sent his ambassadors with presents, the Grand Turk handed Bernardo Bandini, his brother's murderer, over to him. All these things meant that he was very much admired in Italy. Every day his reputation grew because of his prudence and because he was eloquent and sharp in discussion, wise in his decisions, and swift and courageous in action. It is impossible to think of any vices that clouded so many virtues, although he was remarkably entangled in affairs of the heart; he delighted in the company of humorous, witty men, and in childish pranks, more than seemed right in such a great man. Very often he was seen to join in his sons' and daughters' games. When one considered his serious life and his self-indulgent life, one could see two different people joined together in an almost impossible way. The last part of his life was very unhappy because of the illness that plagued him. He was afflicted with terrible stomach pains, and they attacked him so badly that he died in April 1492 at the age of forty-four. No one ever died, not only in Florence but in Italy, who had such a reputation for prudence, or who was so much missed by his country. Heaven gave a number of obvious signs of the great disasters that were to be the result of his death. The highest point of the church of Santa Reparata was hit by a thunderbolt so violently that most of the pinnacle came down, much to everyone's stupor and amazement. All the citizens and all the rulers of Italy mourned his death. They showed this openly, for there was no one who did not send ambassadors to Florence to express their sorrow. The results of his death soon showed whether they had just cause to lament it.

Because with Italy deprived of his advice, those who were left could find no way of appeasing or checking the ambitions of Lodovico Sforza, who governed for the Duke of Milan. As soon as Lorenzo died, these ambitions caused those evil seeds to put forth shoots which no one alive could uproot, and which very shortly caused the present destruction of Italy.

Hugh R. Trevor-Roper, general editor of *The Great Histories Series*, is the distinguished Regius Professor of Modern History at Oxford University. He is probably best known to American readers for his book *The Last Days of Hitler*, which is a classic in the field of modern German history and was the result of official investigations carried out by Professor Trevor-Roper at the behest of British Intelligence in an attempt to unshroud the mystery surrounding the dictator's fate. The book has already been translated into twenty foreign languages. Professor Trevor-Roper is a specialist in sixteenth- and seventeenth-century history and has published several other notable works, including *Archbishop Laud, Man and Events*. He has contributed numerous articles on political and historical subjects to the journals and is familiar to American readers of *The New York Times Magazine* and *Horizon*.

Myron P. Gilmore, editor of this volume, is Professor of History at Harvard and is also Director of Villa I Tatti, the Harvard University Center for Italian Renaissance Studies in Florence, Italy. His published works include *Argument from Roman Law in Political Thought, 1300–1600; The World of Humanism;* and *Humanists and Jurists*.

Judith A. Rawson, translator of this volume, is a lecturer in Italian at the University of Warwick.

Index

Abati family, 60, 75, 81
Acciaiuoli family, 99, 143-44, 159, 160, 161, 229
Acciaiuoli, Agnolo, 207-08, 229, 238, 239-40, 246
Acciaiuoli, Agnolo, Archbishop of Florence, 105, 110, 111, 112
Acciaiuoli, Donato, xi, 282
Acquasparta, Matteo d', Cardinal of Porto, 76, 78
Adams, John, xxx-xxxi, xxxii
Adimari family, 60, 72, 75, 157, 162, 164
Adimari, Antonio, 106, 107, 108
Adorni family, 225, 304
Adorno, Prospero, 281
Adrian VI, Pope, xxxvii
Adriani, Marcello Virgilio, xii, xii*fn*
Agobio, Iacopo d', 95, 96
Agobio, Lando d', 86-87
Alamanni, Boccaccino, 196
Alamanni, Luigi, xxiii, 29
Alberigo, Count, 172, 173
Albert, King of Germany, 87
Alberti family, 95, 128, 155-58, 160, 164-65, 168, 176
Alberti, Antonio degli, 141, 156, 164-65
Alberti, Benedetto degli, 130, 131, 141, 143, 148, 149
downfall of, 155-57, 158
and Giorgio Scali, 148, 151-52, 154, 156, 178
Albizzi family, 47, 106, 118-22, 125-26, 127, 148, 168
Albizzi, Maso degli, 15, 158, 161, 162, 168, 201
Albizzi, Piero degli, 120, 121, 126, 127-29, 132
downfall of, 149, 158

Albizzi, Rinaldo degli, 168, 174-79, 186
and the campaign against Lucca, 187-89, 191, 194, 198
and Cosimo de' Medici, 199-204, 206-12, 222
Alessandri, Cornelia degli, 221
Alexander VI, Pope, xiii, xiv, xvi
Alfonso, Duke of Calabria (son of King Ferrando), 241, 244, 279, 283, 285, 286
and the Ferrarese war, 296, 297, 299-300
occupation of Siena by, 289, 290, 291, 292, 294, 314
and the Pope's war with Ferrando, 307-09
Alfonso, King of Naples and Sicily, 221, 222
Alidosi family, 171, 172, 244
Altopascio, encampment at, 91
Altoviti family, 73, 99, 106, 164, 243
Alviano, Bartolomeo d', 3
Amidei family, 58, 59, 60, 81
Ammuniti, 120, 128-29, 130, 133, 135, 142, 157
under Maso degli Albizzi, 161, 162, 163
Andrea, Giovanni, ix
Andria, Count Novello of, 86
Antonio da Marciano, Count, 302, 306
Antonio da Volterra, 268, 270, 271
Anziani, 61-62, 66
Aquila, 307-08
Arcolano, 186-87
Arezzo, 62, 69, 103, 110, 155, 166
Argyropoulos, 223
Ascesi, Guglielmo d', 104, 109

319

Athens, Duke of. *See* Walter of Brienne

Baldini, Iacopo, 40
Baldovinetti, Mariotto, 207
Balìa, 23, 26, 132, 164, 165, 204, 206, 208
   Cosimo de' Medici's powers of, 215-18, 237-38
   and the reforms of 1382, 153, 156, 157
Bandini, Bernardo, 268-73, 316
Barbadoro, Niccolò, 200, 203, 209, 211, 212
Bardi family, 60, 75
   and the Acciaiuoli, 229
   conspiracies of, 95-97, 103, 106
   and the *popolani*, 112, 114, 115
Bene, Niccolò del, 143, 144
Bentivogli, Antonio, 171
Bentivogli, Giovanni, 235, 313
Bernardi, Taddeo, 51
Bertelli, Sergio, xi*fn*-xii*fn*, xvi*fn*, xvii*fn*, xx*fn*, xxxvi
Biondo, Flavio, xi, xxiii, xxvi, xxvii
Bisdomini family, 60, 76
Bisdomini, Cerrettieri, 104, 109
Black and White parties, 74-85
   in Pistoia, 39
Boccaccio, Giovanni, 116
Boccolino, 311
Bologna, 148-49, 171
   conquest of, xiii, xiv
   See also Bentivogli, Giovanni
Boniface VIII, Pope, 75, 76-78, 80, 81, 82
Borgia, Cesare, xiii, xiv, xvi, xxiv
Borso, Marquis of Ferrara, 233, 234, 235, 241, 243, 244
Braccio da Perugia, 173, 174, 187, 257
Branca, Piero, 83
Brescia, capture of, 181, 184
Brunelleschi family, 60, 76
   Brunelleschi, Berto, 83
   Brunelleschi, Filippo, 195
   Brunelleschi, Francesco, 43, 106
Bruni, Leonardo, xxv, xxvi, xxvii, xxviii
Buondelmonti family, 58-60, 76, 107, 121, 125
Buondelmonti, Uguccione, 106, 108

Buondelmonti, Zanobi, xxiii, 29
Buoni Uomini, 21, 66, 88, 111
Buonromei family, 265

Caesar, Julius, xxi, 4, 57
Calabria, Dukes of. *See* Alfonso; Charles
Cambio, Giovanni di, 151
Campaldino, battle at, 69
Cancellieri family, 74
Capponi, Neri, 215-16
Capponi, Piero, 283
Cardona, Ramondo di, 91
Carlo, Count, 257-58, 268, 283-84
Carmignuola, Francesco, 181, 183
Carradi, Maffeo da, 96
Castiglionchio, Lapo da, 120, 127, 128, 129, 132-33, 144
Castracani, Antonio, 29-31
Castracani, Castruccio
   character of, 49-54
   conspiracy against, 44
   death of, 47-49, 94
   early life of, 30-32
   and the Emperor, 36-37, 40, 48
   Florentines defeated by, 33-35, 41-47, 91-93, 135, 189
   Pisa held by, 37, 44-49, 87, 93
   Pistoia taken by, 39-43, 48, 91, 93
   and the Poggio family, 37-38
   Prato taken by, 43, 88
   and Uguccione, 33-36
   and the Visconti, 37, 48
Catasto, 182-83, 184, 217
Cavalcanti family, 60, 75, 81-82
   and the Duke of Athens, 107-08
   and the *popolani*, 113, 114
Cavicciuli family, 106, 107, 113, 114
   and the conspiracies of 1397 and 1400, 162, 163, 164
Cavicciuli, Boccaccio, 84
Cecca, 313
Cecchi, Baldo, 40
Cennami, Piero, 197
Cerchi family, 60, 74-79, 85, 106, 125
Cerchi, Bonifacio, 44
Cerchi, Veri de', 74, 78, 85
Chabod, Federico, xxxvi
Chamberlains, of France, 12
Chambre des Comptes, 10

Charlemagne, 58
Charles I of Anjou, King of Naples and Sicily, 64, 66, 67, 68, 119
Charles, Duke of Burgundy, 224-25, 227
Charles, Duke of Calabria (son of King Robert of Naples), 43, 44, 47, 92-93, 98, 102
Charles VI, King of France, 14
Charles VII, King of France, 14
Charles VIII, King of France, xiii, xxxvii, 3, 16
Charles of Valois, 77-79
Church
  and Emperors, 58, 62, 67, 93
  and Guelphs, 62, 63, 64, 76
  opposition to, 127-28
  states of the, 255
  See also Pope(s)
Cicero, xi
Cini, Bettone, 105
Città da Castello, 255, 284, 296, 301, 315
Clement IV, Pope, 64, 67
Clement VII, Pope, vii, xxxvii
  See also Medici, Giulio de'
Clough, C. H., xviifn
Cocchi, Donato, 217
Colle, 110, 286
Colleoni, Bartolomeo, 241, 242, 247
Colonization, ancient, 55-56
Colonna family, 296, 301-02
Colonna, Fabrizio, xx-xxi, xxiv
Companies of the People, 24, 80, 82, 83, 87, 90
  and the Duke of Athens, 103
  and constitutional reforms, 111, 112
Company of St. George, 303-05, 309
Conradin, 66
Conseil du roi, 12
Contugi, Giovanni di, 185-86
Coppo Stefani, Marchionne di, xxvii
Council of Basle, 298
Council of the Commune, 93, 142-43
  See also Florence, Councils of
Council of Constance, 222
Credenza, 66
Cremona, diet at, 299
Cyprus, 256

Dante Alighieri, 56, 58, 77, 79, 85
Della Bella family, 60
Della Bella, Giano, 70-71, 85
Della Scala family, 36
Della Scala, Mastino, 97-98
Demetrius, 315
Detmold, C., xviiifn
Diacceto, Pagolo da, 196
Donati family, 58-60, 106, 108, 113, 114
  and the Cerchi, 74-79, 125
Donati, Amerigo, 89, 108
Donati, Corso, 70-71, 76-85
Durazzo, Carlo di, 148-50, 154-55

Emperor(s). *See* German Emperor(s)
England, and France, 5, 9, 14
Ercole da Este, Marquis of Ferrara, 241, 244, 255, 280, 283, 295-96, 298-301
Este family. *See* Borso; Ercole da Este
Eugene IV, Pope, 211-12

Faenza, rulers of, 180, 256, 267, 313, 315
Faggiuola, Uguccione della, 33-36, 53, 83-87
Falconi, Michelagnolo, 47
Farganaccio, 205-06
Federigo, Count of Urbino, 197, 241, 254, 256, 279-80, 296, 298
Federigo, King of Naples, 19
Fedini, Niccolò, 233
Ferrando of Aragon, King of Naples and Sicily, 214, 225, 226, 241, 244, 256-58, 279, 281-82
  and the Ferrarese war, 295-98, 301
  Lorenzo de' Medici's alliance with, 287-91, 294, 310
  and the Pazzi conspiracy, 268
  Pope Innocent's war with, 307-09
  and the Turkish war, 292
Ferrante, Piero, 79
Ferrara, Marquis of. *See* Borso; Ercole da Este
Ferrarese war, 295-301
Ficino, Marsilio, 223
Fiesole, 56, 57, 58, 221
Filippo, Lord of Taranto, 35

INDEX

Flanders, and France, 6
Florence
  Albizzi and Ricci feud in, 118-
    22, 125-26, 148, 168
  alliances of, during the Medici
    regimes, 221, 231, 241,
    255-56, 264, 278-83, 287-
    301, 307-11
  banishment of the Alberti
    from, 155-58, 176
  Bardi and Frescobaldi plot of
    1340 in, 94-97
  Black and White parties in,
    74-80, 124
  Buondelmonti and Uberti feud
    in, 58-60, 125
  Cerchi and Donati feud in,
    74-79, 125
  Colleges of, 21, 22, 25, 82, 90,
    129-32, 140, 142
  constitutional reforms in, xxx,
    15-16, 61-62, 64-66, 68-70,
    73, 93, 109, 111-12, 116,
    147-48, 153, 237
  Corso Donati's influence in,
    79-84
  Cosimo de' Medici's exile
    from, 200-13
  Cosimo de' Medici's party in,
    179, 199, 215
  Cosimo de' Medici's regime in,
    16-19, 215-24
  Councils of, 22-27, 66, 88, 89,
    90, 93, 112, 142-43
  Count Guido Novello's rule of,
    63-65
  Duke of Athens' rule of, xxviii,
    xxix, 92, 98-110, 118, 124,
    135, 147
  Duke of Calabria's rule of, 92-
    93
  excommunication of, 67, 276
  famines in, 113, 127
  feuds and factions in, 214-15
  fire of 1304 in, 80-81
  flood of 1333 in, 94
  Giano della Bella's influence
    in, 70-71
  Giorgio Scali's leadership in,
    147-48, 150-52, 154
  Giovanni de' Medici's influ-
    ence in, 169, 172, 175,
    177-79, 182-85
  Guilds of, 64-65, 68-70, 131-32,
    136-37, 140-48, 153, 158-
    59, 176
  humanism in, xi

instability in, 15-19
interdicts in, 76, 78, 80
King Robert of Naples' rule of,
  85-88, 92
Lando d'Agobio's rule of, 86-
  87
Lorenzo and Giuliano de'
  Medici's regime in, 246-47
Lorenzo de' Medici's regime
  in, 276-78, 287-91, 294-95,
  314-16
Machiavelli's proposals for
  the constitution of, xxiv-
  xxv, 21-28
Machiavelli's role in the government of, xii-xv
Manfred's subjection of, 63-64
Maso degli Albizzi's regime in,
  158, 161, 162, 168
Medici government restored
  in, xii, xiv, xv
Medici rulers of, 16-18, 263
Michele di Lando's leadership
  in, 144-48
nobility defeated in, 68, 116,
  118
origins of, 56-58
Pazzi conspiracy in, 263-75
Piero de' Medici's regime in,
  228-46
plagues in, 116, 285
Priors of, 68, 69, 70
prosperity and prestige of, 69,
  73
public buildings in, 73, 94,
  220, 315
regime of 1381-1434 in, 153,
  154-66, 168
republicanism in, 19-21
Rinaldo degli Albizzi's influence in, 174, 175-79, 187-
  89, 191
Salvestro de' Medici's influence in, 129-31, 141, 148,
  204
Signoria of, 15-16, 21, 22, 25
social conflicts in, 69-73, 88-
  90, 111-18, 136-53
social equality in, 20, 21, 117-
  18, 119, 125
system of choosing magis-
  trates in, 90
taxation in, 173-75, 176, 178,
  181-84, 217
Tommaso Soderini's influence
  in, 246-47, 253

322

Veri de' Medici's influence in, 159-60
Wool Guild of, 137, 141, 142
working-class party in, 148, 150-53, 154, 156, 159, 168, 175-76
See also Ghibellines; Guelphs
Foix, Gaston de, xv
Forlì, 171-73, 244, 311
Fortebraccio, Niccolò, 187, 188, 191
Foscari, Marco, xxvii
France
alliances of, xiii-xiv, 224-25
army and navy of, 2-4, 12
clergy and parishes of, 4-5, 7-8, 12-13
Estates of, 10
and foreign nations, 5-7, 13, 14
governmental offices of, 9-12
invasion of Italy by, xix, xxviii
military defenses of, 7, 10, 12, 13
military power of, xv
nobility of, xxv, 1-2, 8, 20
Parlements of, 10
provincial governors of, 9-10
royal court in, 11-12, 13-14
royal revenues and expenditures in, 8-10
taxation in, 8-9
universities of, 10
wealth of, 4
Francis, Duke of Brittany, 224
Franzesi, Napoleone, 268, 275
Frederick of Bavaria (Hapsburg), 36-37, 40
Frederick II, Holy Roman Emperor, 60, 62
Frederick, King of Sicily, 85
Fregoso family, 302, 304
Fregoso, Agostino, 303, 305, 309
Fregoso, Batistino, 281-82, 302
Fregoso, Lodovico, 289
Fregoso, Tommaso da Campo, 169
Frescobaldi family, 60, 75
and Castruccio, 43
conspiracies planned by, 89, 95-97, 103, 106, 316
and the *popolani*, 114, 115
Frontinus, 57
Fucecchio, battle at, 45-47
Fueter, Eduard, xxviii, xxviii*fn*

Gaeta, Franco, xxiv, xxiv*fn*, xxxvi
Galeazzo. *See* Sforza, Galeazzo; Visconti, Gian Galeazzo
Galeotto, Lord of Faenza, 256, 313
Garigliano, battle of, 3
Genoa, 169, 170, 225, 302
and the Company of St. George, 303-05
rebellion of, 281-82
and the Serezana war, 305-07, 309-11
German Emperor(s), 36-37, 40, 48, 85, 118
and the Church, 58, 60, 62, 67, 92-94, 298
and the Ghibellines, 60-61, 62, 68
Gherardesca, Count Gaddo della, 35, 37
Gherardini family, 60, 75, 81
Gherardini, Lotteringo, 89
Ghibellines
and the Emperor, 60-61, 62, 68
of Florence, after the expulsion of Count Guido Novello, 65-66
of Florence, after Manfred's defeat, 64, 65-69
of Florence, regulation of 1357 against, 119-21, 133
Florentine families of, 60-61
led by Castruccio, 37, 87, 92
led by Manfred, 62-64
led by Uguccione, 33, 83, 85
in Lucca, 31, 32, 33
See also Black and White parties
Ghinazzano, Friar Mariano da, 315
Gia, Iacopo da, 39
Gianfigliazzi family, 60, 76
Gianfigliazzi, Bongianni, 305, 307
Gianfigliazzi, Francesco, 175
Gianfigliazzi, Rinaldo, 159, 160
Gianni, Astorre, 191-94, 199
Giannotti, Donato, xxvi
Gilbert, Allen, xxxvi
Gilbert, Felix, xxxvi
Gino, Neri di, 168, 195, 200, 207, 208
Ginori, Giorgio, 250
Giordano, Count, 63
Giotto, 94

Giotto, Rinieri di, 103
Giovio, Paolo, xii*fn*
Girolamo, Count, 244, 256, 265-69, 295, 299, 301-03, 311-12
Giusto, 185-87
Gonfalonier, powers of, 16, 21-22, 24, 25
  and the *popolani*, 69-70
Gonzaga, Federigo, Marquis of Mantua, 283, 285, 300
Grand Chancellor, of France, 9, 12, 13
Grand Ecuyer, 12
Grand Seneschal, 9, 12
Grandi, 153, 173, 175, 217
Grayson, Cecil, xx*fn*, xxxvi
Gregory X, Pope, 67
Gregory XI, Pope, 126-28
Guadagni, Bernardo, 203-04, 206
Guelphs
  ascendancy of, in Florence, after Manfred's defeat, 64, 66-69
  ascendancy of, in Florence, after 1353, 119-29, 132, 133
  and the Church, 62, 63, 64, 76
  Florentine families of, 60-61, 136
  and King Robert of Naples, 43, 87, 88
  in Lucca, 32, 63, 64, 189, 192
  restoration of, in Florence, after 1381, 153, 159
  suppressed by the Medici and the working-class party, 148, 150, 152, 153, 204
  and the wars of Castruccio, 32-35, 37, 41, 43, 44, 87-88
  See also Black and White parties
Guicciardini family, 201, 209
Guicciardini, Francesco, xxvi, xxx
Guicciardini, Giovanni, 196, 198, 200, 201, 209
Guicciardini, Iacopo, 284, 305, 310
Guicciardini, Luigi, 133, 134, 140, 141, 201
Guilds. *See* Florence, Guilds of; Wool Guild
Guinigi, Cecco, 36
Guinigi, Francesco, 31-32, 52

Guinigi, Pagolo, Lord of Lucca, 32, 37-40, 45, 47-49, 186
  conspiracies against, 188, 197

Hale, J. R., xxxvi
Hannibal, 284
Hawkwood, John, 150, 154
Henry V, King of England, 14
Henry III, Holy Roman Emperor, 58
Henry VII, Holy Roman Emperor, 85
Holy Roman Emperor(s). *See* German Emperor(s)
Humanism, x-xi, xix-xx

Imola, 171, 172, 244
Innocent V, Pope, 67
Innocent VIII, Pope, 303, 307-11
Italy
  destruction of, 289, 317
  disunity of, 7
  French invasion of, xix, xxviii

Joan I, Queen of Naples, 148, 150, 154, 173
John XXIII, Pope, 222
John, Duke of Anjou, 214, 225
John, King of Bohemia, 94
Julius II, Pope, xiii-xv, xxxvii
Justinian, x

Ladislaus, King of Naples, 155, 165, 168, 173, 183
Lamberti family, 60, 81
Lamberti, Mosca, 59
Lampognano, Giovannandrea, 258-61
Landini, Cristofano, 315
Lando, Michele di, 144-48, 154
Lanfranchi, Benedetto, 44
League of Cambrai, xiv
Leo X, Pope (Giovanni de' Medici), xvi, xvii, xxii, xxxvii, 314
  and Machiavelli, xxiv-xxv
Levi, Eugenia, xxvi*fn*
Lioni, Ruberto, 238
Livy, vii, ix, x-xii, xvi, xix, xxvii
Lorraine, Duke of, 299, 300
Lotti, Bernardo, 237
Lottieri, Bishop of Florence, 80
Louis I of Anjou, 154-55
Louis XI, King of France, 224-25, 282
Louis XII, King of France, xiii, xiv, 13, 19

Louis, Duke of Orléans, 13
Lucca, 80, 94, 186, 283
    campaign against, 187-98
    Guelphs in, 32, 63, 64, 189, 192
    under Mastino della Scala, 97-98
    See also Castracani, Castruccio; Guinigi, Pagolo; Uguccione della Faggiuola
Lucretius, xi*fn*-xii*fn*
Ludwig of Bavaria, Holy Roman Emperor, 92, 93, 94
Lupacci, Tommaso, 43

Machiavelli, Bernardo, viii-xi
Machiavelli, Girolamo, 218
Machiavelli, Niccolò
    Arte della guerra by, xx, xxiv, xxxvii
    career of, xii-xv, xxxvii
    Description of the Affairs of France (Ritratto delle cose di Francia) by, xiv-xv, xxxv
    Discorso della guerra di Pisa by, xiii
    Discourse on Florentine Affairs After the Death of Lorenzo (Discursus Florentinarum rerum) by, xxiv-xxv, xxxv
    Discourses on Livy (Discorsi) by, xvi-xxi, xxvii, xxxi, xxxii, xxxv, xxxvii, xxxviii
    History of Florence by, vii, xxv-xxxii, xxxv, xxxvii, xxxviii
    Life of Castruccio Castracani (Vita di Castruccio) by, xxiii-xxiv, xxxv, xxxvii
    The Prince by, xvi-xvii, xx, xxiv, xxxii, xxxv, xxxvii, xxxviii
Magalotti family, 73, 86, 106
Magalotti, Filippo, 155-56
Mahomet, the Grand Turk, 291-92, 295, 316
Malatesta (da Rimini), 98, 219
Malatesta, Gismondo, 219, 244
Malatesta, Roberto, 244, 256, 284, 296-98
Malavolti, Federigo, 205
Malavolti, Giovanni, 196
Mancini family, 73, 106

Mancini, Bardo, 156, 176
Manfred, King of Naples and Sicily, 62, 63, 64, 67
Manfredi, 41
Mannegli family, 60, 75, 114, 157, 162
Mantua, Marquis of. *See* Gonzaga, Federigo
Marignolli, Guerriante, 143
Marius, 57
Martelli, Domenico, 235
Martin IV, Pope, 68
Martin V, Pope, 173, 189
Matthew, King of Hungary, 227, 316
Medici family
    ascendancy of, after 1400, 169
    and the Black and White parties, 80
    characteristics of, 18
    and the *popolani*, 114, 128
    during the regime of the Duke of Athens, 105, 106, 107
    during the regime of Maso degli Albizzi, 159-64, 168, 169
    restoration of, in 1512, xii, xiv, xv, xvi-xvii, xxxvii
Medici, Alamanno de', 161, 178
Medici, Antonio de', 159, 161-62
Medici, Averardo de', 199, 206
Medici, Catherine de', xxii
Medici, Cosimo de', xxv, xxvii, xxxv, 179, 184-85, 199
    and the Acciaiuoli, 229, 239
    and the campaign against Lucca, 188, 199
    character of, 220-24
    death of, 219-20, 224, 227
    government of, 16, 17-18, 19, 28, 215-19
    imprisonment and exile of, 205-11
    marriage alliances of, 221, 264
    opposition to, 200-04
    return of, xxvi, 212-13
Medici, Giovanni de', 169, 172, 175, 177-79, 182-83, 184-85
Medici, Giovanni de' (son of Lorenzo), 314. *See also* Leo X, Pope
Medici, Giovanni di Bernardino de', 98, 99
Medici, Giuliano de' (brother of Lorenzo), 246, 247, 265, 266, 269-71, 275

Medici, Giuliano de' (son of Lorenzo), xvi, xvii, 314
Medici, Giulio de', Cardinal, xxii, xxiv, xxxv, 23, 26, 27, 275. *See also* Clement VII, Pope
Medici, Lorenzo de', xxvi, xxxv, xxxvii, 16, 17, 231, 246-47
  alliances of, 287-91, 294-95, 299, 309, 311
  character of, 316
  conspiracies against, 263, 276-78, 316
  death of, xxvi, xxxii, xxxvi, 316-17
  marriage of, 230, 243
  marriage alliances of, 309, 314
  and Niccolò Vitelli, 255, 284, 296, 301, 315
  and the Serezana war, 306, 307, 310-11
  and the siege of Volterra, 253-54
  and the wars of Pope Sixtus IV, 255, 264, 275-78, 287, 299, 301
Medici, Lorenzo de', Duke of Urbino (grandson of Lorenzo the Magnificent), xvi, xvii, xxii, xxiv
Medici, Piero de', xxxv, 219, 220, 221, 223, 224
  illness of, 243, 245-46
  opposition to, 41, 228-41
Medici, Piero de' (son of Lorenzo), xxxvii, 314
Medici, Salvestro de', 129-31, 141, 145, 146, 148, 153, 168
  death of, 159
  opinions of, 156, 204
Medici, Veri de', 159-60
Melano, Biagio del, 179-80
Micheletto, 198
Micheli, Pier Agnolo, 35
Milan
  French claim to, 13
  social inequality in, 20
  See also Sforza; Visconti
Milan, Archbishop of, 116, 118, 135
Mirandola, Count Giovanni della, 315
monarchy, 19-20
Monreale of Provence, 119
Montano, Cola, 258

Montecarlo, battle at, 33-35
Montenesco, Giovan Battista da, 266-69, 275
Montepulciano, Agnolo da, 315
Montorio, Count of, 307-08
Morozzo, Matteo di, 105
Mozzi family, 60, 72, 75, 115

Naples
  allied with Florence, 287-91, 307-09
  Iacopo Piccinino in, 226
  invaded by Carlo di Durazzo, 148-50, 154
  taken by Manfred, 62
  at war with Florence, 165, 183, 221
  See also Ferrando of Aragon; Robert
Nardi family, 37, 247
Nardi, Bernardo, 247-51
Nerli family, 60, 75, 113, 115
Neroni, Dietisalvi, 228-29, 234-35, 237-38, 240, 243, 248
Neroni, Giovanni di, Archbishop of Florence, 238, 240
Nicholas III, Pope, 67, 68
Nicholas de Tudeschis, Abbot of Sicily, ix, x
Nigi, Nerone di, 168, 200
Novello, Count Guido, 63, 64, 65
Nuto, Ser, 144

Oddo, Count, 174-80
Olgiato, Girolamo, 258-62
Olschki, Cesare, viii, viiifn
Opizi, Giorgio degli, 32-33
Ordelaffi family, 171, 244
Orsini family, 67, 296, 301-02, 308
  and the Medici, 230, 243, 314
Orso, Francesco d', 311-12
Ostrogoths, 58
Otto di Guardia e Balìa, 23, 26, 206
Otto della pratica, 21, 22
Otranto, capture of, 292, 295, 297

Palandra family, 247, 248
Palavisini, Anastagio, 36
Palla, Battista dalla, xxii
Parlements, 10
Paul II, Pope, 227, 244
Pazzi family, 60, 106, 113, 114
  and the Black party, 76, 83

conspiracy of, **xxvi, xxxvii,**
265-75, 290
and the Medici, 221, 264-65
Pazzi, Francesco de', 264-74
Pazzi, Guglielmo de', 221, 264,
274, 275
Pazzi, Iacopo de', 264-69, 273-75
Pazzi, Rinato de', 264, 268, 274
Pergola, Agnolo della, 172, 179,
180
Perugia, 113, 257, 284-86, 315
Perugia, Baglione da, 104, 315
Perugia, Braccio da, 173, 174,
187, 257
Peruzzi family, 73, 99
Peruzzi, Ridolfo, 209-12
Pescia, 188, 196
Petrarch, Francesco, **xi, xix**
Petrucci family, 314
Petrucci, Cesare, 248-51, 272
Philip of Macedon, 54
Piccinino, Iacopo, 225, 226, 256
Piccino, Niccolò, 174, 180-81,
197-98
Piero (brother of King Robert of
Naples), 35, 85, 86
Piero, Friar, Cardinal of Santo
Sisto, 255
Pietrasanta, siege of, 305-07
Pino, Zanobi del, 180
Pisa
attacked by Roberto da San
Severino, 282-83
campaign against, 165, 166
conspiracy in, 198
and the Duke of Athens, 103
early settlement of, 56
reconquest of, xiii-xiv
rule of Castruccio in, 37, 44-
45, 47-49, 87, 92-93
rule of Uguccione in, 33, 35-
36, 85
and the siege of Lucca, 97-98
University of, 315
Pistoia
Castruccio's occupation of,
39-43, 48-49, 91, 93
family feuds in, 74, 247, 250
Guelph domination of, 33, 62
rebellion of, 110
Pistoia, Carmine di, 316
Pitti family, 115
Pitti, Luca, 217-19, 229, 235-36,
238, 247
Pius II, Pope, 219, 222, 227
plague epidemics, 116, 285
Pliny, 57

Poggibonsi, encampment at, 284,
286
Poggio family, 37-38
Poggio Bracciolini, Giovanni
Francesco, xxv-xxviii
Pompey, 57
Pope(s)
and antipope, 93, 94
at Avignon, 40, 118, 126
and Emperor, 58, 67, 92, 298
policies of, 287
See also Church; names of
individual popes
Popolo minuto, 104, 136-37, 142,
147-48, 153, 158
Possente, Bastiano di, 39
Prato, 43, 88, 247-51
Prato, Niccolao da, 80, 81
Prévôt de l'hôtel, 11
Proposto, 130
Pucci, Antonio, 306-07
Pucci, Puccio, 199, 206

Raab, Felix, xxxvi
Ravenna, battle of, xv, 3-4
Riario, Raffaello de', Cardinal,
269-71, 279
Ricci family, 128, 162, 164, 168
and the Albizzi, 118-22, 125,
126, 127, 148
Ricci, Rosso di Ricciardo de', 98
Ricci, Uguccione de', 120, 121,
126, 127
Ridolfi, Antonio, 291
Ridolfi, Lorenzo, 175
Ridolfi, Piero, 314
Ridolfi, Roberto, xi*fn*, xvi, xx*fn*,
xxiv*fn*, xxvi, xxxvi
Rimini. *See* Malatesta
Robert, King of Naples, 33, 35,
37, 40, 53, 85
Florence defended by, 43, 85-
88, 92, 98, 124
Roman history, study of, x-xi
Machiavelli's use of, vii, xii,
xvi-xxi, xxviii
Rome, ancient
nobility and people of, 117-18
origins of Florence in, 57-58
Rome, modern
Pope Eugene IV expelled from,
211
sack of, in 1527, xxxvii
social strife in, 40, 296-97,
302-03
Rossi family, 60, 75, 106, 114-15
Rossi, Bandino de', 43

Rosso, Antonio del, 196, 197
Rucellai family, 106, 107, 221
Rucellai, Naddo, 98, 99
Ruffoli, Ubaldo, 69
Rustichelli, Francesco, 103

Saggineto, Filippo da, 92
St. George, Company of, 303-05, 309
Salerno, Giannozzo da, 148-49
Salviati, Alamanno, 195
Salviati, Francesco, 95
Salviati, Francesco, Archbishop of Pisa, 264, 266-68, 270-72
Salviatis, Iacopo, 268, 272, 314
San Friano, Niccolò da, 140
San Miniato, 37, 38, 44-45
San Severino, Roberto da, 251, 281-82, 288, 295-96, 299-300, 308-09, 311
Savonarola, Girolamo, xiifn, xxxvii
Scali family, 60, 75, 106, 164
Scali, Giorgio, 128, 130, 147-48, 168, 204
  and Benedetto Alberti, 154, 156, 178
  downfall of, 150-52
Seravezza, sack of, 191-94
Serezana, 170, 302, 303-11
Serezanello, 36, 310-11
Serraville, battle at, 41-44, 46
Sforza family
  expulsion of, 281-82
  restoration of, 288-89
  and the Visconti, 13, 226
Sforza, Francesco, Duke of Milan, 196-98, 221, 224, 225-27, 231
Sforza, Galeazzo, Duke of Milan, 225, 227, 231, 241-42, 244
  assassination of, 258-62
  in Florence, 251-52
Sforza, Gian Galeazzo, Duke of Milan, 244, 260, 279-81, 300
Sforza, Lodovico, 281, 288-89, 295, 299-301, 310, 311, 312
  ambitions of, 317
  and Louis XII of France, 19
Sicilian wars, 77, 79, 92
Siena, 62, 63, 113, 186, 257-58
  occupied by the Duke of Calabria, 283-85, 291, 292, 294

social disorders in, 314
Signoria, power of, 15-16, 21, 22, 25
Simonetta, Cecco, 281, 288-89
Sinigaglia, murders at, xiv
Sixtus IV, Pope, 244
  alliances of, 255-58
  and the Pazzi conspiracy, 264, 266-69
  wars of, 275-302
Soderini, Niccolò, 201, 229, 233-36, 238, 240, 243
Soderini, Pagolantonio, 310
Soderini, Tommaso, 201, 280, 281
  and Lorenzo de' Medici, 233-34, 236, 246-47, 253-54, 288
Soldanieri family, 60, 65
Spain, and France, 6
Spini family, 76
Spini, Benedetto degli, 162
Spini, Geri, 72, 83
Spinoli, Gherardino, 94
Stinche, 82, 108
Strozzi family, 106, 149, 164
Strozzi, Andrea, 113
Strozzi, Carlo, 120, 127, 128, 131, 132, 149
Strozzi, Giovan Francesco, 240
Strozzi, Lorenzo di Filippo, xx
Strozzi, Palla, 186, 208-12, 240
Strozzi, Tommaso, 128, 130, 141, 143-44, 148-52, 178
Sulla, 57
Switzerland, and France, 6-7

Tacitus, 57
Tassino, Antonio, 288, 289
Tedesco, Niccolò, x
Tegrimi, Niccolò, xxiii
Tiberius, Roman Emperor, 57
Tornabuoni family, 221, 222, 235
Tosa, Giovanni della, 43, 103
Tosa, Rosso della, 83
Tosa, Simone della, 86, 93
Totila, King of the Ostrogoths, 58
Turks, 219, 222, 227, 244, 283
  capture of Otranto by, 291-92, 295, 297

Uberti family, 73
  and the Buondelmonti, 58-60, 125

Ghibelline politics of, 37, 60, 62-64
Uberti, Farinata degli, 63-64
Uberti, Tolosetto, 82
University of Paris, 10
University of Pisa, 315
Urban VI, Pope, 149, 154
Urbino, Count of. *See* Federigo
Uzano, Niccolò da, 168, 169, 176, 179
  and the campaign against Lucca, 188, 189-90
  restraining influence of, 200-03

Vailà, battle of, 3
Valori, Taldo, 95
Velluti, Donato, 208, 209
Venice
  alliances against, xiii-xiv, 241, 295-96, 298-301
  allied with Florence, 181, 183-84, 198, 221, 253, 255-58, 279-80, 283, 290-91
  attack on Florence by, 240-41
  attacked by the Germans, 311
  early settlement of, 56
  and Genoa, 303
  and the Medici, 206, 221, 231, 240-41
  and the papacy, 227, 255, 295
Vespucci, Agostino, xiii
Vespucci, Guid' Antonio, 282, 294
Vettori, Francesco, xvi
Vettori, Piero, 310
Villani, Giovanni, xxiii, xxvii, xxviii-xxx, 56
Villari, Pasquale, xxviii, xxviii*fn*

Visconti family, 31, 32, 91, 97-98
  wars of, 15, 116, 118, 158, 163, 165, 169-74, 179-84, 188
Visconti, Bernabò, 127, 158
Visconti, Carlo, 258-61
Visconti, Filippo, Duke of Milan, 165, 169-73, 181, 183-84, 186, 188, 221
  and the campaign against Lucca, 190, 196-98
  and Iacopo Piccinino, 226
Visconti, Gian Galeazzo, Duke of Milan, 13, 92, 158, 163, 165
Visconti, Matteo, 37
Visconti, Valentina, 13
Vitelleschi, Giovanni, 211
Vitelli, Niccolò, 255, 284, 296, 301, 315
Viviani, Iacopo, 188-89
Volterra
  conquest of, 62
  rebellions of, 110, 184, 185-87, 252-55
  siege of, 254

Walter of Brienne, Duke of Athens, xxviii, xxix, xxx, 92, 98-110
  conspiracies against, 105-10, 112
  tyranny of, 118, 124, 135, 147
White party. *See* Black and White parties
Whitfield, J. H., xxxvi
Wool Guild, 137, 141, 142

Zagonara, capture of, 172-73, 179